A

NEW RENDERING

OF THE

HEBREW PSALMS

INTO

ENGLISH VERSE

WITH NOTES, CRITICAL, HISTORICAL AND BIOGRAPHICAL,
INCLUDING AN HISTORICAL SKETCH OF THE FRENCH,
ENGLISH AND SCOTCH METRICAL VERSIONS.

BY

ABRAHAM COLES, M.D., LL.D.

AUTHOR OF DIES IRÆ IN THIRTEEN ORIGINAL VERSIONS;
OLD GEMS IN NEW SETTINGS; THE LIFE AND TEACHINGS OF OUR LORD IN VERSE
THE MICROCOSM AND OTHER POEMS, ETC.

WIPF & STOCK · Eugene, Oregon

Wipf and Stock Publishers
199 W 8th Ave, Suite 3
Eugene, OR 97401

A New Rendering of the Hebrew Psalms into English Verse
With Notes, Critical, Historical and Biographical,
Including an Historical Sketch of the French, English
and Scotch Metrical Versions
By Coles, Abraham
Softcover ISBN-13: 978-1-6667-6100-9
Hardcover ISBN-13: 978-1-6667-6101-6
eBook ISBN-13: 978-1-6667-6102-3
Publication date 10/4/2022
Previously published by D. Appleton Company, 1888

This edition is a scanned facsimile of the original edition
published in 1888.

CONTENTS.

INTRODUCTION:

    I. THE PSALMS—THEIR CHARACTER, - - - v

    II. HISTORICAL SKETCH OF THE FRENCH, ENGLISH AND SCOTCH METRICAL VERSIONS OF THE PSALMS, - xiv

    III. NOTES, CRITICAL, HISTORICAL AND BIOGRAPHICAL, xxvi

    TESTIMONIES TO THE EXCELLENCE OF THE PSALMS, -

THE PSALMS—A NEW RENDERING OF THE WHOLE INTO ENGLISH VERSE, - - - - - - - - 1-291

INTRODUCTION.

I.—THE PSALMS—THEIR CHARACTER.

THREE thousand years ago the Hebrew Decachord, "The Tenstringed Law," was boldly swept by Prophet-fingers. The sweetness of the music has filled the world. The chords are vibrating yet. "Voice and Verse, those sphere-born harmonious sisters, wed their divine sounds," fitly preluding,

> " That undisturbéd song of pure concent,
> Aye sung before the sapphire-colored throne
> To Him that sits thereon,
> With saintly shout and solemn jubilee;—
> Where the bright Seraphim in burning row,
> Their loud uplifted angel trumpets blow,
> And the Cherubic hosts, in thousand quires,
> Touch their immortal harps of golden wires,
> With those just spirits that wear victorious palms,
> Hymns devout and holy psalms
> Singing everlastingly."

The inspiration of the Psalms is not pagan and feigned; not merely poetic, but really and truly divine. We believe them to be in a high and special sense God-inspired. The Muse is avowedly "Heavenly"—the same

> . . . "That on the secret top
> Of Oreb and of Sinai did inspire
> That Shepherd who first taught the chosen seed
> In the beginning how the heavens and earth
> Rose out of chaos."

Undoubtedly the Psalms were written for our learning, and were meant for all time. So long as man is man they must have a function for him. Other things grow old, but these do not. Other things die, but these live. Cut across the arteries of their life anywhere, and they bleed. We listen and we hear a heart beating and throbbing, timed to our own. No mirror reflects the features more faithfully than these do the heart and life of man. They cover all varieties of human experience. No joy, no sorrow, no fear, no hope, but find there suitable expression. All heights and depths are explored. "Heaven hides nothing, nor the deep tract of hell." The realism is intense.

For however inspired and "enriched by the Eternal Spirit with all utterance and knowledge," we are sure that the Singer is one of us — is a man of like passions and like organs — so that, if by virtue of his prophetic office, he is able to telescope the heavens, even the heaven of heavens, and see farther than we, he, nevertheless, is compelled to see with our eyes; and since he sees not for himself alone but for others, and it is made his duty to make full report of all he sees, his discoveries can have, we suppose, no higher meaning for him than for us. For knowing only in part, he prophesies only in part. The organ of prophecy with which he is gifted, being restricted in its exercise and utterance, can go just so far and no farther.

We value the Psalms for what they are, and not for what they are not. It does not affect the question of their inspiration, that "the song is partial;" that they do not contain all truth; that some things were kept back, we must believe, purposely and for wise reasons. We are told, "It is the glory of God to conceal a matter" — the foolishness of God is wiser than man — for everything there is a time. It is enough to know that the All-Wise judged it best to make His revelations gradual, to let the twilight precede the dawn, the dawn the sun-rising. This being according to the analogy of nature, why should it be thought strange that certain truths should have been kept in abeyance — that, for example, a clear, explicit and positive affirmation of the doctrine of the Future Life should have been withheld in those first ages, so that even inspired men were left in comparative ignorance? That their ignorance was absolute is not asserted. Their belief may have been defective, but it never amounted to a disbelief. That they had an apprehension more or less distinct of a Conscious Hereafter, both for the righteous and the wicked, Psalms

INTRODUCTION.

16 : 11; 17 : 15; 49 : 14, 15, may be cited in proof. The doctrine, moreover, was so bound up with other beliefs implying it, that it was a necessity of reason. For we find it everywhere assumed as a fundamental truth, that righteousness shall be rewarded and wickedness punished; that though the bad prosper in life, and have no bands in their death, there is for them an unfulfilled retribution.

No one can forsee all the applications and bearings of the simplest truth. The discoverer of electricity had little prescience of the astonishing uses to which it would be put. In this respect, the child of to-day knows more of its powers than the wisest philosopher had dreamed of a few years ago. As it was with the philosopher, so it was, we have reason to believe, with the prophet. He was half-ignorant of what he taught. "He builded better than he knew."

Of the prophet we may not know even the name; nor is it important that we should. It is the message, not the messenger, that concerns us. We, upon whom the ends of the world have come, have clearly one advantage. We have witnessed the fulfillment of many things which prophetic vision only dimly descried and imperfectly understood. Time, in his onward flight, has overtaken the thing predicted, and left it behind. The mills of Providence grind slowly, but constantly and surely, and the event prophesied, at the proper moment, punctually happened. Then it was that all enigmas were solved and all uncertainties cleared up. When the sun arises, "All the stars hide their diminished heads." Among those born of woman, there was none, no prophet greater than John the Baptist, but the least in the kingdom of heaven is greater than he. He is exalted to a higher dignity of privilege and knowledge. But it is in vain that the sun shines if we wilfully close our eyes. Amid noonday's splendors we can, if we choose, dwell in darkness. Aside from Revelation we know how inconsequent a being man is. We who live in the full enjoyment of those things, which ancient worthies saw afar off and were glad, fall behind them in many ways. How the ardor of their devotion shames the coldness of ours! What love to God did they express! What trust in Him! What zeal for His worship! What attachment to His law! What hungerings and thirstings after righteousness! Considering that all this was true of men, who, so far from having our light, dwelt in comparative darkness, knowing little of God and His truth — we blush the more. With motives to righteousness so inferior (He not having yet come who brought life and immortality to light), they nevertheless pursued it as the supreme good, never doubting that well-being depended on well-doing. Without knowing that God so loved the world as to give His only-begotten Son, they still loved Him with a rapturous affection. Without understanding the dear and affecting reasons which justified the gratuitous imputation, they could wonder at the grace and rejoice in the blessedness of the man to whom the Lord imputed righteousness without works. While all this goes to prove the falsity of the allegation that the service of God is a mercenary transaction, and that the worshipper is selfishly devout, having his eye fixed on the recompense of reward — it enhances the value of those joyful anticipations of Christian truths which make their harp sound so sweetly in Christian ears. The creed of the heart is often in advance of the intellect, for therein is resident the " prophetic soul." Trust is more than theory, and love than knowledge. The Psalms do not need any modern manipulation to fit them for Christian Worship.

Prayer is the child of need. Standing on

> " The great altar-stairs
> That slope through darkness up to God,"

prayer is sometimes, even in good men, little better than

> " An infant crying in the night,
> An infant crying for the light,
> And with no language but a cry."

But the Psalms are a perpetual rebuke to all skeptic confusions. To the Hebrew bard God was the Supreme Reality. He was an example to all ages of Trust. He felt it good to trust in Him; to throw all his burdens at His feet. He never doubted in darkest hours that He cared for him. He endured as seeing Him Who is invisible. God's Face was so clearly mirrored in his heart that he saw its varying expression. He saw it now dressed in smiles, and now in frowns. If the frown was the projection of conscience, it was no less the frown of God. If he sometimes mistook outward calamity, sickness, low spirits, for tokens of Divine displeasure, that must be ascribed to the imperfection of his knowledge. It was important that he should realize that God's love was not a weak favoritism — something to presume on. He came with all boldness to the Throne of Grace, pushed forward by the urgency of his need. He was absolutely sincere. He exemplified an actual approach of a human soul to its Maker; and thus the mouth of man was brought close to the ear of God. We are sure the words he spoke were pleasing and acceptable words; that the cry of penitence and the prayer for pardon were heard and answered. We are impressed with the sublimity of the spectacle. We are more convinced than ever, that the soul on its knees is the right posture; and that to refuse worship is to do violence to the fitness of things, and to incur proportionate guilt and loss.

Man's superiority over all the creatures that surround him consists in this: That he alone is capable of religion. The tie that unites him to his Maker is not only one of creatureship but sonship. To sever this tie, to ignore his divine relationship—with feet standing on the steps of the Eternal Throne to refuse to mount, what madness! In the lapse of the centuries man's relation to God has undergone no change. The relation is one of character. A right relation is full of blessedness. All sin, all misery springs from a wrong attitude. It is easy to see how, to a creature "so fearfully and wonderfully made"—so complex in himself and so related to every thing else— this must be so. It is easy to understand, how all the ministers of good to which he stands related should become the ministers of evil ; how, through a false adjustment, every avenue of pleasure should be made an avenue of pain ; how completely atheistic folly and the insanity of wickedness should be able to frustrate the best designs of Infinite Beneficence; how effectually health and happiness can be made exiles and outcasts from the Human Organism by indulgence in that which is forbidden. Van Helmont conceived the existence of an immaterial principle, which, present from the beginning, presides over the development of the body, and over all organic phenomena.

Besides this chief one, which he called Archeus, and located in the upper orifice of the stomach, he admitted several subordinate ones, one for each organ, each of them being liable to anger, caprice, terror, and every human feeling. While this may be fanciful in form, it is substantially true. The approaches to the Tree of Life were not more jealously guarded by Cherubim and flaming sword, than is the gateway to every particular cell that goes to make up the totality of the organs, by the guardian powers whose office it is to resent and resist the entrance of what is alien and hurtful. Woe to the individual if this vital constabulary, instituted in the interests of order and virtue, should be overpowered. A watchful instinct resident in the stomach sounds the alarm when the body demands food; and manifests terror and rage when compliance is too long delayed. What powerful disgusts and repugnances and efforts at rejection attend the introduction of some irritant poison, instead of wholesome nourishment! No one can say, but what this is necessary for the safety and welfare of the body. That punishment should follow in the footsteps of violated law is the best proof we have of Creative Love and Wisdom. The connection between sin and suffering is not arbitrary. It is simply cause and consequence. The conditions of *being* are not more absolutely fixed than those of *well-being*. We are bound to the universe by innumerable ties, and we cannot sever a single one. In this sense we are helpless; in another, we are all powerful, for we have the power of adjusting the manner of our relation, so as to make it normal or abnormal, right or wrong, false or true. Nothing in Nature is evil of itself. Take what you will—take fire if you please. It burns you or warms you according to your actual position to it. In itself it is the most friendly of powers; you could not live without it. Through a long life, up to the present moment it has been to you a minister of good. But this will not prevent this very hour the manifestation of a terrible resentment should you dare to trifle with it—to cross so much as a line the proper limit of your approach. Its genial heat will then be converted into wrathful flame and consume you to ashes.

The Psalms are full of bold anthropomorphisms. In the second Psalm, for example, derisive laughter, and wrath are attributed to

Deity. Admitting that this is speaking after the manner of men, and that the terms employed are not to be too strictly interpreted, there is no room for doubt as to their meaning. They fitly and powerfully express the divine antagonism to all evil and evil-doers. That this does not misrepresent Him is conclusively proved by what we see of Him in Nature. It is true that anger in man is not the same as anger in God—inevitably so, for the quality of anger depends upon character. There are we know diversities of anger even among men. The anger of a good man is not the anger of a bad one.

Anger to be right must be moral. It must be void of malice. It must be justified by the occasion. It must not be in excess. When it is the pure expression of the sentiment of Justice there is nothing holier. It thus approximates to what we may suppose anger to be in the Divine Mind. It is a measured and righteous indignation against sin. It is the repulsion of Infinite Purity from that which is not pure. Not only is it compatible with Love, but it is one of the forms in which Infinite Love manifests itself. Its inexorableness is the inexorableness of Love, or Law, which is but another name for Love. Penalty, which is an essential constituent of Law, is a kind of anger. For Law as found in Nature, we repeat, everywhere resents violation. Anger is the defensive property of things. Every atom is armed with it. The minutest insect has its sting. Every thing is sovereign in its own sphere with rights and prerogatives of vengeance. Individual sanctities may not be invaded. Out of this arises, as said before, an universal police necessary to the conservation of order throughout the Universe. Look where we will, we find that every thing has two aspects or faces—one all smiles, the other all frowns; and it depends very much upon ourselves which is turned towards us. So far as we can discover, the God seen in Nature and the God declared in Revelation are the same God. He is not more the God of vengeance in the one than He is in the other. He undoubtedly is so in both; but we will not be guilty of the folly of closing our eyes to the proofs of His goodness. They are scattered everywhere throughout the universe, but what a divine thing it is, to have it put in human speech, and compressed in three words, God is Love.

The Divine Government is not more august than it is lovely. It exists for the good of the governed. The meanest subject is God's darling. All the powers of the Universe, and His almightiness are pledged for his protection and safety, so long as he remains loyal and law-abiding. But suppose he does not remain so, what happens then? Only what happens in every well ordered human government under like circumstances. To the loyal and obedient, Law is paternal and benign. It is a shield and a high tower. But not so to its violators. To them it wears a changed aspect, full of dreadful menace. To the end that it may appear to all men that it does not bear the sword in vain, it is not slow nor slack to punish. It arrests and brooks no resistence. It consigns to dungeons. It hangs on the gallows. Can it be that this is the self-same power that one moment before the crime was committed was firmly and solemnly pledged for the felon's safe-keeping, protesting that not a hair of his head should be injured? Even so. The Law stands upright, but the transgressor holds towards it an inverted position, and by virtue of this inversion he is emptied of all his rights under the Law. Law is not simply preceptive—it is command backed by penalty. This is true of man's law, and it is true of God's law.

Human government sometimes undertakes to pardon, and to reëstablish the criminal in his former relations: but, to remove the falsity of a corrupt nature, to correct the insane inclination of the heart to evil. transcends her power. Here the analogy fails between human government and the divine. What is not possible to man is possible to God. He can both pardon and save. He can make the guilty soul pure, and the sick soul well. For not only has He provided remedies to heal the flesh but to heal the spirit also; and thus, by a true restoration to old relations, man is made just the same as if he had never sinned.

Physicians in the treatment of disease rely on an automatic force or tendency, denominated *vis medicatrix Naturæ*, which, if it does not in every case suffice for cure, always aids it. Conscience may be said to answer to this in man's moral and spiritual economy, operating as a *vis medicatrix* in the recovery of a sick soul. While not adequate alone to meet all the exigencies of man's desperate condition, with "his whole head sick and his whole heart faint," it continues to be the indispensable fulcrum upon which the lever of Help must rest. Salvation is a return to wholeness, or holiness, without which no man can see the Lord. The Psalmist celebrates the felicity of "the man whose iniquity is forgiven, whose sin is covered—to whom the Lord imputeth not iniquity," or as Paul construes it, "imputeth righteousness without works." Regeneration can only mean a readjustment of right relations of the soul of man to the Universe and its Maker. Found in his place and in harmony with his surroundings, then, as Herbert sings:

> " Man is all symmetry,
> Full of proportions, one limb to another,
>   And to all the world besides.
>   Each part may call the farthest, brother;
> For head with foot hath privy amity,
>   And both with moons and tides.
>
> " Nothing hath got so far,
> But man hath caught and kept it as his prey;
>   His eyes dismount the highest star;
>   He is in little all the sphere.
> Herbs gladly cure our flesh, because that they
>   Find their acquaintance there.
>
> " For us, the winds do blow,
> The earth doth rest, heavens move, and fountains flow;
>   Nothing we see but means our good,
>   As our delight, or as our treasure;
> The whole is either our cupboard of food,
>   Or cabinet of pleasure.
>
> " The stars have us to bed:
> Night draws the curtain, which the sun withdraws.
>   Music and light attend our head.
>   All things unto our flesh are kind,
> In their descent and being; to our mind,
>   In their ascent and cause.
>
> " More servants wait on man
> Than he'll take notice of. In every path,
>   He treads down that which doth befriend him
>   When sickness makes him pale and wan.
> O mighty love! Man is one world, and hath
>   Another to attend him."

II.—METRICAL VERSIONS OF THE PSALMS.

FRENCH, ENGLISH AND SCOTCH.

THE earliest attempt of which we have any record to turn the Psalms into English Verse was made in the Thirteenth Century, and was known as the Northumberland Psalter. It was followed in the next Century by another, the work of Richard Rolle, the Hermit of Hampole. The Council of Toulouse in 1229 interdicted the Bible to the laity, but made an exception in favor of the Psalter. Periods of religious revival in all ages have been favorable to the growth of Sacred Song. The Psalms themselves may be regarded as the intense outcome of the religious life of ancient Israel, as displayed in the individual or the nation, while they served to signalize and punctuate different epochs and special crises in the history of the Jewish people. The historic books of the Bible, it is safe to say, do not give so clear an insight into the character of those remote times as the Psalms. David's history is a very eventful one, and full of romance, and is well calculated to excite a lively interest; but the story of his life, without the lyric supplement supplied by the Psalms, would be divested of its greatest charm. Prose deals, for the most part, with the outward and objective; and usually practises reserve in regard to what is subjective and private. Not so with Poetry, particularly Lyric Poetry. That delights in self-revelations. It has to do with the facts of the inner life. It keeps nothing back. It is the soul on fire. It kindles others. The little spark becomes a spreading conflagration. The poet, not infrequently, is the truest and best historian.

It has been often exemplified in modern times, that nothing lies so near the popular heart, and is so fitted to awaken its enthusiasm, as Song. A wise man said long ago, " If a man were permitted to make all the ballads of a nation, he need not care who should make its laws." This was peculiarly true when the people knew only what

INTRODUCTION. xv

was stored in their memories. Verse, making knowledge portable and pleasing, would naturally be more valued then, than in an age of printed books and multitudinous newspapers. But the first effect following the invention of printing was to awaken an insatiable curiosity in regard to the writings handed down from antiquity, especially the Holy Scriptures, leading to a demand for translations in the vernacular, and preparing men to give them a boundless welcome as soon as they appeared. Metrical Versions of the Psalms in the mother-tongue not only attended the ushering-in of the Reformation, but aided materially in bringing it about. Their history as pertaining to different countries is full of interest.

In FRANCE, the earliest of these was that of Clement Marot, who, even in our day, has been described as the most agreeable, if not one of the greatest, poets of France, and a figure of all but the first importance in her literary history. He was born in 1495 and died in 1544. He was *Valet de Chambre* to Francis I., and accompanied him in his disastrous Italian campaign. He was wounded and taken prisoner, but soon liberated, and was again in Paris in 1525. Accused of heresy, he was thrown into prison. After his release, finding his liberty again in jeopardy, he fled to Geneva. Here he added Twenty Psalms to the Thirty already published. They were set to music by the celebrated composer Goudemel, the master of Palestrina, a musical composer of still greater celebrity. Goudemel was a Protestant, and was one of the victims of the massacre of St. Bartholomew. Marot's translations were very popular. The powerful influence which the book exercised on contemporaries is not denied by any one. The great persons of the Court chose different pieces, each as his or her favorite. They were sung in Court and city; and they are said, with probable exaggeration, but with a basis of truth, to have done more than any thing else to advance the cause of the Reformation in France. At a later period, having been proscribed by the Sorbonne,* their use became almost exclusively confined to the Protestants. An edition of his *Fifty Psalms* was

---

* It is remarkable that as late as 1563 an edition was printed at Lyons, "*Avec privilege*," during the reign of Charles IX., so that the order interdicting their use was probably later.

published in Geneva in 1543, to which Calvin prefixed a long Preface. The particular Psalms translated by him were: Psalms 1 to 19, 22, 23, 24, 25, 32, 33, 36, 37, 38, 43, 45, 46, 50, 51, 72, 79, 86, 91, 101, 103, 104, 107, 110, 113, 114, 115, 128, 130, 137, 138, 143 = 50. The date of composition affixed to Psalm 1. is 1540. The renderings are in a variety of metres. Some of the beautiful airs to which they were set still survive. Subsequently to Marot's Fifty, Calvin added Two, and Theodore Beza the remaining Ninety-Eight — thus the French Psalter was made complete. The whole was known as Marot and Beza's Version, but still oftener, perhaps, was spoken of as Marot's alone.

It became to the Huguenots their most precious Manual of Devotion. They learned the verses by heart, and taught them to their children. It was in vain that the singing of them was forbidden — they continued to sing them at the peril of their lives. When driven from their homes, hunted and persecuted, they broke the silence of the Desert with their murmured melodies, and betrayed their hiding-places by an irrepressible utterance. In their battles for the Rights of Conscience, they used them to nerve their hands and fire their hearts. They beguiled the weariness of long marches by the music of their words; and in loud chorus they shouted some sacred Battle Hymn as they rushed, forgetful of danger, with irresistible *élan* against the enemy; and in the crowning close, when victory perched on their banners, some remembered Psalm of Praise and Thanksgiving burst simultaneously from ten thousand lips. They found consolation in them under disappointment and defeat. Their attachment to them triumphed over the rack. They sang them in prison and on the scaffold. Condemned to the galleys, they lightened slavish toil by timing the stroke of their oars to their chanted favorites. They employed them to sweeten exile, and to hallow new homes. Translations of them were made into almost all the languages of Europe. The first Scotch Psalter of 1565 derived many of their metres and tunes from this source.

In ENGLAND the first complete Metrical Version of the Psalms in the mother-tongue was that known as Sternhold and Hopkins. Though the Version went by their name, they were the authors of only a part. The object was, says old Fuller, in his quaint and witty fashion, to " make the Psalms portable in men's memories, verses being twice as light as the same bulk of prose " — slyly adding that the translators would seem to have " drunk more of Jordan than of Helicon during their labors."

Thomas Sternhold was Groom of the Robes to Henry VIII. and Edward VI. He was born about 1500 and died 1549. He was noted at Court for his poetical talents and extreme piety. Wishing to provide a substitute for the profane songs in vogue, he undertook a translation of the Psalms, hoping that they might become popular with the courtiers. He completed only thirty-seven (which were published in 1549, after his death), with seven by Hopkins, under the title of "*All such Psalms of David as Thomas Sternholde, late Grome of the Kinges Majestyes Robes, did in his lyfe-time drawe into Englyshe Metre.*" The Version was made complete, and was published in 1562, as " *The Whole Book of Psalms collected into English Metre by T. Sternhold, J. Hopkins, and Others, conferred with the Ebreu, with apt Notes to sing them withal,*" — under which title it was annexed to the " Book of Common Prayer," and adopted under Elizabeth as the Metrical Version to be used by the Church of England. It continued to be so used for 135 years (until superseded by the " New Version " of Tate and Brady, first published in 1696), during which time it is said to have passed through at least three hundred and nine distinct editions. Such was the attachment of the people to it, that they regarded it as little less than inspired. Even its faults of grammar and rhythm became sacred in their eyes, and they were intolerant of the slightest change. The Non-conformists continued to use it down to the time of Watts.

It was customary in the successive editions of the work to distinguish the author of each version contributed by the initials of his name — T. S. standing for Thomas Sternhold; J. H. for John Hopkins, of whom little is known except that he graduated at Oxford in 1544, and was a clergyman and schoolmaster; W. K. for William Keith, a Scotchman, an exile with Knox in 1555, and chaplain of the English forces at Havre in 1563; W. W. for William Whitingham, a brother-in-law of Calvin, and minister of the English refugees at Geneva;

N. for Thomas Norton, translator of Calvin's Institutes; M. for John Markand; H. W. for Henry Wisdome; T. C. for some person unknown, unless John Craig be meant. In the later editions some of these names do not appear as contributors, and there are various changes in the attribution of authorship. In the Baskerville edition of 1762 there are assigned to T. S. 42; to J. H. 27; to W. W. 14; to W. K. 6; to T. C. 1.

In regard to the " New Version," it was first published under the title of an " *Essay of a New Version of the Psalms of David, consisting of the first Twenty, by N. Brady and N. Tate*" (8 vo. 1605). This was succeeded by " *The Book of Psalms, A New Version in Metre fitted to the Tunes used in the Churches, by N. Tate and N. Brady,*" (1696). Nahum Tate was born in Dublin in 1652 and died in London 1715. After the death of Shadwell in 1692, he succeeded him as poet-laureate. He was associated with Dryden in the authorship of " Absalom and Ahithophel," the second part being chiefly his composition. He produced several dramatic works, among which was an alteration of " King Lear " from Shakespeare, which long held the stage to the exclusion of the original. Nicholas Brady was born in 1659 and died in 1726. He was partly educated at Oxford, and partly at Trinity College, Dublin. He was the author of a tragedy, and numerous sermons. Just prior to his death he published a poetical translation of Virgil. His reputation however rests chiefly on the part he took in the Metrical Version of the Psalms. The Version of Tate and Brady is still retained in the Book of Common Prayer, both in England and in this country. In regard to the comparative merits of the two Versions, while all must admit that the New is a great improvement upon the Old in smoothness and correctness of versification, the advantage, it is thought, in some cases at least, is more than counterbalanced by a falling off in vigor and raciness, and the loss of a certain homely quaintness and antique flavor, which constituted no small part of the charm of the earlier Version. The rendering in the older Version is confessedly unequal, and in some of the Psalms is, no doubt, rude, disjointed and uncouth, and thus has furnished the occasion for much cheap wit and ridicule.

Sternhold and Hopkins' Version had had, for more than seventy years, entire possession of the field, when in 1636 appeared "*A Paraphrase upon the Psalms of David, by George Sandys, set to New Tunes for Private Devotion; and a Thorough-Bass for Voice and Instrument, by Henry Lawes, Gentleman of His Majesty's Chapel Royal,*" which received high commendation. Dryden calls him " the ingenious and learned Sandys, the best versifier of the former age." James Montgomery styles his Version as " incomparably the most poetic in the language." That Sandys' poetry and Lawes' music combined should have failed to obtain popularity, is thought remarkable. Lawes wrote the music to Milton's " Comus," in which he also acted the part of Thyrsis, and the poet's allusion to the musician is well known (Comus 494):

> " Thyrsis, whose artful strains have oft delayed
> The huddling brook to hear his madrigal,
> And sweetened every musk-rose of the dale."

To him, too, Milton addressed the sonnet:

> " Harry, whose tuneful and well measured song
> First taught our English music how to span
> Words with just note and accent."

George Sandys (or Sandes), the seventh and youngest son of Edwin Sandys, Archbishop of York, according to the Archbishop's own entry, " was born the 2nd day of March at six of the clock in the morning in 1557." After having spent some time at Oxford, he set out on his travels in 1610, of which he published an account in 1615, with a dedication to Charles I., then Prince of Wales. The work attained great popularity. He visited the Holy Land, and the picture he gives of the East in his time, particularly of Jerusalem, is specially interesting and valuable. He was but a short time at home. In 1606, a charter of incorporation had been granted to the Adventurers of London to begin their first plantation and seat in any place upon any part of the Colony of Virginia. Under date of July 24, 1621, Sir Francis Wyat is mentioned as Governor, and George Sandys as Treasurer. It is interesting to know that the greater part of his Translation of " Ovid's Metamorphoses " was composed under great difficulties in the Colony, and that it was the first considerable book written in America. Besides the Psalms he wrote a poetical Paraphrase of the Book of Job, of Ecclesiastes, upon the Song of Solomon, Lamentations of Jeremiah, etc., all excellently done. He died in 1643 aged 66.

Tate and Brady's Version, already noticed, followed in 1696. Then we have Dr. John Patrick's "*Psalms of David in Metre*," which appeared in 1698, from which it is said Dr. Watts borrowed. It is a book the writer only knows by report; and is unable to say therefore how far it is original. In 1709 followed Isaac Watts' "*Imitations* (not Versions) *of the Psalms.*" His method was a new one. It virtually consisted in converting the Psalm into a Christian Hymn. It was a Christian graft on a Jewish root. The song was made into a sermon. In this form it easily lent itself to the purposes of Christian worship, but in order to make it serve this end, some violence was necessarily done to the original. It has met however with such favor as to have become a model to all later attempts at versification of the Psalms. While it may have its advantages, they are not, it is thought, of so pronounced a character as to forbid a new essay, in which the poet, availing himself of all the results of modern scholarship, shall give an English Version of the Psalms in their original form, without interpolation or alteration of any kind, after the old manner. Twelve years before, in 1707, Watts published his *Hymns* in Three Books. In his original Preface to his Psalms he acknowledges his indebtedness for ideas and even expressions to Denham, Milbourne, and Tate and Brady. From Patrick he is said to have taken most. In the Lenox Library may be found Franklin's Edition of Watts' Hymns, 1741; Joel Barlow's amendments to his *Psalms*, 1785; and Timothy Dwight's improvements to *both*, 1800. Isaac Watts was born in 1674, died in 1748, aged 74.

"*The Psalms Translated or Paraphrased in English Verse, by James Merrick,*" was published in 1766. Bishop Horne in his "Commentary on the Psalms" frequently refers to it in terms of high commendation, and quotes from it. Its chief fault is said to be diffuseness. The author was born in 1720 and died in 1769. While he was at Oxford he was the tutor of Lord North. His poetical fable, " The Chameleon," has been often printed.

Coming nearer our own times, we have " *The Book of Psalms Translated into English Verse, by Edmund G. March, London, 1832.*" John Keble — author of " The Christian Year," which had appeared fourteen years before — published in 1839, " *The Psalter, or Psalms of David in English Verse,*" dedicated by permission to the Lord Bishop of Oxford. It took the name of the " *Oxford Psalter.*" He remarks in his Preface: " The Versions commonly used, notwithstanding much that is meritorious, are confessedly deficient each in an important qualification. That of the Elizabethan age wants force; that which dates from the Revolution fidelity. The Translator much fears that the general character of his Version will be found to partake of harshness and obscurity, to a far greater degree than he could wish; yet he is not without hope that (with the permission of those in authority) it may be found occasionally useful for congregational singing." The hope so modestly expressed was not fulfilled. His biographer, Sir J. T. Coleridge, accounts for the coolness of its reception by its deficiency in the singing quality. It reached however in England a Fourth Edition (1869). Singularly enough, it would seem hardly to have found its way to this country, and is comparatively unknown.

In SCOTLAND the first Version employed in the Churches after the Reformation was mainly that of Sternhold and Hopkins, but not exactly, for forty-one had different renderings by various authors. The first complete Version was printed at Edinburgh in 1564 by order of the General Assembly and was continued in use till 1650. It was the Psalm-book of Knox, Walsh, Melville, etc. From this sprung the Version now in use. The Westminster Assembly, in 1643, undertook the task of selecting a New Version. After comparison with other Versions it adopted that of Francis Rous (or Rouse) and appointed a committee to confer with him on changes and emendations. While Rouse's Version was made the basis, a number of translations drawn from the old Scottish Psalter and other sources were substituted for his. After much preliminary pains-taking, there appeared in 1650 " The Psalms of David in Metre: Translated and diligently compared with the Original Text and former Translations; More plain, smooth and agreeable to the Text than any heretofore; Allowed by the Authority of the General Assembly of the Kirk of Scotland, and appointed to be sung in Congregations and Families." This Version has continued in use until the present time. Dr. James Beattie, the author of *The Minstrel*, attributes to it "a manly, severe simplicity, without any affected refinement." Dr. Chalmer thinks it has "a charm peculiar to itself." Dr. Robert Lee describes it as "sometimes rugged, occasionally sinking to doggerel, but upon the whole faithful, vigorous and good — equal if not superior to any other." Sir Walter Scott says, "Its expression, though homely, is plain, forcible and intelligible, and very often possesses a rude sort of majesty which would be ill exchanged by more elegance." The Marquis of Lorne in 1877 added to this Version, a Version of his own, bound up in the same volume.

Having noticed the chief of the Complete Versions of the Psalms, it may be interesting to glance at some of the partial ones executed by distinguished hands. Sir Philip Sidney (b. 1544, d. 1586), one of the most conspicuous figures at the Court of Elizabeth, the *preux chevalier* of his time, made a Translation of a part of the Psalter "into sundry kinds of verse," in conjunction with his accomplished sister, the Countess of Pembroke—"Sidney's sister, Pembroke's mother." It extended to the 43rd Psalm. As none of Sidney's writings were published in his life-time the date of the composition is uncertain. It was first printed in London in 1823. The worth of these paraphrases, which have all the author's sincerity, directness, and sweetness of rhythm has been recognized by Mr. Ruskin who has edited them under the title of *Rock Honeycomb* in the the second volume of his *Bibliotheca Pastorum*.

In 1625, Lord Bacon published a small volume dedicated to "his friend Mr. George Herbert," entitled "*Translations of Certaine Psalms into English Verse.*" The actual number was seven, viz., Psalms 1, 12, 90, 104, 126, 137 and 149. He wrote them during a fit of sickness in 1624. He evidently thought well of them, for, contrary to custom, he lost no time in giving them to the public. He seems to have tried both methods, the literal and the free—in the one case keeping as close to the text as possible, adding no more than the necessities of metre required, in the other combining with paraphrastic freedom an exegetical purpose, representing a kind of poetical commentary.

Sir Thomas Wyatt made a paraphrase of the *Seven Penitential Psalms*. The Fourteenth and Twentieth Psalms, versified by Queen Elizabeth and King James, have been preserved.

John Milton in 1648, did into metre *nine* of the Psalms (Pss. 80-88), and in 1653, *nine* others (Pss. 1-8). At the age of fifteen he versified Psalms 114 and 136, making *twenty* in all. They continue to be published, and form a part of his Poetical Works.

Dean Swift wrote in pencil in a copy of Gibb's Poetical Version of the first eighteen Psalms, " I warn the readers that this is a lie, both here and all over the book; for these are not the Psalms of David, but of Dr. Gibb." The grounds of the Dean's furious dislike is not stated.

James Montgomery, besides being the author of numerous Hymns, published in 1822, " *Songs of Zion, being Imitations of the Psalms.*" He says in the Preface: " In the following imitations of portions of the true '*Songs of Zion*," having followed in the track of none, he would venture to hope that by avoiding the rugged literality of some and the diffusive paraphrases of others, he may, in a few instances, have approached nearer than either of them have generally done to the ideal model of what devotional poems, in a modern tongue, grounded upon the subjects of ancient Psalms, yet suited for Christian edification, ought to be."

Since the above was in type, two other complete versions have come under the writers notice: In April, 1854, the Venerable Edward Churton, Archdeacon of Cleveland, published a version known as the " *Cleveland Psalter.*" In 1882 appeared still another metrical version by William Digby Seymour, Q. C., LL. D. There are other omissions. Mr. Henry Fish discovered in the well-known handwriting of Charles Wesley, among the archives of a certain English College, translations lacking about twenty-four of the entire number of Psalms, presumably his own, but curiously enough containing Tate and Brady's rendering of Ps. 136. It forms the principal part of the *Wesleyan Psalter*, which has been published in this country. Mention should have been made likewise of "The Book of Psalms, Translated into English Verse," by George Burgess, Bishop of Maine, New York, 1840.

Richard Baxter (B. 1615, D. 1691) is said to have published a metrical version (probably of a part only) of the Psalms which was issued a year after his death. Joseph Addison (B. 1672; D. 1719), the well-known author of two much admired paraphrases of the Nineteenth and Twenty-third Psalms, is said, upon doubtful authority, to have contemplated a metrical version of the entire number, had he lived. Anne Steele (B. 1716; D. 1778), whose name has an honored place in all Modern Collections, wrote, it is said, 144 Hymns and 34 Psalms. On account of the great looseness of the language employed, one cannot always be sure what is meant, when a person is spoken of as having made a version of the Psalms, whether an entire version is intended or only a partial and fragmentary one. The writer's list includes those versions that have come under his notice; it is not pretended that it comprehends all.* The synopsis is given below of the versions, complete and partial, in chronological order:

Complete,		Partial,	
	Sternhold and Hopkins'..1562		Sir Thomas Wyatt's......1540
"	George Sandys'...........1636	"	Sir Philip Sidney's.........1583
"	Scotch Version (Rous's)..1643	"	Lord Bacon's..............1625
"	Tate and Brady's.........1696	"	John Milton's.........1648, 1653
"	John Patrick's............1698	"	Richard Baxter's...........1691
"	Isaac Watts'..............1719	"	Charles Wesley's........ ..1778
"	James Merrick's..........1765	"	Anne Steele's..............1778
"	Edmund G. Marsh's.....1832	"	James Montgomery's.....1822
"	John Keble's..............1839		
"	Bishop Burgess's.........1840		
"	Archdeacon Churton's...1854		
"	Marquis of Lorne's.......1877		
"	W. D. Seymour's.........1882		

In regard to the Version here given, 'The book must be its own

---

* It is stated that the first printing press in America was put up at Cambridge, in 1639, by Stephen Day, and the first book printed upon it was "The Psalms in Metre, faithfully translated for the use, edification and comfort of the saints, in public and private, especially in New England, printed at Cambridge in 1640." The Pilgrim Fathers entered on their records, "Stephen Day, being the first that

defense.' If all attempts, hitherto made, have, as some allege, been failures, this, at the worst, can only add one to the number. We are told by a recent writer, "Poetical translations of the Psalms postulate their own failure. Parallelisms cannot be cramped into eights and sixes."* Keble in the Preface to his own Version says: "It was undertaken with a serious apprehension, which has grown into a full conviction, that the thing attempted is, strictly speaking, *impossible.*" These strong expressions are adapted, certainly, to impress one with the great difficulty of the task, and to deter all but the most bold from ever engaging in it. But surely something can be said on the other side. The first writer quoted, admits, "that the Psalms may not only be understood but profoundly *felt*, by those who have not earned the privilege of following them in the divine original." It is fortunate that this is so, considering how small is the number who have earned this privilege. It is not at all surprising, that many should prefer the prose renderings of the Prayer Book and the Bible, on æsthetic and other grounds, for in them we have preserved the peculiar verse-structure of the Hebrew original in a great degree. Ewald compares its parallelisms to the "alternate beat of wings"; and Herder speaks of it as "that language of the heart, which has never said all, but ever has something more to say." All this is true. But it is difficult to see why the meaning, which after all is the essential thing, cannot be conveyed equally, or almost as well, in another form. In regard to Metrical Versions, imperfect as they have been, all history for the last three hundred years is full of attestations to their value and efficiency. Witness Marot's Version, which wielded such a mighty influence in bringing about the Reformation in France. Witness the Scotch

set up printing, is granted three hundred acres of land, where it may be convenient without prejudice to any town." Below is a verse of one of the Psalms in the Indian tongue, as printed for their use by Eliot in 1663:

"Kesuk Kukootumushteaumoo
God wussohsumoonk
Mamahehekesuk wumahtuhkon
Wutanakausnonk."

* *The Witness of the Psalms to Christ and Christianity, by William Alexander, D. D., D. C. L., Bishop of Derry, 1876.*

Version. No one would wish to deny the important part it has played in the religious life of the Scotch people.

And then we know that the melodious prose of the Psalter, produced about the same time as the bald rhymes of Sternhold and Hopkins' Version, was no match for them in the race for popular favor, indicating the people's preference for measured verse conjoined with rhyme, suitable for singing. It is asserted, that to so great an extent were the Reformers, singers, that 'psalm singer' and 'heretic' became synonymous terms. The term, Lollard, by some is derived from *lollen* to sing softly, whence it may be inferred, that the earlier reformers rested under the same reproach as the later. It is not wise certainly to despise an instrument of such power. Admitting that Hymn-making has been overdone, and that the Psalms have been too much neglected of late years,* and that a return to them is desirable, the question arises how can this be best

---

* Dr. Binnie, in the last edition of his work: "The Psalms: Their History, Teachings and Use," London, 1886, cites various honored names, representative of different branches of the Church, in favor of a return to the church use of the Psalms, now so generally displaced by Hymns. *Right Hon. William E. Gladstone* says: "In the Book of Psalms, for well nigh three thousand years, the piety of saints have found its most refined and choice food. . . . There is the whole music of the heart when touched by the hand of the Maker, in all its tones that whisper or that swell, for every hope and fear, for every joy and pang, for every form of strength and languor, of disquietude and rest. . . . It is a particular and privileged Book." The late *Isaac Taylor*, in his book "*The Spirit of the Hebrew Poetry*," 1861, expresses himself with great decision: "It is but feebly, and as afar off, that the ancient liturgies (except so far as they are mere copies of the original) come up to the majesty and the wide compass of the Hebrew Worship such as is indicated in the 148th Psalm. . . . It would not be possible—it has never yet seemed so—to Christianize the Hebrew anthems—retaining their power, their earth-like riches, and their manifold splendors. . . What are modern hymns but so many laborious attempts to put in a new form that which, as it was done in the very best manner so many years ago, can never be done well again." *Edward Irving*, in his "*Essay on the Book of Psalms*," says: "There has grown up in these lean years a miserable notion that the Psalms are not so appropriate for expressing the communion of the Christian Church, for the reason that they contain allusions to places and events which are of Jewish and not of Christian associations. Why do they not, upon the same principle, weed out the Jewish allusions of the Four Gospels and the Epistles? But it as poor in taste, as it is wrong in feeling, and bold in execution."

brought about. Care needs to be taken not to defer too much to the preferences, not to say prejudices of a class—scholars, for example. Because what is pleasing to them may be 'caviare to the general': and inasmuch as it is the great public whose tastes and inclinations are to decide in the matter, it is important to ascertain if possible what those are. A rhymed version in various metres, and set to proper tunes, all ideally perfect, would be likely to meet the exigency; but, alas! perfection is so rare and so difficult. The Psalms chanted do not seem well adapted for general use. It may be very delightful for me to sit and hear

> " The pealing organ blow
> To the full voiced quire below,
> In service high and anthems clear,
> As may with sweetness through my ear
> Dissolve me into ecstacies,
> And bring all heaven before my eyes,"—

but the trouble is, that all this requires skilled performers and other things. For congregational singing, it is doubtful whether anything will take the place of the Hymn, or metric Psalm. To make this more sweet and tunable should be the object of every new rendering. The writer is well aware of the imperfections of his work. He knows as well as anyone can tell him how far he falls below the ideal of what a version ought to be. His *aim* has been to be literal, but not so literal as to convert rich prose into poor verse; to be a faithful but not too punctual an interpreter; to get as close to the Hebrew Original as possible, and preserve, as far as the two idioms would allow, the precise form and color of the Hebrew thought; to transfer, wherever he could, the exact phraseology, hallowed and familiar, of the Received or Revised Version: and to use no more words than sufficed to express the meaning of the Text. By comparison he has found that his lines do not take up more than two-thirds of the space occupied by Sternhold and Hopkins' Version. The fidelity of the Scotch Version is remarkable.

He would be glad to think he has equalled it in that respect. Something is due to ease and fluency, but he would not be thought guilty of supposing that he could improve on the Inspired Original. The pedestrian Muse that is plain and simple, and is content to walk humbly with the Text, and does not try to soar above it — to be louder than the thunder, or sublimer than the storm — can claim a merit of her own, and ought not to be despised on account of her rustic qualities. Every good Version has an exegetical value, and may be the most useful of commentaries. A word to the critics. They are doubtless aware that there are disputed readings which divide learned Hebraists, and that, in comparing the Version with the Text, it is but fair that this fact should be kept in mind.

> " Great Almighty, King of Heaven!
>   And one God, in persons three;
> Honor, praise and thanks be given,
>   Now and evermore to Thee:
> Who hast more for Thine prepared,
> Than by words can be declared.
>
> " Therefore as Thy blesséd Psalmist,
>   When his warfares had an end,
> And his days were at the calmest,
>   Psalms and Hymns of praises penned —
> So my rest from Thee enjoyed,
> To Thy praise I have employed
>
> " And with Israel's royal singer,
>   Teach me so Faith's Hymns to sing;
> So Thy ten-stringed Law to finger,
>   And such music thence to bring,
> That by grace I may aspire
> To Thy blesséd angel choir."

III.— NOTES — CRITICAL, HISTORICAL, AND BIOGRAPHICAL.

THE inspired Lyrics which go to make up the Hebrew Anthology, called the Book of Psalms, are the product of different ages. They extend over a period, it is estimated, of five hundred years. The whole consist of *Five distinct Collections*, made at different times, in the order in which they now stand. Each is closed by a Doxology. Hence comes the division into FIVE BOOKS. Of the *First* Collection made (Pss. 2-41) all but three are expressly noted as David's, and these may have been his also. Of the *Second* (Pss. 42-72) seven are by the sons of Korah, a Levitical family of singers; 1 by Asaph; 19 by David; 3 writer unnamed; 1 by Solomon. Of the *Third* (Pss. 73-89) eleven are by Asaph; 4 by the sons of Korah; 1 by Ethan. Only the Eighty-sixth is ascribed to David. Of the *Fourth* (Pss. 90-106) the Ninetieth is by Moses, and the 101st and 103rd are by David. Of the *Fifth* (Pss. 107-150) fifteen are by David; 1 by Solomon; 28 writer not given. *The Pilgrim Songs* were fifteen in number (Pss. 120-134). The exact time when these Collections were made is not known. All the Psalms with only thirty-three exceptions have *Titles* or *Inscriptions* prefixed indicating the writer; or the one to whom it was committed for Temple use; or its character, as a psalm, a song, a prayer, etc.; or the occasion on which it was composed; or the tune or melody to which it was sung; or the accompanying instrument.

The Psalms have been divided into four historical periods. 1. Those written before David's accession to the throne. 2. Those during his reign. 3. Those subsequent, down to the Captivity. 4. During the Captivity, and after the Return. The moral results of David's influence as an inspired teacher of religious truth are aptly set forth in the following lines:

> " It softened men of iron mould;
> It gave them virtues not their own.
> No ear so dull, no heart so cold,
> That felt not, fired not to the tone,
> Till David's lyre grew mightier than his throne."

Herder claims, that every Psalm has an historical back-ground; and Goethe says, all good poems are called forth by an occasion. The Rev Dr. Maclaren of Manchester, England, in an interesting little volume entitled," *The Life of David as Reflected in his Psalms*," makes eloquent use of this principle. He divides his life into epochs: " His early years up to his escape from the court of Saul; his exile; the prosperous beginning of his reign; his sin and penitence; his flight before Absalom's rebellion, and the darkened end." He seeks to find out the Psalms belonging to each of these periods, and arranges them accordingly. He shows how aptly the historic dovetails with the experimental, and how the two serve to mutually illustrate and explain each other.

The shepherd boy became a king. His life therefore takes in a vast sweep — filled with strange and exciting events. But to know only these outward details is to know only half. Fortunately in his Psalms we have the other half. There was no feeling of his heart, no secret of his breast, he did not confide to his lyre. He was placed in many trying situations, and experienced many signal deliverances, and it was his wont, to punctuate each with a song. In laying his heart bare before God, he bared it to all the world. All is genuinely human. The utterances are self-evidently sincere. They are true to life, and, being so, are representative and prophetic, and have " germinant fulfilments."

David was a prophet, and spoke by Divine inspiration. He says of himself: " The Lord spoke by me, and His word was in my tongue " (2 Sam. 23 : 2). It is well for us that the prophet was also a man, even such a man, clothed with our weakness, sharing our infirmities, tempted as we are even to falling into sin. It is evidently a mistake to conceive of him as dwelling always in the light of a superior knowledge, speaking at all times with an infallible utterance qualified by no ignorance — for, outside of a special illumination for a special purpose, we have every reason to believe that he was left as much in the dark as we are. If the Bible had been written by angelic pen, it is doubtful whether it would have been of much use to us.

While an extended commentary would be out of place, a few brief

Notes, chiefly explanatory, it is hoped may be useful. Moreover, in view of the important part which the Psalms have played in History and the Lives of men, a collection of the scattered facts, illustrative of the truth of this, is adapted to form a chapter of much interest.

Ruskin says, The Psalter contains in the first half of it, the sum of personal and social wisdom. The 1st, 8th, 14th, 19th, 23rd and 24th Psalms, well learned and believed, are enough for all personal guidance; the 48th, 72nd, and 75th have in them the law and the prophecy of all righteous government; and every real triumph of natural science is anticipated in the 104th.

PSALM I.—It could not have been by accident, that this Psalm was placed first in the Collection, for it is evidently prefatory and exordial. It sums the whole. The doctrine it emphasizes is the doctrine of the whole. The very first word stirs the heart like a trumpet. It is the swift glad answer to the question of questions, which everybody is asking: Who is happy? Where is happiness to be found? The Porch undertook to locate and define it, but failed. It was and is, Philosophy's despair. Poetry apostrophizes to no purpose. "O Happiness, our being's end and aim." Riches says, It is not in me. Honor says, It is not in me. Learning says, It is not in me. Pleasure says, It is not in me. Where is it then? Where, O where? Echo answers, Where? Some call the proud, happy. Are they so? No! Vanity of vanities, saith the Preacher. Here the true word breaks in like a burst of sunshine. Inquire no farther. The Happy Man is the Righteous Man; and no other. Should you wish an answer more in detail, the introductory verses of the Sermon on the Mount, will give it you. Righteousness is the soul's health. Carlyle says truly: "A healthy body is good; but a soul in right health — it is the thing above all others to be prayed for; the blessedest thing this earth receives of Heaven." Never was there a Preface so brief that contained so much as this First Psalm.

PSALM II—Stands at the head of the objective Messianic Psalms to which the Forty-fifth and the One Hundred and Tenth also belong. Four speakers are introduced, indicating its dramatic character. 1. The rebels; 2. Jehovah; 3. The Anointed; 4. The Psalmist. For its Messianic application, see Acts 4: 24-30.

PSALM III·—The historic occasion was David's flight before his son Absalom (2 Sam. 15: 14, 17, 30).

Ver. 3. *My glory and the lifter up of my head.* One might almost think that Horace had borrowed from David, when he compliments Macenas as " his patron and sweet glory " — *O et præsidium et dulce decus meum.*

" The French Protestants in the time of their persecution had psalms adapted to their varied circumstances. The Third Psalm was for the stationing of sentinels to keep watch against sudden attack; when the danger was over, and they could worship in safety, they sung the 122nd."—*Rev. John Ker, D. D.*

PSALM IV.—Relates to Absalom's revolt. By "the sons of men ' [man] would be meant the leaders of the conspiracy against David's kingly right, or "glory," who had been especially "set apart" by God as His "favored" or "beloved * one," (for so the term "godly" may be rendered). They are counselled "to stand in awe and sin (rebel) no more;" and revolving silently and alone their guilt and folly, repent and return to their allegiance. The desponding inquiry, "Who will show us good?" indicates the gloominess of the outlook, but the Psalmist was buoyed up with a pious confidence which filled him with joy and peace.

It was a rule in the Syrian Churches, that no person could be ordained sub-deacon until he had learned the Psalter by heart. Jerome mentions, that he had learned the Psalms when he was a child, and sang them constantly in old age. In the first centuries of the Chris-

* Maclaren thinks, "It was prophetic instinct which made Jesse call his youngest son by a name, apparently before unused — David, (Beloved) ".

tian Church, the Psalms were in general use. *Augustine*, born in 354, was converted when he was in his 33d year, under the preaching of Ambrose, Bishop of Milan. In his "Confessions" referring to this period, he exclaims, "O, in what accents spake I unto Thee, my God, when I read the Psalms of David." He makes mention of the *Fourth Psalm* in particular. The subject of his " Enarrations," (a kind of running commentary) was the Psalms. His custom was to embrace an entire Psalm in one discourse. He was ignorant of Hebrew, and allegorized too much, but his " Enarrations" were read and prized for a thousand years.

PSALM V.—Joab, prompted by jealousy, assassinated Abner (2 Sam. 3: 27), and subsequently his rival, Amasa, (2 Sam. 20: 10). David complains that although King, " the sons of Zeruiah are too hard for me." Joab is the probable subject of the bitter reference in verse 5, where he is called "the bloody and deceitful man"—and other parts of the Psalm would seem to apply to him.

PSALM VI, Verse 3.—"But Thou, O Lord, how long?" In its Latin form, *Domine, quousque?* it is said to have been the favorite ejaculation of Calvin in times of suffering, and especially of painful sickness. This is the first of the so-called PENITENTIAL PSALMS. The other six are the 32d, 38th, 51st, 102d, 130th, and 143d.

Dr. Philip Schaff, in his " History of the Christian Church" (Vol. III, p, 905) says of *St. Augustine;* " The last ten days of his life he spent in close retirement—in prayers and tears, and repeated readings of the *Penitential Psalms*, which he had caused to be written on the wall over his bed, so that he might have them always before his eyes. He closed his life 25th August, 430, in the 76th year of his age in the full possession of his faculties."

Strangely enough, *Catherine de Medici*, the queen mother of Charles IX, the prompter, and real author of the Massacre of St. Bartholomew, which numbered fifty thousand victims—chose this Psalm to give expression to her worldly disappointment.

The Wife of Thomas Carlyle, sick in body and mind, gives vent to her feelings in language drawn from this Psalm, entering in her

Journal, 1855, verses 2-4: "Ah, me! 'Have mercy upon me, O Lord, heal me, for my bones are sore vexed, my soul is also sore vexed: but Thou, O Lord, how long?'" In the sketch of his wife's history, written three years after his wife's death, Carlyle relates, how, about the above-named time (1855 or 1856), "The sufferings of our poor little woman, which must have been great, though she whispered nothing of them, reached their nadir—internal sufferings and dispiritments. To whatever owing, my little darling was extremely miserable! Of that year there is a bit of private diary by chance left unburnt, and not to be destroyed, however tragical and sternly sad are parts of it." See *Carlyle's Reminiscences, by Froude.*

PSALM IX.—Furnishes an example of what may be called *topical parallelism*, after the Hebrew manner. There is a division of the Psalm into two parts, with an orderly *repetition of topics* in the second part. The whole Psalm is a review of God's gracious dealings in driving back the invading heathen A grateful acknowledgment of former deliverances (vs. 1-6) is followed by expressions of trust in regard to the future (vs. 7-12) with consequent petitions (vs. 13, 14): then there is a return to the same topics, the same recollections of the past, anticipations of the future, and prayers for present and immediate help.

Five scholars of Lausanne devoted to the Reformation were arrested in France, 1553, and burned in the Place des Terreaux at Lyons. On their way to execution they sung with a loud voice this Psalm.—*Ker.*

PSALM X.—The character here drawn answers in so many respects to Joab that it is difficult not to believe that David had him in his eye as a typical case of audacious wickedness.

PSALM XI.—Is somewhat dramatic in form like Psalm 2d. The advice of faint-hearted friends to fly (vs. 1-6) is followed by a passionate rejection of the counsel as a wicked distrust of God.

PSALM XII, Ver. 5.—"*For the oppression of the poor,*" etc., was the text of Dr. Fabricius before Gustavus Adolphus, when he took Augsburg after a severe fight. A solemn thanksgiving was held in the principal church, and religious liberty was proclaimed, while the ferocious Tilly, after his defeat retired, breathing out threatening and slaughter.—*Ker.*

PSALM XV.—Professor Wilson (Christopher North) in his "Lights and Shadows of Scottish Life," in describing the affecting scene of the Elder's death-bed, tells us, the minister took the Family Bible, and kneeling, said: "Let us sing to the praise and glory of God a part of the *Fifteenth Psalm*, and he read with a tremulous and broken voice those beautiful verses:

> "Within thy tabernacle, Lord,
> Who shall abide with thee ?
> And in thy high and holy hill
> Who shall a dweller be?" etc.

PSALM XVI, Vers. 2, 3.—"*My goodness extendeth not to Thee, but to the saints.*" Later versions from the Hebrew differ from the A. V. and each other. That reading has been adopted that seemed most plausible. Ver. 4, "*Hasten after*" is more exactly rendered *wedded* or *united* to another God.

This Psalm was the last Scripture read by *Hugh M'Kail* the evening before his execution in the Grassmarket of Edinburgh. He was a young man of fervid nature, with much ability and culture, was educated at the University of Edinburgh and in Holland, and was licensed to preach at the time of the treacherous overturn of the Constitution of the Church of Scotland, by Charles II, Middleton and Sharp. His last sermon was preached while 400 Presbyterian ministers were being driven from their churches, Sept. 8, 1662 He is the chief figure in a pen-picture of the Covenanters by Sir Walter Scott.—*Ker.*

PSALM XVII, is full of passionate appeal, alternations of hope and fear. Vs. 14, 15 are worthy of the New Testament.

Alexander Hume, of Hume, closed his life, singing the last verse (Scotch version) of this Psalm. His death was one of the most cruel murders of the time.—*Ker*.

PSALM XVIII.—For another copy of this Psalm see 2 Sam. XXII. Of the two copies, this is supposed to have been the earlier, and to have been composed by David in his youth. Revised by him in his later days, he sent it to the chief musician in its slightly altered form. The rabbins reckon up seventy-four differences between the two, but they are very minute. It is admitted that there is nothing grander in Poetry than this Psalm. Grand in many ways, it is grandest in its motive. It is the flashing splendor of the underlying thought which dazzles and amazes. The majesty of the scene does not consist so much in the material concomitants, the tempestuous terror and pomp of the descent, as in its moral purpose. Take this away, and there remains, to be sure, a magnificent description of a thunder storm, distinguished by bold metaphor and striking diction, but that is all. To appreciate its unparalleled sublimity, we need to raise ourselves to the height of the poet's great argument, and conceive the Deity, as the Supreme Judge and Ruler of the Universe, coming forth in person, and putting in operation this unspeakable machinery of terror, just because Right had been struck down in the person of his servant, and a cry has risen to Him for help and deliverance. What gave effect to the cry, was not the dignity of the suppliant, for God is no respecter of persons. "The poor man cried, and he also was delivered." So dear, in fact, is Right to the heart of God, so essential is it to the stability of His throne, that, if it were necessary, He would summon from the farthest limits of His empire, the requisite powers for its enforcement and vindication in behalf of the meanest of his subjects.

For He makes every just cause His own. This He does from a necessity of His being. Well it is so. If a just God is dreadful, what a horror would be a God not just! God cannot be just without being good; nor good without being merciful. Goodness comprehends both Justice and Mercy. One regulates the other. Shakespeare is warranted, therefore, in saying that Mercy is

> "An attribute to God Himself;
> And earthly power doth then show likest God's,
> When Mercy seasons Justice."

God's Government is paternal. He loves, and pities, and punishes. To the merciful He will show Himself merciful; to the upright he will show Himself upright; to the pure He will show Himself pure. (Vers. 25, 26)—

> "So dear to Heaven is saintly Chastity,
> That when a soul is found sincerely so,
> A thousand liveried angels lacky her."

Love Virtue !—

> "She can teach you how to climb
> Higher than the sphery chime;
> Or if Virtue feeble were,
> Heaven itself would stoop to her."

The words, from vers. 17-19, were sung upon the scaffold by four sons of the Huguenots. They were the last martyrs of the Desert—who suffered as late as 1762, under the reign of Louis XV. Near to Nismes, in a solitary spot, there is to be seen the Cave where the assemblies of the Desert were held. At Aignes-Mortes is the Tower of Constance, which served as a prison for the Protestant ladies who refused conversion to Catholicism. Some remained nearly forty years in this sepulchre without seeing or hearing from a friend.— *Ker.*

PSALM XIX.—There are two voices—one inaudible—declaring the *glory* of God, the other audible, declaring His *will*. It forms a fit companion piece to Psalm VIII. We have thus a day-piece, and a night-piece by the same hand. The pastoral life is favorable to meditation. Spent in the open air, all natural sights and sounds grow familiar. David in both Psalms recalls the peaceful time, when, a shepherd lad, already skilled in the use of his rustic lyre, and accustomed to give vent to his pious rapture in holy song, he lay on summer nights on the pleasant hill-sides of Bethlehem watching his flock and, looking up, saw "the heavens sowed with stars, thick as a field;" and as the night wore away saw the grey dawn, and the kindling fires of day-break, till, all at once, the sun, the regent of day, shot suddenly up from behind the mountains of Moab—

> " Jocund to sun
> His longitude through heaven's high road."

PSALM XX.—Is an expression of loyal attachment to David, the sovereign, by the army. Dr. Maclaren thinks it may have been connected with David's organization of "the service of song." He imagines the army drawn up for action, that prays for the king; who, according to custom, brings sacrifices and offerings before the fight. Then, as they wave their banners, they send up the shout, " In the name of our God we will set up our banners!" Then the king speaks, rejoicing in his soldiers' devotion, and accepts it as an omen that his sacrifice has not been in vain. " Now I know Jehovah saveth His anointed." Then the chorus of the host exclaims, as they look across the field to the chariots and cavalry of the foe (forces which Israel seldom used), "Some trust in chariots and some in horses, but we will remember the name of the Lord our God." Ere a sword is drawn, they see the enemy scattered. " They are brought down and fallen, but we stand upright." Then with the prayer, " Jehovah, save! let the king hear us when we call," they dash forth to victory.

PSALM XXI—This Psalm, it is said, was sung as a Coronation Ode throughout England by the overtrustful Presbyterians at the restoration of Charles II.

PSALM XXII.—This is *by* David but surely not *of* David. It only then becomes intelligible, when it is accepted as a prophecy of a suffering Messiah. It is not inaptly called by Spurgeon, *The Psalm of the Cross*.

PSALM XXIII.—The tranquilizing effect of this sweetest of all Pastorals, compared with which all others that were ever written are puerile and poor, is felt by every reader. It deserves to be set to some heavenly tune by some angelic composer, for no

> "Inferior hand or voice could hit
> Inimitable sounds."

For want of this let it be sung only to ideal music—

> "Heard melodies are sweet, but those unheard
> Are sweeter; therefore, ye soft pipes, play on,
> Not to the sensual ear, but, more endeared,
> Pipe to the spirit ditties of no tone."

Sir Charles Bell arrived at the seat of Mr. Holland, Hallow Park, on the 27th of May, 1842. He was apparently in good health, but suffered from heart-disease (Angina pectoris). One or two recent attacks of "anguish of the chest" had made him more than usually awake to the associations which the quiet churchyard might naturally prompt. He spent some pleasant hours in sketching the beauties of the scenery. "This is a sweet spot," he said, "here I should like to rest till they come to take me away." During the evening he descanted upon that masterpiece of art, the "Last Supper," of Leonardo da Vinci, an engraving of which lay before him, and repeated the passage from the Gospel. After retiring, as was his wont, selections from the Scriptures and the Prayer Book were read to him, and he chose the *Twenty-third Psalm*. After a few hours of sleep he awoke with a frightful spasm, asked to be supported, and immediately expired.—*Quarterly Review*.

When *Edward Irving* was on his death-bed he repeated the 23d Psalm in Hebrew. Ver. 4, *Thy rod and Thy staff they comfort me*, were the dying words of the great Scottish philosopher, *Sir William Hamilton*. When *Dr. Alexander Duff*, the Indian Missionary, lay dying, and apparently unconscious (Feb., 1878) his daughter repeated to him the *Twenty-third Psalm*, and he responded at the end of each verse.

Heinrich Heine, who had been a pantheist and scoffer, was laid for years on what he called his *mattress sepulchre*, and took to reading the Bible, especially the Psalms. One of the very last of his poems addressed to his wife, bears traces of this *Twenty-third Psalm*. It begins thus—

> " My arm grows weak: Death comes apace,
> Death pale and grim; and I no more
> Can guard my lamb as heretofore.
> O God! unto Thy hands I render
> My crook; keep my lambkins tender,
> When I in peace have laid me down
> Keep Thou my lamb, and do not let
> A single thorn her bosom fret,
> And guide where pastures green and sweet
> Refresh the wanderer's weary feet."—*Ker*.

PSALM XXIV is divided into two portions: the first half replies to the question, "*Who shall ascend the Hill of the Lord, and who shall stand in His Holy Place?*" The second half deals with the inquiry, "*Who is the King of Glory?*" It is regarded as a Processional Hymn, of choral structure. The first half was to be sung during the ascent to City of David, the second while standing before the Gates, responsive singing attending the march, the Levites bearing the Ark, and the multitude streaming after.

Philip Melancthon, when dying, caused to be read the *Twenty-fourth*, Twenty-fifth and Twenty-sixth Psalms, the 53d of Isaiah, 7th of John and 5th Romans. * * Upon being asked by his son-in-law if he would have anything else, he replied: "ALIUD NIHIL—NISI CŒLUM!"—*Nothing else—but Heaven!* At a quarter of an hour before seven o'clock, 9th April, 1560, at the age of 63, he gently breathed his last.—*Dr. F. A. Cox's Life of Philip Melancthon.*

We learn from Ranke's "History of the Popes," that during the later sittings of the Council of Trent, in 1562, the subject of congregational psalmody, and the administration of the sacraments in the mother-tongue was brought up by the representatives of the Emperor Charles V, and the King of France. The proposition, urged by the Cardinal of Lorraine and the French Prelates, "that the Psalms may be allowed to be sung in the French language in full congregation," was rejected. The inhibition continued until the Edict of Nantes, 1598, authorizing Protestant worship at Paris and elsewhere. In that year

INTRODUCTION. xli

Catherine of Navarre, assembled a large company in the Palace of the Louvre, on which occasion the Psalm first sung was the *Twenty-Fourth Psalm*.

PSALM XXVI.—Louis XIV, the dupe of a cruel and mistaken policy, where the blunder was as conspicuous as the crime, had through long years harried and oppressed his Huguenot subjects. Then came the infamy of the dragonades. The cavalry (dragoons) took possession of the southern provinces, and established their quarters in the dwellings of the Huguenots. These booted missionaries devoured their substance, but made few converts. At last came the Revocation of the Edict of Nantes, Oct. 22, 1685. The religious worship of the Calvinists was now forbidden; their churches were torn down; their schools closed; and their preachers banished from the land. When the emigration of the people increased to a formidable degree, this was forbidden under punishment of the galleys and the forfeiture of goods. But despite all threats and prohibitions, upwards of 500,000 French Calvinists carried their industry, their faith and their courage to Protestant lands. Pineton, of Chambrun, one of these exiles, relates, that when he and his companions came in sight of Geneva, they sang with tears of joy the *Twenty-sixth Psalm*, from the eighth verse to the close.

PSALM XXIX.—We have here another marvelous description of a thunderstorm. Having its starting point somewhere on the Mediterranean, it sweeps with irresistible force, whirling and smiting, over the length and breadth of the Land, from Lebanon and Sirion (Herman) on the north, to the wilderness of Kadish (Petra) on the south. Poetry can no further go. But, like the *Eighteenth Psalm*, it owes its awful and unequalled sublimity less to the storm than to God, who is present in the storm. We forget the storm, and think only of Him. It is God we see and hear. Great masses of cloud, black as night, charged with tempestuous winds, lightning and rain— are seen coming up from the sea, now agitated to its lowest depths, and rolling great waves towards the shore. The crash of thunder, peal after peal, is heard. It is God speaking. "The voice of the

Lord is on the waters ; the God of glory thundereth; the Lord is on many waters." The air thickens; the blackness spreads; the path of the cyclone is strewed with a thousand wrecks. "It breaks the cedars of Lebanon, yea, the Lord breaketh the cedars of Lebanon." The mountain itself is made to rock—"to skip like a calf, Lebanon and Sirion like a young unicorn." The voice of the Lord forks the lightning—"divideth the flames of fire." Meanwhile, two hundred miles away in the far south, "The voice of the Lord shaketh the wilderness, the Lord shaketh the wilderness of Kadish; the voice of the Lord maketh the hinds to bring forth prematurely, and strips the forests." All at once we hear countless voices out of the clouds and above them, shouting Glory! Glory! and a fearless child lying in a sheltered nook, a delighted witness of the spectacle

> " Of the most terrible and nimble stroke
> Of quick, cross-lightning;"

claps hands, and cries, bonnie! bonnie! and we too, borne upward by the ecstacy of the hour, join the "mighty ones," invoked in the beginning, in ascribing to the Lord the glory due unto His Name— unalterably assured, that He "who sat enthroned at the Flood, and sitteth King forever," serene and calm, "will bless the people with peace." Milton knew of this description—he could hardly have hoped to rival it:

> " And either tropic now
> 'Gan thunder, and both ends of heaven: the clouds
> From many a horrid rift, abortive poured
> Fierce rain with lightning mixed, water mixed with fire,
> In ruin reconciled, nor slept the winds
> Within their stony caves, but rushed abroad
> From the four hinges of the world, and fell
> On the vexed wilderness, whose tallest pines,
> Though rooted deep as high, and sturdiest oaks
> Bowed their stiff necks, loaden with stormy blasts,
> Or torn up sheer."
>
> —*Paradise Regained, B. IV., l. 409-419*

PSALM XXX.—Among those who suffered in the Netherlands during the first governorship of the cruel Alva was *John Herwin*. At the place of execution he sang the *Thirtieth Psalm*. He was first strangled and then burned to ashes. Ver. 5 was among the latest sayings of *Rev. John Brown*, the commentator.—*Ker*.

PSALM XXXI.—Verse 5, "*Into Thine hand I commit my spirit. Thou hast redeemed me, O Lord God of truth;*" or as we have it in the Latin Vulgate, *In manus tuas, commendo spiritum meum: redimisti nos, Domine, Deus veritatis.* These words (the first part at least) were the last spoken by our Lord on the Cross. The first martyr, Stephen, addressed them to the Lord Jesus during his stoning; and many Christian martyrs since have breathed confidently the same words, at the stake and on the scaffold. In the private chamber too,

> "When unto dying eyes
> The casement slowly grows a glimmering square,"

has taken place the same solemn committment of his spirit by this and that good man, distinguished for important services rendered to mankind—

> "He gave his honors to the world again,
> His blessed part to heaven, and slept in peace."

Doubtless,
> "'T is a vile thing to die,
> When men are unprepared, and look not for it "—

(We quote by preference, from the poets rather than the preacher). Shakespeare says further of death:

> "Thou know'st 'tis common; all that live must die,
> Passing through nature to eternity." . . .
> "Why, what is pomp, rule. reign, but earth and dust,
> And, live we how can, yet die we must."

Another poet moralizes:

> "The glories of our birth and state
>   Are shadows, not substantial things;
>   There is no armor against fate—
>   Death lays his icy hands on kings; * * *
>   All heads must come
>   To the cold tomb—
>   Only the actions of the just
>   Smell sweet and blossom from the dust."

"The Last Words of Eminent Persons" are always invested with melancholy interest. It has often happened, that men, not known to be devout, when brought (unexpectedly, it may be) face to face with death, have not been ashamed to make an open avowal of their secret belief in the reality of religion by a cry for mercy, and a commending of their soul to the Christian's God. However we may wish the cry had been made earlier, and been clear from all suspicion of superstitious fear, we are bound to respect it always as something inexpressibly pathetic. Because of their appropriateness, the words of our text have been more frequently used perhaps than any others. We have room only for a few names.

John Huss was burned alive, July, 1415. When he came to the stake, he threw himself upon his knees and prayed: "*Into thy hands, O Lord, I commit my spirit. Thou hast redeemed me.*"

Christopher Columbus was born at Genoa, 1445-6, and died at Valladolid, May 20th, 1506, aged 70, worn out by neglect, poverty and disease. His last words were, "*In manus tuas, commendo spiritum meum: redimisti nos, Domine Deus veritatis. — Irving's Life of Columbus.*

Lady Jane Grey, beautiful, accomplished and good, who was executed 1554, at the age of 17, a victim to the rashness and ambition of her misguided parents, uttered these words as she laid her neck on the block.

The same prayer is attributed to *Mary Queen of Scots*, just before she was beheaded, February 8, 1557.

Francis Quarles (B. 1592; D. 1644) when dying, spake in Latin to this effect: O sweet Saviour of the World, let Thy last words upon the cross be my last words in the world—Into Thy hands, Lord, I commend my spirit.—*Clissold's "Last Hours of Christian Men."*

It is told of the *Emperor Charles V* (Charles I of Spain, B. at Ghent, 1500; D. 1558), that, having had mock funerals performed in behalf of his father, mother and wife, long dead, each on a different day, at which he attended, preceded by a page bearing a taper, and joining in the chant in a very devout manner out of a tattered prayer-book, he asked his confessor whether he might not now perform his own funeral—in other words, whether it would not be good for his own soul. The monk said it certainly would; and on the following day, the 30th August, as the monkish historian relates, this celebrated service was actually performed. The high altar, the catafalque, and the whole church shone with a blaze of wax lights; the friars were all in their places, at the altars and in the choir, and the household of the emperor attended in deep mourning. The pious monarch was there, attired in sable weeds, and bearing a taper, to see himself interred, and to celebrate his own obsequies. While the solemn mass for the dead was sung, he came forward, and gave his taper into the hands of the officiating priest in token of his desire to yield his soul into the hands of his Maker. The funeral rites ended, the emperor dined in his western alcove. [One cannot help feeling that there is something very grotesque and ghastly in this acting one's own funeral, so much so, as to suggest the existence of a taint of insanity.]

Three weeks afterward, on September 20th, he had been attended by his confessor and by the preacher Villalva all the previous night, who frequently read aloud at his request, passages from Scripture— usually from the Psalms—his favorite one being Psalm XC. He asked for the eucharist. Having had great difficulty in swallowing the sacred morsel, he opened his mouth and made Quixada see if it had all gone down. It spite of his extreme weakness, he followed all the responses as usual, and repeated with great fervor the whole verse, *In manus tuas, commendo spiritum meum: redemisti nos, Domine, Deus veritatis.* The clock had just struck two when he expired.— *Sterling's " Cloister Life of the Emperor Charles V."*

Motley, in his History of " The Rise of the Dutch Republic," relates, that on June 3, 1568, *Counts Egmont and Horn* were brought from Ghent to Brussels, and lodged in the Broodhuis. On the 4th, the Duke of Alva pronounced sentence against both on an unsupported charge of high treason. The Countess of Egmont hearing of the sentence fell at the Duke's feet, and implored mercy for her husband. He, with heartless and incredible irony, reassured her that on the morrow he should be *released.* The Count, when informed that his death was to take place in the morning, expressed great surprise and indignation at the cruel and unjust sentence. On his way to execution he read aloud the *Fifty-first Psalm.* Having ascended the scaffold he said the Lord's Prayer. Kneeling upon the cushion he drew a little cap over his eyes, and folding his hands together, cried with a loud voice, "*Lord, into thy hands I commit my spirit.*" The executioner then severed his head from his body at one stroke. A moment of shuddering silence succeeded. A dark cloth was now quickly thrown over the body and the blood; and, within a few minutes, the *Admiral, Count Horn*, was seen advancing, his bald head uncovered, and his hands unbound. He calmly saluted each of his acquaintances. Casting his eyes upon the corpse, he asked if it was the body of Egmont. He did not kiss the crucifix, but knelt upon the scaffold to pray. Then drawing a Milan cap completely over his face, uttered in Latin, the same invocation that Egmont had used, *In manus tuas,* etc., and submitted his neck to the stroke.

Froude, in his "History of England," gives this account of the execution of *Anne Boyelin,* in 1536. The queen walked firmly to the front of the block. When the few preparations were completed, she turned to the spectators, and said: "Christian people, I am come to die. And according to law, and by law, I am judged to death; and therefore I will speak nothing against it. I am come here to accuse no man, nor to speak anything of that whereof I am accused and condemned to die. * * Thus I take my leave of the world and of you; and I heartily desire you all to pray for me. O, Lord, have mercy on me. *To God I commend my soul!*" These words, says Stowe, "she spoke with a smiling countenance," which done, she kneeled down on both her knees, and said: " *To Jesus Christ I commend my soul;*" and with that word the hangman of Calais smote off her head at one stroke with a sword. Her body, with the head, was buried in the quire of the chapel.

Lord Thomas Cromwell, B. 1490, D. 1540. The concluding part of his last prayer was in these words: "Grant, merciful Savior, that when death hath taken away the use of my tongue, yet my heart may cry and say unto Thee, *Lord, into thy hands I commend my soul. Lord Jesus receive my spirit. Amen.*" With these words on his lips he was beheaded.

George Wishart was executed for heresy March 1st, 1546. He was led to the fire, with a rope about his neck, and a chain of iron about his middle. When he came to the fire, he said these words thrice: "Oh, thou Savior of the world, have mercy upon me. Father of Heaven, *I commend my spirit into thy hands.*" He was put upon a gibbet and hanged, and then burnt."—*Froude's History of England.*

In Michelet's *Life of Luther*, we read, that he arrived at Eisleben, the 28th January, and though already ill, joined in all the conferences until the 17th February, when he was too ill to go out. At supper he spoke much of his approaching end; and some one asking him if he thought we should recognize each other in the other world, he rejoined that he thought so. On returning to his chamber, he slept without waking for an hour and a half. It was now eleven o'clock. When he awoke he said to those in attendance, "What, still sitting up by me; why do you not go to rest yourselves?" He then commenced praying, and said with fervor, "*In manus tuas,*" etc. Later he repeated three times following, "*In manus tuas,*" etc. Suddenly his eyes closed and he fainted. Soon after he expired. He was born 1484 and died 1546.

Monday, Nov. 24th, 1572, was the last day that *John Knox* spent on earth. His biographer, Dr. M'Crie, tells us: "In the afternoon he desired his wife to read the 15th Chapter of First Corinthians. 'Is not that a comfortable chapter?' said he, when it was finished. 'O, what sweet and salutary consolation the Lord hath afforded me from that chapter.' A little after he said, 'Now, for the last time, *I commend my soul, spirit and body*, (touching three of his fingers), *into thy hands, O Lord!*' About eleven o'clock he expired, without a struggle. On Wednesday, Nov. 26th, he was interred in the churchyard of St. Giles. The regent pronounced his eulogium in these emphatic words, 'There lies he who never feared the face of man.'"

Torquato Tasso, was born at Sorrento, 1544, died at Rome, 1595, on the evening of the intended ceremony of crowning him Prince of Poets, by Pope Clement VIII, who was a great admirer of his genius. A contemporary account states that, his end drawing near, no one was admitted to his chamber, except his confessor, and some fathers of approved learning and sanctity, who sung Psalms, one with another, Tasso joining in so far as his failing breath would allow. So he remained all night till the next day, when feeling himself giving way, he began to chant the words, *In manus tuas*, etc., but had not strength to finish the verse.—*Milman's Life of Tasso.*

PSALM XXXII.—This is the second of the *Penitential Psalms*. No leaf from the book of David's experience, all blotted as it is with tears, is so fraught with comfort as this. It shows that the Evangel of the Old Testament, if less clear in its utterances as to the justifying reasons and grounds of the grace, differs in no essential respect from the Evangel of the New. We have here in David a typical exemplification of the possibilities of remedial mercy — the blessed freeness of Divine forgiveness in a real case, and the one method set forth of obtaining pardon. Here is one, who had been raised to a bright eminence above all men of his time, 'the observed of all observers,' 'the cynosure of neighboring eyes,' the anointed head of the Theocracy, and representative of the True Religion

"Into what pit thou seest,
From what height fallen."

It has been well said, "Nobody pays for a little pleasure in evil at so dear a rate, or keeps it for so short a time, as a good man." In such an one Conscience is a terrible power. There is no peace for him night nor day. His mind is "filled with scorpions," condemned

"Upon the torture of the mind to lie
In restless ecstacy."

When David says: "While I kept silence, my bones waxed old, through my roaring all the day long," he only tells us what we know must have been. But when he said, "I will confess my transgression unto the Lord," forgiveness followed—the word of healing. O, the blessedness of it. For this shall everyone to the end of time pray, and seek the Lord while He may be found. No doubt this Psalm was written later than the 51st.

PSALM XXXIII.—Vers. 16, 17, seem to point to a deliverance from some formidable heathen power that employed cavalry.

PSALM XXXIV.—This is one of the Alphabetical Psalms, and, like the rest, didactic in character.—See Notes to Ps. 37 and 119.

During the middle ages the copying of the Psalter was a favorite employment in the religious houses. *St. Columba*, who had spent a long life in incessant labors among the Celtic and Gothic tribes, occupied his leisure hours in his beloved Iona in multiplying copies of the Psalms. His biographer relates, that the day on which he died, June 9, 597, he was at work on the *Thirty-fourth Psalm*, and had got as far as the tenth verse, "The young lions do lack and suffer hunger; but they that seek the Lord shall not want any good thing.'

PSALM XXXV.—Ver. 15, "*In my adversity*," *i. e.*, "in my sickness, or when I was taken ill."

PSALM XXXVII.—An Alphabetical Psalm. See Note. Paul Gerhardt's widely known and admired Hymn, "*Befiehl du deine Wege*" is founded on the fifth verse: "*Commit thy way unto the Lord; trust also in Him; and He shall bring it to pass.*" It was first printed in 1656. John Wesley's translation, consisting of sixteen verses, is well-known; and as a part or as a whole, may be found in most of our modern Hymn Books:

> " Commit thou all thy griefs,
> And ways into His hands.
> To His sure trust and tender care,
> Who earth and heaven commands."

Gerhardt composed, it is said, 133 Hymns. A large number have been translated into English verse by John Wesley and others. The singing of his hymns as well as Luther's, was a powerful means of advancing the Reformation.

The first Lutheran Church in Philadelphia was opened in 1743, with Gerhardt's Hymn.

Robert Baillie, says Dr. Ker, was condemned to death at Edinburgh, Dec. 24, 1648. He was the great grandson of John Knox, was called the Scottish Sidney, and was feared and hated by the Government of the time for his religious and political opinions, though no unlawful act could be laid to his charge. The evening before his execution he bade his son to trust in the testimony of the Psalmist (Ps. 37: 25). "I have been young, and now am old, yet have I not seen the righteous forsaken, nor his seed begging bread." The son proved worthy of his father, rose to high office in the State after the Revolution; and the descendents of Robert Baillie are found among some of the noblest families of the kingdom.

PSALM XXXIX.—Ewald speaks of this Psalm as "The most beautiful of all the elegies of the Psalter."

PSALM XLII.—Lord Fairfax (B. 1611; D. 1671) was attacked by a fever which carried him off in a few days. The last morning of his life he called for a Bible, and read the *Forty-second* Psalm.—" *The Book of Death.*"

PSALM XLVI.—This forms the basis of Luther's celebrated Hymn, *Ein' feste Burg ist unser Gott*, "A safe stronghold our God is still," which was written in 1529, in a time of darkest peril. Some one has called it 'Luther in Song,' the rugged and fit embodiment of one 'whose words were half battles.' It was a recruiting energy of immense efficiency during the whole progress of the Reformation. It made brave men braver. It ennobled service and sacrifice. It rendered the faint-hearted, fearless, unflinching and invincible—lifted them up to the height of heroes and martyrs, fighting or suffering. Each soldier, as he sang it, felt his heart leap. It taught him, that if life was dear, there were other things still dearer—that a pure doctrine and worship were well worth dying for; that the way to gain life was to be willing to lose it.

Crusades for the recovery of the Holy Sepulchre belonged to the past. Unnumbered lives and incalculable treasure had, once upon a time, been sacrificed in a frenzied struggle for the possession of an empty tomb. No higher honor, no greater merit could be imagined than to have

> " Fought
> For Jesu Christ, in glorious Christian field,
> Streaming the ensign of the Christian cross,
> Against black Pagans, Turks and Saracens."

Here is a returned knight of whom it is told, that

> " Worn out with works of war, retired himself
> To Italy, and there at Venice gave
> His body to that pleasant country's earth,
> And his pure soul unto his Captain, Christ,
> Under whose colors he had fought so long."

But times had changed, and worthier objects claimed the attention of men. It was not now the possession of the Holy Sepulchre, but the possession of the Holy Scriptures which was the great point of dispute—the *casus belli* that split the nations into hostile camps. The train was all laid, waiting for the electric spark, which this Lyric of Luther partly supplied, and the effect was proportionate. Heine called it the *Marseillaise* of the Reformation.

Before the battle of Leipsic, September 17, 1631, under the orders of Gustavus Adolphus, the whole army, drawn up in battle array, sung this Hymn of Luther; and after the victory, he thanked God, that the assurance of the concluding line of the second verse, ' Shall conquer in the battle,' was made good. The Hymn was again sung before his last fight at Lützen with Wallenstein, in which, though successful, he was mortally wounded.

PSALM LI, is the third of the *Penitential Psalms*, and is known as the "*Miserere*," this being the initial word in the Latin Version of the Psalm: *Miserere mei, Deus,* "Have mercy upon me, O God." Here is a cry for mercy that has gone, and is going up, continually, from innumerable death-beds. No one has a right to brand it as weak or cowardly. It is admitted that there is a fear of death, which is simply instinctive and common to all animals, and that if this were all, it were nothing. But, indisputably, man holds a relation to death which is distinctive and peculiar. Endowed with "intellectual being, thoughts that wander through eternity," it to him is necessarily a thing of mysterious and mighty import. He cannot well avoid asking the question, What is it? What does it mean?

The most skeptical is obliged to admit, that Death is an unsolved problem—that, in all philosophical speculations respecting it, there is a residuum of doubt, sufficient to cause anxiety. It is the unthinking alone that have no misgivings. Infidel negations, not being based on knowledge, amount to nothing. They are mere assumptions. It is unseemly bravado for anyone to say: "I have no fear of death, nor any anxiety about what lies beyond it." To speak thus is evidence of foolishness, not of wisdom.

The fool may say in his heart, There is no God, but how does that help his case? Suppose there is none, what then? There is still room for innumerable imaginable hells. Buddhism, eliminates the gods, but finds place for 136 Buddhist hells, places of punishment, into which the bankrupt in merit is immediately born when he dies—the shortest term of suffering being ten millions of years, and the longest being almost beyond the power of even Indian notation to express. It would seem therefore, that a bad man can ground no comfort on the presumption that no God exists, so long as there are Buddhist and Agnostic possibilities of intolerable suffering without one. What state can be worse than to stand on the brink of unknown abysses, with no Power to pray to!

Without reference to the question of probation after death, who would not rather, like David, fall into the hands of God, than into the hands of men? Much more, who would not prefer to bide his chances for weal or woe in the next world, subject to the disposition of a Being, declared to be, "A God merciful and gracious, slow to anger, abundant in goodness and truth, forgiving iniquity, transgression and sin, but by no means clearing the guilty"—than to be delivered over to the crushing and grinding forces of blind mechanic laws, and an unfeeling irresistible destiny.

As God is unchangeable, what He is, He will continue to be? So much is certain. What bearing this has on the question of probation after death, and the duration of future punishment, it may not be impertinent to inquire, quite fearlessly, up to a certain point, beyond which we have no right to go. When a prurient and unwarranted curiosity leads us to pry into matters which do not directly concern us, and which God has not seen fit to reveal, He checks and shames our presumption by the mildness and condescension of His lofty challenge, "Shall not the Judge of all the earth do right? Cannot you trust Me? Must I give an account of all My doings to you beforehand?" What reply did Christ make when questioned as to the number who should be saved, and the precise time of the end? If one might be so bold, as to turn the sweet courtesy and grace of the Divine answer into the coarseness of our every-day speech, it would run somewhat in this wise: "I may not tell you. It is none of your business." Surely, if I believe in a God at all, I can afford to trust Him, without any assurances and guarantees beforehand.

Do you not know, my brother, has it not been told you, God is Love? Out of the immeasurable Ocean of Doubt rises this Rock of Certainty. Its shining pinnacles pierce the Heavens. This Rock is Christ, which is only another name for Divine Love in Divinest manifestation. Upon this Rock, fixed and everlasting, it is your privilege and mine to stand. What if billows beat below, they cannot mount to these serene altitudes! What if darkness encompass us, thick and impenetrable, we are comforted with the assurance that it hides nothing that can harm us, since Love is there in the darkness! Why then is man wretched? Whence comes his misery? Why do our *Misereres* ascend? Where lies our danger? Where but in ourselves, and from ourselves? If all were right within, all would be right without.

> " He that hath light within his own clear breast,
> May sit in the centre, and enjoy bright day:
> But he that hides a dark soul and foul thoughts,
> Benighted walks under the mid-day sun,
> Himself is his own dungeon."

What we need is an internal salvation — to be saved *from* our sins. To be saved *in* our sins is impossible. For what would that involve? Nothing short of this: Order, which is Heaven's first law, would be broken Not a single link in all that chain which binds the universe to the Eternal Throne but would be shattered. Manifestly a dissolution of the tie which unites cause and effect necessitates chaos, the negation of government, and the annihilation of the Godhead. For God could not be otherwise than he is, and be at all. We see, therefore, how irrational is the hope, that we shall ever be able to handle fire with impunity, so long as fire is fire and flesh is flesh. An impure man wants to reap the rewards of purity — to gather grapes of thorns. He wishes to be happy, but is unwilling to comply with the conditions of happiness. The mountain must come to Mahomet, since Mahomet will not go to the mountain.

If we had not abundant proof of this perversity all around us, nay, a degree of it in ourselves, we would not be able to credit it. In some cases it would seem to reach a stage where it is incurable. Evil tends to perpetuate itself. Habit confirms obduracy. Reform becomes more and more difficult, the longer a man lives in sin. It would be hard to turn Methuselah into new paths. Millennial depravity is dreadful to think of.

The law of tendency no doubt is for the unrighteous to remain unrighteous — the filthy to continue filthy.

> " Suppose God should relent
> And publish grace to all, on promise made
> Of new subjection; with what eyes could we
> Stand in His presence humble, and receive
> Strict laws imposed to celebrate His throne
> With warbled hymns, and to His Godhead sing
> Forced hallelujahs: how wearisome
> Eternity to spend in worship paid
> To one we hate!"

The object of this line of thought is to show, that we have not so much reason to fear God as to fear ourselves. The danger of our perdition is not from without but from within.

The argument in favor of a posthumous probation proves too

INTRODUCTION.   lv

much. We encounter at the outset this difficulty: If Divine fairness requires that all men should be treated alike; that no one should be permitted to have any advantage over another; that the opportunities which have been accorded to some, should be extended to all—particularly the opportunity of accepting the salvation offered through Christ—so that an absolute equality of privilege should be secured to every human being who has lived or shall live — then, it is manifest, that the new trial will need to reach backward and forward so as to comprehend almost the entire human race. *Qui bono?* Besides, if there is to be a probation after death, it must clearly be a probation different from the earthly one. It can be more favorable, or less favorable, but it cannot be the same, for the scene and circumstances of the trial are not the same. To a disembodied spirit whence shall come those fleshly lusts, which in this life war so fiercely against the soul? That the ordeal is to be less severe, and the result more favorable, militate against those passages of Scripture which speak of peril, great and imminent, which men are urged to escape from, declaring and protesting, *now* is the accepted time, and *now* is the day of salvation   What is the use of a new opportunity with no different issue?

Possibly, some of our Creeds are too narrow and need enlarging. Of God and His ways, how little do we know. He has revealed Himself only in part. So much as was necessary for us to know, He has told us, and little or nothing beyond. But we are only a small part of His great family. We know what He is to our world, but not what He is to other worlds. We have therefore no right to say that He is shut up to but one way in His dealings with His creatures. We may be convinced, that. if He has other ways, not one of them is so dear and wonderful as that revealed to us through Jesus Christ. No doubt every way He has devised is like Himself, divinely perfect, and suited to the case. Bewildering speculations about the final fate of the heathen are useless, if not worse than useless. We know that the Gospel is necessary to them, otherwise we would not be commanded to take it to them, or send it. Our duty toward them ends with this life. What will become of them beyond this life, that is God's matter, not ours. And well it is so. It is not for man to say what is right—to instruct the Judge, or anticipate Him.

INTRODUCTION.

Judgment is the highest function of Godhead. The first requisite is omniscience, and nobody is Omniscient but God. Problems which are difficult to us, are not difficult to Him. He has Divine solutions for all enigmas. No man, nor body of men, with the combined wisdom of all the angels, would be competent to pass sentence on a single human soul. But God is able to do so easily and infallibly, so that no creature in the universe shall have just cause of complaint against his Maker in the end. That poor wretch — who has lived amid depraved surroundings ever since he was born; who is of corrupt lineage, vicious, so to speak, almost from necessity — will he be allowed to plead these adverse influences? He will. Whether he pleads them or not, they shall plead for him. The Supreme Judge will take every thing into account. He will unravel the entire web of his life to the last thread and fibre; will follow up the taint of a bad ancestry back to Adam, if need be; and will temper justice by the extenuating circumstances of his whole history, so that justice and mercy and every attribute of His Godhead shall be vindicated and glorified in the sentence.

It is enough to know that the Judge of all the earth will do right. In no way can we so honor Him as to trust Him—to trust Him implicitly—to say with a filial heart, "Father, Thy will be done." Our duty is to trust Him always and to the end. Were we standing on a precipice, and heard God's voice saying, "Throw thyself down"—and could be sure that it was His voice, and not Satan's, we need not hesitate, knowing that we shall fall into the arms of God—yea, even though our body should be mangled and crushed at the foot, our soul shall be safe in Him.

It is instructive to observe how differently good men deport themselves in their last moments. One might suppose that Christian heroes and martyrs would have no occasion to use the words of this Psalm, but it is remarkable how large a number of those whose lives have been spent in devoted service, have, *in extremis*, sent up this last cry for mercy. No doubt it is largely an affair of temperament, and proves little or nothing. Bunyan, in his immortal Allegory, illustrates this in the cases of Christian and Hopeful, while crossing together the River of Death.

Of all that has been said, this is the sum. From some cause or other, man's nature is out of joint. What he needs is a change of will, a change of affection, a change of spiritual relations, a change from discord to harmony, so that, inasmuch as, at the first, in a higher sense than Pythagoras intended or imagined,

> " From harmony, from heavenly harmony
> This universal frame began;
> F.om harmony to harmony,
> Through all the compass of the notes it ran,
> The diapason closing full in man,"

there may be, at last, a restoration to pristine musical consent and agreement, without one jarring note. In the mean time, let our *miserere*, if need be, go up, not doubting, if sincere, that it will be heard. The dying thief, we know, was heard in the last hour, but how much better is it to seek, and experience the blessedness of " the healing benediction " at once, than to wait. Or should there be those inclined to holy mirth, let them sing psalms.

PSALM LV.—Whether or not, Mary Queen of Scots, was privy to the murder of her husband, Darnley, has been always a vexed question. Froude supplies us with this story: " When the Queen quitted Darnley's bedside, after being more than ordinarily lavish, as it seemed, of her fondness, she let drop one fearful sentence. The Earl, though it was late, was in no mood for sleep; and Mary's last words sounded awfully in his ears. ' She was very kind,' he said to Nelson, ' but why did she speak of Davie's (Rizzio) slaughter?' Just then Paris came back to fetch a fur wrapper which the Queen had left, and which she thought too pretty to be spoiled. ' What will she do?' Darnley said again, when she was gone, ' It is very lonely.' The shadow of death was creeping over him; he was no longer the random boy, when, two years before, he had come to Scotland, filled with idle dreams of vain ambition. Sorrow, suffering, disease and fear had done their work. He opened the Prayer Book and read over the *Fifty-fifth Psalm*, which by a strange coincidence was in the English service for the day (Sunday, February 9, 1567) that was dawning. The last words that passed his lips were vs. 1-5 of this Psalm, which read: 'Hear my prayer, O Lord, and hide not Thyself from my petition. My heart is disquieted within me, and the fear of death hath fallen upon me: Fearfulness and trembling are come upon me. It is not an open enemy that hath done me this dishonor, for then I could have borne it. It was even, thou, my companion, my guide, and my own familiar friend.' Forlorn victim of a cruel time! Twenty-one years old—no more. At the end of an hour he went to bed with his page at his side. An hour later, they two were found lying dead in the garden under the stars. The house had been blown up with gun-powder."—*Froude's "History of England."*

PSALM LXVII. has been called "The Lord's Prayer of the Old Testament."

PSALM LXVIII.—Called by the Huguenots the "Song of Battle," and often sung by them, amid the storm of conflict, (French Version). Here is the beginning (as given in "*Les Psaumes de David mis en Vers Francois,*" published in 1807):

> Que Dieu se montre seulement,
> Et l'on verra dans un moment
>   Abandonner la place,
> Le camp des ennemis épars,
> Epouvanté de toutes parts,
>   Fuira devant sa face.
> On verra tout ce camp s'enfuir
> Comme l'on voit s'evanonir
>   Une épaisse fumée:
>   Comme la cire fond au feu,
>   Ainsi des mechans devant Dieu,
>   La force est consumée, etc.

As this Psalm is not found among those that Marot translated, the version here given is probably Beza's, slightly altered.

The following account of the Battle of Dunbar, fought September 3, 1650, is taken from Carlyle's *Life of Oliver Cromwell:* The small Town of Dunbar stands on one of those projecting rock-promontories with which the shore of the Frith of Forth is niched, forming a grim barrier of whinstone, sheltering it from the chafing and tumbling of the German Ocean. Landward rises, some short mile off, a long hill of considerable height, called the Doon or Doon Hill.

On this Hill lies David Leslie with the victorious Scotch army. Cockburnspath with its ravines has been seized on Oliver's right and made impassable. Behind Oliver is the sea. Lesley's force is 23,000, Oliver's about half as many. Lesley commits the mistake of coming down to the base of the Hill, edging with a portion of his army towards the right to cut off the enemy's retreat on that side. At the sight of this movement, Cromwell determines to profit by the advantage it affords, and to anticipate the enemy's attack by attacking first. All things being in readiness (the night has been wild and wet) for the attack to be made at earliest daybreak, the trumpets sound and there is cannonading along the whole line. The Scots too are on the wing, and awake. At the end of an hour's fighting the Scotch give way and run. Just then over the Abb's head and the German Ocean bursts the first gleam of the level sun, and Cromwell is heard to say, in the words of the *Sixty-eighth Psalm*, "Let God, arise, let His enemies be scattered"—or, in Rous's metre,

> "Let God arise, and scatteréd
> Let all His enemies be
> And let all those that do Him hate
> Before His presence flee!"

Even so. The Scotch army is shivered to utter ruin; rushes in tumultuous wreck, hither, thither. Before entering on the pursuit, Oliver orders a halt, and all sing the *Hundred and Seventeenth Psalm*, uplifting it to the tune of Bangor, and rolling it strong against the sky:

> "O give ye praise unto the Lord,
> All nati-ons* that be;
> Likewise ye people all, accord
> His name to magnify.
>
> For great to-us-ward ever are
> His loving kindnesses:
> His truth endures forevermore:
> The Lord O do ye bless.

* To be pronounced in three syllables.

PSALM LXXI.—*Robert Blair*, the grandfather of Robert Blair, the author of *The Grave*, called this "My Psalm."

Philip de Morney, an illustrious friend and champion of the Huguenots, on his death-bed desired the *Seventy-first Psalm* to be read to him.

PSALM LXXVI.—Charles Kingsley, when sailing up the Rhine, and looking on the strongholds of the old freebooters, writes: "How strange that my favorite Psalm about the hills of the robbers (hills of prey) should have come in course the very first day I sailed up the Rhine."

PSALM LXXIX.—Fourteen Protestants of Meaux, arrested at a meeting, sang this Psalm as they went to death.

PSALM LXXXV.— When Richard Cromwell was installed Protector, Dr. Thomas Godwin preached, at the opening of Parliament, January 27, 1659, a sermon, taking for his text, Ver. 10, "Mercy and truth are met together; righteousness and peace have kissed each other."

PSALM XC.—Herder calls it, "that Ancient Psalm, that Hymn of Eternity." Vers. 1-4 is the burial song of the Russian Church.

John Hampden (B. 1594; D. 1643), at the beginning of the Civil War, was fatally wounded in a skirmish with Rupert's cavalry between Thame and Oxford. In great pain and almost fainting he reached Thame where his wounds were dressed. After nearly six days of cruel suffering he died. He was buried among the hills and woods of Chiltern. Many troops in the neighborhood followed the beloved body to its grave, with arms reversed, drums and ensigns muffled, and heads uncovered, singing the *Ninetieth Psalm* as they went, and the 43rd as they returned.— *Forster's* "*Lives of British Statesmen.*"

PSALMS XCVI, XCVII, XCVIII.—Dr. William Alexander, Bishop of Derry, says, "We have in these Psalms the pæans of all creation."

PSALM C.—No Psalm has been more sung. It gave name to the tune known as Old Hundred composed by William Franc in 1553 — sometimes attributed to Luther, but he only changed and improved it.

Bishop Heber speaks of having been greatly moved at hearing Thirteen Hundred native Christians — at a Tamul service in Tangore, India — all join in singing this Psalm in their own tongue.

PSALM CI.—David was engaged in the task of ordering his household. Ver. 3, *house*. The king's house in an Eastern monarchy included the government of his army, and the administration of justice.

Ernest, the pious Duke of Saxe-Gotha, the founder of the Saxe-Gotha family (B. 1601; D. 1675) used to send a copy of the Psalms to unfaithful officials, so that when any magistrate had done wrong, it became a proverb, " He will certainly receive the Prince's Psalm to read ": " Mine eye shall be upon the faithful of the land," etc. He was the intimate friend of Gustavus Adolphus.

PSALM CII.—Is the Fifth of the Seven Penitential Psalms. Dr. Ker remarks, there is no grander missionary hymn than Vers. 13-22.

PSALM CVII.—Contains, according to one hypothesis, the thanksgiving of exiles (Ver. 3) not yet returned to Jerusalem, but already escaped from the thraldom of Babylon. The main body of the Psalm was probably sung only by the leader, the chorus joining in the refrain. " O that men would praise the Lord," etc.

PSALM CXVI.—This Psalm was a great favorite with Dante. He introduces it into his *Purgatorio* as sung by a hundred spirits just arrived under the conduct of an angel :

> '*In exitu Israel de Egypto*,'
> All with one voice together sang, with what
> In the remainder of that hymn is writ —

and he speaks elsewhere, in his prose writings, of the 114th Psalm as the voice of thrilling joy.

PSALM CXV.—*Henry V.* entered France by Calais with an English army. It was already much wasted and reduced in numbers by sickness, when the battle of Agincourt took place on St. Crispian's Day, 1415. The French army, four times the number of its opponents, was overthrown, and the flower of the French chivalry either fell in the field or were taken prisoners. After the battle was over, Henry ordered the chaplain to read the 115th Psalm; and at the words, " Not unto us, but unto Thy name give the glory," the king and cavalry dismounted, and they and all the host prostrated themselves on the ground. Shakespeare puts it thus:

> " O God, Thy arm was here,
> And not to us, but to Thy arm alone
> Ascribe we all.—When without stratagem,
> But in plain shock, and even play of battle,
> Was ever known so great and little loss
> On one part and the other?— Take it, God,
> For it is only Thine!" —*Henry V., Act IV., Scene VIII.*

Basing-House, Pawlet, Marquis of Winchester's mansion, stood at a small distance from Basingstoke in Hampshire. It was a very important royal stronghold, and had stood siege after siege for four years. The Lieutenant-General, Cromwell, gathering all the artillery he could lay hold of, stormed and took it. Carlyle tells, that he had spent much time in prayer the previous night; and as he seldom fought without some text of Scripture to support him, he rested on the eighth verse of the 115th Psalm.

The Turks marched, plundering and devastating, to the walls of Vienna. The capital seemed lost. The Imperial army commanded by Charles of Lorraine, in conjunction with a Polish force under the heroic king, John Sobieski, defeated the Turks, and relieved the beleaguered city, September 12th, 1683. The battle-song of the Polish king, sung on the occasion, was *Non nobis, Domine.* The battle was a turning-point in history. The Turkish power, previously so formidable, as to threaten the overrunning of Europe, was effectually broken.

PSALM CXVII.—Sung by Cromwell and his army after the battle

of Dunbar, September 3, 1650, and known afterwards by the Puritans as the Dunbar Psalm.

PSALM CXVIII.—The biographer of Clement Marot tells, that he presented the Emperor Charles V., as he was passing through France, with a copy of his Psalter, who gave the poet 200 doubloons, and asked him to complete his translation, praying him to send him as soon as he could the translation of the 118th Psalm, as he loved it much. It took rank with the 68th as the battle-song of the Huguenots.

When William of Orange landed at Torbay in 1688, he asked Carstares to conduct service. He prayed and gave part of the 118th Psalm to be sung, in which all the troops along the beach joined; and this act of devotion, it is said, produced a sensible effect.

The 17th verse, "I shall not die but live, and declare the works of the Lord," was the last utterance of *Philip Berthelier*, a noble Genevese. At the time that Bonivard was committed to the dungeon of Chillon, 1519, for defending the liberty of his native city, Berthelier was beheaded on an island at the outlet of the Lake of Geneva.

Ver. 22, "The stone which the builders," etc., was the text of Ebenezer Erskine's sermon, preached October 10, 1732, before the Synod, which led to the formation of the Secession Church.—*Ker*.

PSALM CXIX.—Is the most perfect specimen of the Alphabetic or Acrostic Psalms—Bishop Cowper calls it "a Holy Alphabet"—not amiss, perhaps, if we consider that the Primer of the Divine Law is the first book to be learned, beginning with the heavenly A, B, C of obedience.

Ver. 9. "Wherewithal shall a young man cleanse his way? By taking heed thereto according to Thy word." Henry Scougal, author of *The Life of God in the Soul of Man*, was so impressed with these words that he became a Christian minister—and later, Professor of Theology, King's College, Aberdeen. He died in 1679 aged twenty-eight.

Ver. 20. Chalmers says, while he could not speak of the raptures of Christian enjoyment, he thought he could enter into the feeling of the Psalmist, "My soul breaketh for the longing it hath unto Thy judgments at all times."

Pascal singled out ver. 59 as pivotal: "I thought on my ways, and turned my feet unto thy testimonies." He used to say that, "with the deep study of life, this Psalm contained the sum of all Christian virtues."

Ver. 83. *bottle in the smoke.* The bottle being of skin would shrivel and burn in the smoke like leather—an apt metaphor for one, the sap of whose life was dried up by trouble.

Ver. 92. "Unless Thy law had been my delight, I should have perished in mine affliction," is written on Luther's Bible by his own hand. The date is 1542.

Ver. 97. Henry Martin says, "I experienced a solemn gladness in learning this part, 'MEM,' of the 119th Psalm."

Ver. 105. "Thy word is a lamp unto my feet." This is the text prefixed to a little book called *The Lantern of Light*, which was the favorite reading of the Lollards before the Reformation. The Lollards of England and Scotland were charged with reading the Bible in their mother-tongue—Wickliffe's translation—and with esteeming it above any instruction they received from the priests. On this account they were called *Biblemen.—Ker.*

Ver. 164, "*Seven times in a day will I praise Thee.*" In the fourth century, the number of *Canonical Hours* for daily devotion was enlarged from three to seven in accordance with the above; but they were strictly kept only in the cloisters, under the technical names of *matina*, about three o'clock, A. M.; *prima*, about six, A. M.; *tertia*, nine, A. M.; *nona*, three, P. M.; *vesper*, six, P. M.; *completorium*, nine, P. M.; and *mesonyctium* or *vigilia*, midnight. Usually two nocturnal prayers were added.

William Wilberforce writes in his diary, 1819, "Walked from Hyde Park Corner repeating the 119th Psalm."

John Ruskin, in "Fors Clavigera" says, "It is strange that of all the pieces of the Bible which my mother taught me, that which cost me most to learn, and was, to my child's mind, most repulsive, the 119th Psalm, has now become, of all, the most precious to me in its overflowing passion of love for the law of God."

PSALM CXX.—This is the first of a Collection of Fifteen Psalms, (Pss. 120-134), each bearing the title, Pilgrim Song, literally, Song of

Ascents, Song of the Goings-up, namely, to the Holy City, "whither the tribes go up" (Ps. 122: 4). Many, perhaps most, were written with another design, and selected for this purpose because of their suitableness. The goings-up might relate to the going up from Babylon at the close of the Captivity, or from different parts of Palestine. Three annual pilgrimages to the Holy City were required by the Law. These were usually made in large companies, with singing on the route.

PSALM CXXIV.—A Pilgrim Ode. Ver. 6, *The snare is broken, and we are escaped*, referring to the deliverance of the Jews from their captivity in Babylon.

Attempts have been made to chronologize the Psalms. "*The Psalms Chronologically Arranged, by Four Friends*," adopt the arrangement of Ewald, " as full of suggestive thought, edifying, and generally satisfactory." But however acute and learned, the element of conjecture enters too largely to entitle it to more than a limited acceptance. According to this, the present Psalm marks the beginning of a period extending from the rebuilding of the Temple. The destruction of Babylon by Cyrus freed Israel from the thraldom of the Chaldeans. The nation, once careless of the law, after this grew tenacious of its very letter; once rigorously exclusive, they now saw their ideal in the king who should enroll all the world as citizens of a spiritual Jerusalem. The future duty of the nation was, to make themselves ready for his advent.

The above scheme arranges the Psalms covering this period in the following order: Pss. 124, 129, 125, 126, 127, 128, 133, 122, 87, 134, 137, 118, 125, 106, 138, 92, 93, 95, 100, 97, 99, 96, 98, 67, 68, 66, 91, 139, 44, 74, 79, 80, 132, 89, 60, 85, 83, 78, 81.

PSALM CXXIX.—An outburst of joy at deliverance from captivity. A Pilgrim Ode.

PSALM CXXXIV.—A Temple-hymn. Ver. 2, *by night*, the priests lodged round about the House of God, and some were employed day and night. The lamps were kept burning all night. The last of the Pilgrim Odes.

PSALM CXXXVII.—The hopes of a revival of the ancient empire of David intensified the patriotic zeal of the nation. This feeling vents itself on the Edomites who had joined the invading hosts of Nebuchadnezzar in that fatal 'day of Jerusalem' and had received a portion of the land as a reward for their share in the destruction of Jerusalem. Contrast the apparent bitterness of this Psalm with the comprehensive spirit of the 87th Psalm.—*Four Friends.*

PSALM CXXXIX.—Ver. 8, *parts of the sea*, indicates that it was written in Palestine. Ver. 17, *Thy thoughts, i. e.*, counsels, contrivances, devisings, divine adaptations of means to end, illustrated in creation, particularly in the structure of organized beings, culminating in man.

PSALM CXLV.—An Alphabetic Psalm.

PSALM CXLVII.—The rebuilding of Jerusalem and the restoration of the ancient ritual had inspired the nation with new hopes.

EMINENT WITNESSES TO THE EXCELLENCE OF THE PSALMS.

"This book is the most beautiful (*elegantissimus*) in the world."--*Melancthon.*

"These songs, not in their divine argument only, but in the very art of composition, may be easily made appear over all this kind of poesy to be incomparable.'
—*Milton.*

"What is there necessary for man to know which the Psalms are not able to teach?"—*Hooker.*

"The effect of the Psalms on the character of the Huguenots was wonderful. * * We need to-day a generation nourished on this *marrow of lions.*"— *Lelievre.*

"Songs which like the Psalms have stood the test of three thousand years may well be said to contain in them the seed of eternity."—*Tholuck.*

"David is the first of the poets of feeling—the king of lyrists, . . . Read Greek or Latin lyrics after a psalm—they turn pale."—*Lamartine.*

"The Psalms have been called *the abstract* or *summary of both Testaments.*"— *M. Henry.*

"The Psalms can make a life of trial a life of joy."—*Johannes Von Müller.*

"Even the French Deists, the theo-philanthropists, sworn enemies of the Bible, could only make out their liturgy by the help of the Psalms."—*Hengstenberg.*

"David struck tones that were an echo of the sphere-harmonies and are still felt to be such. * * Read a psalm of David, then go to the opera, and hear, with unspeakable reflections, what things men now sing."—*Thomas Carlyle.*

"All the wonders of Greek civilization heaped together are less wonderful than is the simple book of Psalms—the history of the human soul in relation to its Maker."—*W. E. Gladstone.*

"This book has no equal in the expanse of time which it reflects, beginning with the wanderings in the wilderness, 1450 years before Christ, and reaching down to the building of the sacred temple, 800 years later. * * If it is the peculiarity of the classic, that the oftener it is read the more beautiful and full of meaning it becomes, then are the Psalms classic in the highest degree."—*Delitzsch.*

"Not only for its contents but its form, is the use of the book of Psalms a benefit to the spirit of man. In no lyric poet of Greece or Rome can we find so much instruction or comfort, and in none such a variety and rich change of the poetic mood. These flowers can be carried to every clime and every soil, and they bloom in fresh youth. It is a Book of Song for all ages."—*Herder*.

"The Bible itself is an old Cremona; it has been played upon by the devotion of thousands of years, until every word and particle is public and tunable."—*Emerson*

If we keep vigil in the church, David comes first, last and midst.—*St. John Chrysostom*.

"What various and resplendent riches are contained in this treasury (Book of Psalms), it were difficult to find words to describe. I am in the habit of calling it 'The Anatomy of all parts of the soul,' for not an affection will any one find in himself, an image of which is not reflected in this mirror. Nay, all the griefs, sorrows, fears, misgivings, hopes, cares, anxieties, in short, all the disquieting emotions with which the minds of men are wont to be agitated, the Holy Ghost hath here pictured to the life."—*Calvin*.

The Hebrew Psalms

IN ENGLISH VERSE.

THE PSALMS.

BOOK I.

PSALM I.

O HAPPY is the man who hath
   Not walked in counsels of deceit;
Who stands not in the sinner's path;
   Who sits not in the scorner's seat;

2 But in the statutes of the Lord
   Finds evermore a new delight;
Feasts on the sweetness of His word
   In meditation day and night.

3 Like to a tree that's planted near
   Unfailing streams that feed the root,
Midst foliage that's never sere,
   He brings forth seasonable fruit.

Whate'er he does shall grow and thrive;
His joyful soul shall leap and laugh:
4 Not so th' ungodly—winds shall drive
Them far away like empty chaff.

5 They shall not in the judgment stand;
Their path leads downward to the pit:
6 But known of God, at His right hand
The righteous shall in honor sit.

PSALM II.

WHY do the nations rage,
Imagine a vain thing?
2 The rulers plot against the Lord
And His Anointed King?

3 "Let us break off their bands,
Their cords," say they, "divide."
4 He who sits high in heaven shall laugh,
Their vain attempts deride.

5 He speaks to them in wrath:
"Though ye rebel, I still
6 Immovably have set My King
On Zion's Holy Hill."

7 "I will declare My Lord's
Unchangeable decree—
He said: 'Thou art My Son, this day
Have I begotten Thee;

8 "'Ask Me, and I will give
   The nations for Thine own;
And I will make earth's utmost bounds
   The limits of Thy throne:

9 "'Those that resist Thy sway,
   Should any be so rash,
With iron rod, like vessel frail,
   Thou shalt in pieces dash.'"

Therefore, be wise, ye kings,
   Ye judges of the earth;
Serve ye the Lord with fear, and mix
   Much trembling with your mirth.

O kiss the Son! Beware
   Slight kindlings of His ire,
Lest ye should perish in the way
   When once His wrath takes fire.

PSALM III.*

O LORD! how many foes
   In arms against me rise;
2 How many say of me, "No help
   For him in God there lies."

---

* David having crossed the Jordan, halted for the night with his party on the way to Mahanaim; and rising early (recovered now from his first depression) wrote, we may suppose, this MORNING HYMN; and before the next bivouac, the EVENING HYMN that follows, Psalm iv. See Introduction.

3 But Thou, Lord, art my Shield,
  My Glory and Good-will—
4 I called, and Thou didst answer me
  Out of Thy Holy Hill.

5 I laid me down and slept,
  For Thy sustaining arm
Was underneath my head; I woke
  Refreshed and free from harm.

6 I will not be afraid
  Though myriads me oppose:
7 Rise, save me, for Thou smitten hast
  On the cheek-bone my foes,

And broken hast their teeth:
8   Salvation is from Thee—
Lord! let Thy blessing evermore
  Upon Thy people be.

PSALM IV.

DELAY not answer when I call,
  God of my righteousness!
Thou didst, ere this, me disenthrall
  When I was in distress.
Now pity, Lord, and for me care,
Incline Thine ear and hear my prayer.

2 How long, ye sons of men, will ye
    My kingly right despise?
  How long will ye love vanity,
    And follow after lies?
3 The Lord, who loved* and set apart,
  Will hear me, for He knows my heart.

4 O stand in awe and fear to sin!
    With your own heart commune
  Upon your bed, by night shut in,
    While silence fills the room.
5 Offer ye sacrifices just,
  And in Jehovah put your trust.

6 Many there be who say: "Ah, who
    Will show us any good?"
  Light of Thy face lift up anew,
    And I'll have all I would.
7 Their joy shall not compare with mine,
  Who have a glut of corn and wine.

8 In fearless peace I'll lay me down,
    And go at once to sleep :—
  Though slumber deep my senses drown,
    Since Thou, Lord, watch dost keep,
  I know I'm safe where'er I dwell,
  In palace or in lonely cell.

---

* The name David means "Beloved."

PSALM V.

GIVE ear unto my words, O Lord!
    My moaning heeded be:
3 To Thee each morn I'll duly pray,
    And watch and wait for Thee.
4 For Thou art not a God that hath
    In wickedness delight;
Evil shall not with Thee abide,
5   The proud stand in Thy sight.

6 All evil doers Thou dost hate;
    Wilt slay them that speak lies;
The bloody and deceitful man
    Is odious in Thine eyes.
7 But in Thy numerous mercies, I
    Will in Thy House appear;
And toward Thy Holy Temple, Lord!
    Will worship in Thy fear.

8 Lead me, O Lord, because of those
    Who watch to see me slide:
Make plain Thy way before my face,
    Nor let me turn aside.
9 No truth is in their faithless mouth,
    Wide yawns a gulf within,
Their throat's an open sepulchre,
    They smooth their tongue to sin.

10 God! hold them guilty. Let them fall,
    By their own counsels felled:

In their transgressions thrust them out,
   Who have 'gainst Thee rebelled.
11 Let all be glad who trust in thee;
   Be happy lips unsealed;
12 For Thou the righteous wilt surround
   With favor as a shield.

PSALM VI.

REBUKE me not in anger, Lord!
   Correct but not consume:
Let not Thy just resentment flame;
   Give gentle pity room.

2 Have mercy, Lord! for I am weak;
   O heal me and restore!
With anguish all my bones are vexed,
   My soul is troubled sore.

3 But Thou, O Lord, how long? Return;
4   My soul deliver; make
My threatened life Thy care; me save,
   For Thine own mercies' sake.

5 Of Thee no memory is in Death,
   The blotting out of days—
In Sheol who will give Thee thanks,
   Or celebrate Thy praise?

6 I with my groanings weary am ;
   I make each night my bed
A kind of sea* in which I swim,
   All drenched with tears I shed.

7 Mine eye is shrunk, it wastes away
   Through weeping o'er my woes ;
It prematurely waxes old,
   Because of all my foes.

8 Depart from me, ye evil men !
   Jehovah is aware
9 Of all my sighing, and hath heard
   And will receive my prayer.

10 My foes shall all confounded be ;
   Be filled with sudden shame ;
They shall return in headlong haste
   Along the way they came.

PSALM VII.

LORD my God, in Thee I trust,
   Save from all those who pursue me ;
2 Lest that lion-like th' unjust
   Rend and tear me and undo me ;
   And they triumph who o'erthrew me,
Lying prostrate in the dust.

---

*" Nightly my couch I make a kind of sea."—*Milton*.

3 If, my God, I ill have wrought ;
    If my hands are found to blame ;*
4 If I him have wronged in aught
    Who my friend was to my shame ;
    If I rescued not the same,
Who is now my foe for naught ;

5 Let him then pursue my soul ;
    Overtake it in its flight ;
Trample it ; my glory roll
    In the dust in public sight ;
    I will not dispute his right,
But will justify the whole.

6 Lord, now in Thy anger rise ;
    Lift Thyself against the rage
Of my foes, who ill devise,
    And unrighteous warfare wage ;
    Wake for me ; for me engage—
Just Thy judgments are and wise.

7 Let all people round Thee gather,
    While Thou speakest from the sky ;
Let them stand and listen—rather
    Let them on their faces lie—
    After this return on high,
Thou who art th' Eternal Father.

8 Judge me by my righteousness,
    Mine integrity within :

---

* See 1 Samuel xxiv. 11.

I would ask nor more nor less,
      Sure I shall acquital win.
9   Make the sinner cease from sin,
   And his wickedness confess;

   But establish innocence:
      For Thou, righteous God, dost try
   Hearts and reins, and wilt me, hence,
      Vindicate and justify:
10   I on Thee, my Shield, rely—
   Th' upright's safety and defence.

11 God a just Judge is, and hath
      Indignation every day:
12 If men turn not, in His wrath
      He will whet His sword to slay;
13   Bend His bow, prepare straightway
   Tools of death to sweep His path.

   He His arrows fiery makes,
      For the wretch who multiplies—
14 Travailing constantly—and wakes
      To conceive iniquities,
      And bring forth a brood of lies,
   Hissing, venomous as snakes.

15 He with malice digged a pit,
      And so, rightly in my stead,
   Tumbled headlong into it;
16   All the mischief he has bred

    Shall descend on his own head—
    Retribution just and fit.

17 I, Jehovah the Most High
    Will adore and magnify:
    Will His righteousness proclaim,
    Harping praises to His name.

PSALM VIII.

O LORD, our Lord, in all the earth,
    How excellent Thy Name!
Thou it hast blazoned on the heavens
    In characters of flame.

2 By mouth of sucklings hast ordained
    An armory of light,
With Truth's celestial weapons stored
    To vindicate the Right.

  On weakest things hast founded strength—
    The babes' believing cry—
  Because of foes, to silence them
    Who hate Thee and deny.

3 When I behold Thy heavens, the work
    Of Thine own fingers, Lord!
The moon and stars which Thou hast fixed
    By Thine almighty word,—

4 O what is man that Thou for him
    Such love shouldst manifest?
  Shouldst condescend to visit him
    And be Thy creature's guest?

5 For Thou hast made him next Thyself—
    This brother of the clod—
6 Hast crowned him with dominion that
    Befits a son of God:

  Hast given him lordship o'er Thy works,
    Put all things under him—
7 All flocks, all herds, all beasts, whate 'er
8   Doth walk, or fly, or swim.

9 O Lord, our Lord, in all the earth
    How excellent Thy Name,
  Whose glory in the heavens is set
    In signature of flame.

PSALM IX.

I WITH my whole heart will praise,
  And recount Thy wondrous ways:
Joy in Thee, O Thou Most High!
Sing Thy Name and magnify:

3 For my enemies turned back,
  Finding Thee upon their track;
  At Thy dreadful presence they,
  Stumbling, perished in the way.

4 Thou, O Lord, my right and cause
  Hast maintained, upholding laws—
  Seated high upon Thy throne,
  Judging righteously alone.

5 Thou hast nations swept away,
  Blotted out their names for aye:
6 Cities, which Thou hast destroyed,
  Lost to memory are and void.

---

7 God sits King—earth at His feet—
  Ever on His judgment seat;
8 He'll the peoples' wrongs redress,
  Judge the world in righteousness.

9 Tower of refuge for th' oppressed,
  A high tower for the distressed;
10 Who Thee know will in Thee trust,
  For Thou ne'er wilt from Thee thrust

  Them that seek Thee, nor forsake
  Such as Thee their refuge make.
11 Sing His praise, His doings tell,
  Who in Zion loves to dwell.

12 When for blood He shall inquire,
   Burn His anger will like fire!
   For the poor man's cry is not
   By th' Omniscient Judge forgot.

---

13 Pity, Lord, whose quickening breath
   Raises from the gates of death.
   See what sufferings on me wait,
   From the hands of them that hate!

14 Save me, that Thy praise I may
   In the gates of Zion pay.
   I will then with heart and voice
   In Thy saving health rejoice.

---

15 Sunk are nations in the pit
   Themselves made, God ordering it—
16 Justly ill their own foot fared,
   In their own net caught and snared.

17 Back the wicked shall be turned,
   Reaping the reward they earned:
   Perish shall in Sheol yet
   Nations all that God forget.

18 For the needy and the meek,
   Who from God assistance seek,
   Shall not always be unheard,
   Nor their hope for aye deferred.

19 Rise, Lord, let not man assail
  Right's strong bulwarks and prevail.
  Nations that against Thee fight
  Let them judged be in Thy sight.

20 Let the terror of Thine arm
  Fill their souls with just alarm;
  And with trembling let them then
  Know themselves to be but men.

PSALM X.

LORD, why standest Thou afar?
  Why dost Thou Thyself thus hide?
From Thy presence why debar
  Those by hopeless trouble tried?

2 In his pride the wicked still
    Is engaged in hot pursuit;
  'Gainst the poor contriving ill,
    Ceasing not to persecute.

3 Let his cunning serve him not,
    In his own devices caught—
  Glorying in plunder got,
    God is banished from his thought.

  Swayed by greed that God condemns,
    He, a worshipper of gain,
  God renounces, yea, contemns,
    Fuller license to obtain.

4 Hear the boaster proudly say:
   "I've no fear God will require;
There no God is to repay,
   I will have my heart's desire."

5 Always firm against the right
   He Thy judgments dares contemn;
They're above him out of sight—
   As for foes he puffs at them,

6 Saying, "I shall ne'er be moved;
   No calamity I fear."
7 Cursing by his mouth's approved,
   Guile and cruelty are dear.

8 He in hamlets lies in wait;
9   Like some savage beast of prey,
Lurks in ambush, watching late,
   Hapless ones to seize and slay.*

Draws the poor man in his net,
10   Crushes him remorselessly:
11 God, he fancies, doth forget—
   Hides his face—will never see.

12 Rise, O Lord, lift up Thy hand;
   Let the poor remembered be;
Let the proud one understand
   Thou his wickedness dost see.

*See 2 Samuel iii. 27; xx. 10.

13 Why should he Thy justice flout?
　　Saying, Thou wilt not require;
That Thou seest leave no doubt,
　　Make him feel Thy righteous ire.

14 Make him know 't was at his cost,
　　He the fatherless did harm:
Let each wicked scheme be crost,
15　Shatter Thou his lifted arm!

　　Thorough inquisition make
　　　　Of the evil he has done—
　　It pursue and overtake,
　　　　Punish it till there is none.

16 Sits Jehovah on His throne,
　　A just sceptre in His hand,
All the nations, overthrown,
　　Perish shall from out His Land.

17 Thou of meek hearts art the stay;
18　Thou the orphan wilt redress,
That vain man, a child of clay,
　　Henceforth may no more oppress.

PSALM XI.

I PUT my trust in God my King:
　　How counsel ye then dastard flight?
How say ye to my soul, "Take wing,
　　And safety seek in mountain height,

2 "For lo, the wicked bend the bow,
　　They to the string their arrow suit;
　Hid in the dark, that none may know,
　　They ready stand at thee to shoot.

　"The labor of thy hands is void;
　　In vain thou dost the work pursue;
3 If the foundations are destroyed,
　　What can the righteous man then do?"

4 The Lord is in His Temple,* why
　　Should we take counsel of despair?
　His throne is fixed above the sky,
　　No earthly power can reach it there.

　Enough to know, His eyes behold,
　　His eyelids try the sons of men—
5 He proves and purifies the gold,
　　And naught deceives his searching ken.

6 Upon the wicked He shall rain
　　Snares, fire and brimstone, as of yore;
　The portion of their cup is pain,
　　Is, was, and shall be evermore.

7 For that the Lord is righteous, He
　　Loves righteousness, and evil hates:
　The upright man His face shall see,—
　　Immortal honor him awaits.

---

* The Tabernacle, which contained the Ark, is so called 1 Samuel i. 9; iii. 3.

PSALM XII.

HELP, Lord, for these are evil days;
　　The godly cease, the faithful fail;
Lone and deserted are Thy ways,
　And rank impieties prevail.

2 All speech is an exchange of lies;
　　Each with his neighbor plays a part;
They practice smooth hypocrisies,
　With flattering lip and double heart.

3 The Lord will guileful lips destroy;
　　And tongues that say in lordly tone,
4 "Who's over us? We will employ
　　These as we please, they are our own."

5 "Now, will I rise," Jehovah saith,
　　"For those they spoil, whose bread they scant,
Who pine for safety, fearing death—
　And give them that for which they pant."

6 His words are pure, mean what they say,
　　As silver seven times purified,
7 "He shall them keep, though vice bears sway,
8 　Though strut the vile in robes of pride.

PSALM XIII.

HOW long wilt Thou, Lord, me forget?
　　Wilt Thou Thy face forever hide?
2 How long shall daily sorrows fret?
　　My foe exalt his head of pride?

3 Hear, Lord! revive my fainting breath,
　　Lighten mine eyes whose light has failed,
　Now, lest I sleep the sleep of death,
4 　　Lest my foe boast, "I have prevailed."

5 But I have trusted Thee, and still
　　In Thy salvation will rejoice;
6 And for Thy bounteous goodness will
　　Attune to Thee both heart and voice.

PSALM XIV.

BESOTTED pupil in that school,
　　The darkened reason of a fool!—
　He, proud of his ancestral clod,
　Saith in his heart, "There is no God."

　No wonder from such evil root,
　There springs abominable fruit:
　Mad revelers at Nature's feast.
　Men grow more beastly than the beast.

2 The Lord looked down from heaven to see
 If any bowed to Him the knee;
 If there were any understood,
 And there was none, none that did good.

3 They all had gone aside, all had
 Become corrupt and wholly bad.
4 Are evil-doers void of sense
 As well as of all innocence?

 They, like wild beasts with ravin red,
 My people eat as they eat bread;
 They on the Lord disdain to call—
5 But, lo, great tremblings on them fall.

 For God, now with the righteous seen,
 His arm laid bare, doth intervene;
6 And counsels, that were put to shame,
 Are made triumphant in His Name.

7 O that salvation might with power
 Come out of Zion at this hour!
 When back from thraldom God shall bring,
 Then Jacob shall exult and sing.

PSALM XV.

WHO shall inhabit, Lord, Thy Tent?
 How nobly born? Of what descent?
Who in Thy Holy Mount abide,
To what imperial race allied?

Not to the great ones of the earth,
Of princely blood, of royal birth;
Not to the haughty and the proud,
Is this high privilege allowed.

2 But he who walks uprightly here,
Whose words are true, whose heart's sincere,
With slanderous tongue does not offend,
Basely betray or wrong a friend;

3 Aids not his neighbor to defame;
4 Who towards the vile feels only shame,
But honors those that fear the Lord;
Swears to his hurt and keeps his word;

5 Makes no hard terms for money lent;
No bribes takes 'gainst the innocent—
Who does these things, he enter may
God's House, and permanently stay.

PSALM XVI.

PRESERVE me, for in Thee I trust,
    I said: "My God Thou art;
2 My good, my only good, I have
    No good from Thee apart,

3 Ev'n as Thy saints, the excellent
    In whom is my delight."
4 Their sorrows shall be many who
    With other gods unite:

I their drink-offerings of blood
  Will not pour out; nor take
Their hateful names upon my lips,
  Nor mention of them make.

5 The Lord the portion is of my
    Inheritance and cup:
  His favors are so numerous,
    I cannot count them up.

Thou wilt maintain my lot—my lines
  In pleasant places fall:
A goodly heritage have I
  For, having Thee, have all.

7 I bless the Lord Who counsels me;
    At night when I awake,
  I hear Him whisper in the dark
    Words that me wiser make.

8 The Lord is always in my sight—
    With Him at my right hand,
9 I never shall be moved, therefore,
    Glad thoughts my heart expand.

10 My flesh shall dwell secure, my soul
     Not left to Sheol be:—
   Thou wilt not let Thy Holy One
     The least corruption see.

Thou wilt me show the path of life !
  I'll to Thy presence soar,
Where there is fullness of all joy—
  Pleasures forevermore.

PSALM XVII.

HEAR Thou the right, O God !
  Unjustly I'm arraigned :
Sit judge, and listen to my prayer,
  That comes from lips unfeigned.

2 I make petition, let
  My sentence come from Thee :
And let Thine eyes behold what things
  Belong to equity.

3 Thou hast my heart oft proved ;
  Hast come to me at night,
Hast tried me, and hast nothing found
  At variance with right.

4 As for the works of men,
  I, governed by Thy word,
Have kept myself aloof, and been
  From violence deterred :

5 Have held fast to Thy paths ;
  My feet have firmly stood :
6 Incline, O God, Thine ear to me,
  And hear, for Thou art good.

7 Thy wondrous kindness show,
 O Thou who savest those
 That put their trust in Thee from all
 Who rise up and oppose!

8 O guard me, keep me as
 The apple of the eye;
 Under the shadow of Thy wings,
 Let me for shelter fly,

9 From deadly foes that spoil
 And compass me around—
10 They proudly speak, they watch each step
11 To hurl me to the ground.

12 He like a lion is,
 That's greedy for his prey—
 Like a young lion that lies hid
 Along the public way.

13 Arise, O Lord, confront,
 Cast down and overthrow!
 Deliver by Thy sword and hand
 From the ungodly foe,—

14 From men whose portion's here,
 Whose cravings Thou dost fill,
 Who live, enjoy, and what is left
 They to their children will.

15 As for myself, Thy face,
    In righteousness I'll see;
  And when I with Thy likeness wake
    I satisfied shall be.

PSALM XVIII.

I LOVE Thee, Lord! my Strength,
    My Fortress and High Tower;
2 To Thee, my Rock, my Shield, my Trust,
3   I fly in danger's hour.

5 The snares of death and hell
    Around my feet were spread;
4 And floods of wickedness rose high,
    And filled my soul with dread.

6 I called upon the Lord
    In my extreme distress;
  He heard my voice, and came attired
    In robes of righteousness.

7 Trembled the earth and shook,
    By mighty terror seized;
  The mountains' deep foundations quaked,
    Because He was displeased.

8 His nostrils issued smoke,
    His mouth devouring fire,
  And glowing coals were kindled by
    The hotness of His ire.

9 He bowed the heaven of heavens,
   In gloomy pomp came down;
  Thick darkness was beneath His feet,
   But darker was His frown.

10 He on a cherub* rode,
   He on the swift winds flew,
11 He darkness made His hiding-place
   That no eye could pierce through.

  Dark waters and thick clouds
   Were round about Him cast,
12 Then at the brightness of His face
   The charged clouds bursting passed.

13 He thundered in the heavens,
   The Highest gave His voice;
14 His lightnings scattered them who vexed
   The person of His choice.

---

* The prevalent notion, that by *Cherubim* is meant a superior order of Celestial Intelligences, finds more support, it is safe to say, in Paradise Lost than in the Scriptures. In view of the description there given it seems surprising that any one should ever have been in doubt as to their purely symbolic character; for while as real beings they would be judged monstrous and impossible, understood as simply hieroglyphical and pictorially illustrative, all difficulties vanish, and we are delighted to see how luminous the name becomes studied in its true meaning. In the present Psalm, verse 10, we read: *"And He rode upon a Cherub and did fly, yea, He did fly upon the wings of the wind."* Here the Cherub is made expressly identical with the swift wind. While the term is used in this place in the singular number, and with a limited meaning, it furnishes, we venture to think, a reliable clue to the right interpretation of the symbol in its more complex form, as the mystic tetramorph, described by Ezekiel — the four-faced, four-winged Cherubim, every part covered with eyes—with accompanying revolving wheels, suggestive of rapid circular movement, orbit within orbit, exemplified in the

15 At Thy rebuke, O Lord !
   The seas' deep bed appeared ;
   The world's foundations were laid bare
   And all Creation feared.

16 He reached down and me drew
   From whelming waters great—
17 He rescued me from my strong foe
   And them that did me hate.

   They mightier were than I,
18   And met me in the day
   Of my calamity ; but then,
   Jehovah was my stay.

19 He also brought me forth ;
   And by his arm of might
   He rescued me, because I was
   The child of His delight.

---

planetary system. It is but the extension of a part to the whole to make this many-sided figure comprehensive not of the wind only, otherwise the Air, constituting one of the Elements of Nature, but the whole Four, and God immanent in them all. If this view be correct, by Cherubim would be meant, what in modern speech is called Nature, having respect to all the aspects of its unerring perfect four-sidedness; otherwise known as the Universe, Laws of the Universe—the whole cosmic array of Secondary Causes—Force in its endless manifestations—embracing all ministerial agencies, every thing, in fact, that belongs (to use the language of Milton) to 'the throne and equipage of God's almightiness, and what He works and what He suffers to be wrought with high providence in His Church.' Placed over the Sacred Chest which contained the Decalogue, the lid forming the Mercy Seat, the same mysterious symbol is seen under a more simple form—two Cherubim keeping guard over the Law to preserve its sanctity, while God is spoken of as enthroned between or above them in token of His supremacy over all creatures and created things. The bi-formed Pan [the All] half beast, half man, as conceived by the Greeks, representing the universal frame of things, or Nature, is a figure of the same kind, but far less rich and significant.

20 After my righteousness,
    He did reward dispense;
  After the cleanness of my hands,
    He did me recompense.

21 For I have kept His ways;
    And have not wickedly
  Departed from my God, who is
    My sole felicity.

22 For all His judgments were
    Before me night and day;
23 I kept His statutes perfectly,
    Not putting them away.

24 After my righteousness,
    The Lord did me requite;
  After the cleanness of my hands
    In His omniscient sight.

25 Thou to the merciful
    Wilt make Thy mercy sure;
  Wilt with the upright upright be,
    And pure be with the pure;

26 Thou too wilt show Thyself
    Froward to frowardness;
27 For while Thou dost resist the proud,
    The lowly Thou dost bless.

28 For Thou wilt light my lamp,
  Disperse my darkness deep;
29 By Thee I can run through a troop,
  By Thee a wall o'erleap.

30 Most perfect is God's way,
  His word is sure and tried;
 He is a buckler to all those
  Who in His Name confide.

31 The Lord alone is God,
  There is no other Rock;
32 He girds with strength, He suffers naught
  My perfect way to block;

33 My feet, like hinds' feet, makes
  To dizzy heights ascend;
34 My hands He teaches how to war,
  The bow of brass to bend.

35 Thou hast to me the shield
  Of Thy salvation given;
 And Thy right hand hath held me up
  And disciplined for Heaven.

---

36 Thou hast enlarged my steps,
  My free feet have not slipped;
37 I will pursue and overtake,
  Of every hindrance stripped,

      And will not turn again,
        Until the smitten foe
38 Shall fall beneath my conquering arm—
        Be utterly laid low.

39 For to the battle Thou
        Hast girded me with might;
40 And made th' insurgents turn their backs
        In ignominious flight.

41 They cried aloud for help,
        But there was none to save;
      Ev'n to the Lord they cried, but He
        No answer to them gave.

42 Then did I beat them small;
        Away I made them fleet
      As dust wind-driven, I cast them out
        As the mire of the street.

43 Thou from the people's strifes
        Hast freed me, and me made
44 Head of the nations—homage shall
        By strangers be me paid.

45 Those whom I have not known
        Shall hasten to obey;
      They shall submit themselves to me,
        And fear and fade away.

46 Jehovah lives, my Rock;
　　Let Him exalted be!
47 The God of my salvation, who
48 　Avenged and rescued me.

49 Therefore will I give thanks,
　　And will His praises sing,
50 Who wrought this great deliverance
　　For His anointed King.

PSALM XIX.

THE rolling skies with lips of flame
　Their Maker's power and skill proclaim:
2 Day speaks to day, and night to night
　Shows knowledge writ in beams of light.
3 And though no voice, no spoken word
　Can by the outward ear be heard,
4 The witness of a travelling sound
　Reverberates the world around.

In the bright east with gold enriched
He for the sun a tent has pitched,
5 That. like a bridegroom after rest,
Comes from his chamber richly drest,
An athlete strong and full of grace,
And glad to run the heavenly race,—
6 Completes his round with tireless feet,
And naught is hidden from his heat.

7 But, Nature's book sums not the whole:
　God's perfect law converts the soul;
　His sure unerring word supplies
　The means to make the simple wise;
8 His precepts are divinely right,
　An inspiration and delight;
　His pure commandment makes all clear,
9 Clean and enduring in His fear.

　The judgments of the Lord are true,
　And righteous wholly through and through;
10 More to be coveted than gold,
　Of higher worth a thousand fold;
　More sweet than sweetest honey far,
　Th' unfoldings of their sweetness are:
11 They warn Thy servant, and they guard;
　In keeping them there's great reward.

12 Who can his errors understand?
　My secret faults are as the sand:
　From these me cleanse, make pure within,
13 And keep me from presumptuous sin;
　Lest sin me rule and fetter fast,
　And I unpardoned die at last.
14 My words and meditation be
　O Lord, my Rock, approved of Thee.

PSALM XX.

M AY God thee answer in the day
  Of battle-peril and of need!
The God of Jacob thee upstay,
2   And out of Zion help proceed!

3 Have to thy offerings due regard;
   Of thy pure zeal be mindful still;
4 Thy pious faithfulness reward,
   And all thy purposes fulfil!

5 We'll praise thee, victor in the fight,
   And God too, who for thee contests;
  And on our loyal banners write:
   "The Lord fulfil all thy requests."

6 The Lord doth His Anointed save,
   I know, with a salvation grand;
  Ev'n while He asked, God answer gave—
   The saving strength of His right hand.

7 While some in mounted horses trust,
   And some in chariots of war,
  In God, and in a cause that's just,
   Our confidence is greater far.

8 And justly so; for while they lie
   O'erthrown and prostrate and deject,
  Or panic-stricken wildly fly,
   We risen are and stand erect.

9 Jehovah, save! God save the King!
　　Let the King hear us when we call!
　Hosanna! God's high praise we sing,
　　By whom the nations rise or fall.

PSALM XXI.

THE King shall in Thy strength rejoice,
　　And Thy salvation, Lord!
2 The fullness of his heart's desire
　　Thou hast to him outpoured.

3 With gifts and blessings infinite,
　　Thou goest him before,
　Forestalling all his large requests
　　And giving him yet more.

　A crown of purest gold, Thy gift,
　　Doth on his forehead blaze;
4 He asking life, Thou gav'st it him,
　　Ev'n endless length of days.

5 Thou dost on him high honor lay,
　　Great majesty and might,
6 For Thou most blessèd makest him
　　Forever in Thy sight.

　And Thou appointest him to be
　　A blessing to the race;
　Dost gladden him with gladness found
　　Nowhere but in Thy face.

7 For the King trusted in the Lord,
   And he unmoved shall stand :
8 Against all those who bear Thee hate
   Thou wilt display Thy hand.

9 Like to a flaming furnace Thou
   Wilt make them in that hour ;
   God shall them swallow up in wrath,
   A fire shall them devour.

10 Their seed shall perish from the earth,
11   For their intended ill—
   The plot which they devised, they are
   Not able to fulfill.

12 For Thou Thy bowstrings wilt prepare,
   And wilt them put to flight :
13 Be, Lord, exalted in Thy strength,
   So we will harp Thy might !

PSALM XXII.

MY God, my God, O why
   Hast Thou forsaken me ?
My cry sounds shrill throughout a lone
   And dark eternity.

One moment seems an age,
   Mid this desertion drear ;
The empty heavens receive my prayer,
   But there is none to hear.

2 I in the daytime call,
　　My calling is in vain ;
　I am not silent in the night,
　　But yet no help obtain.

3 But Thou most holy art—
　　Amid the praises throned
4 Of Israel, who trusted Thee,
5 　And never was disowned.

6 A worm, and not a man,
　　Reproach I on me draw—
7 All they that see me wag their head,
　　And, mocking, cry : "Ha ! ha !

8 " He trusted in the Lord,
　　That He would him befriend—
　Let Him, since He in him delights,
　　Deliverance extend."

9 But from my birth Thou hast
　　Thy love and care expressed ,
　And madest me to trust, when I
　　Was on my mother's breast.

10 Thou art my Father, God,
　　My stay, my only one—
11 O be not far, for trouble 's near,
　　And helper there is none.

12 O many bulls, strong bulls
    Of Bashan, hem me round;
13 They gape on me, and, lion-like,
    They roar and tear the ground.

14 Like water I'm poured out;
    My bones are drawn apart;
   Like melted wax within my breast
    Is my dissolving heart.

15 My strength is all dried up;
    Fierce thirst inflames my breath;
   My tongue is fastened to my jaws,
    And I am nigh to death.

16 Round me a barking crowd
    Of evil-doers meet—
   With murderous and cruel nails
    They pierce my hands and feet;

17 They on my anguish gloat;
18   My garments, at the last,
   They part among them, and they lots
    Upon my vesture cast.

19 Haste to my help, my Strength!
    Cast off each cruel clog—
20 My soul deliver from the sword,
    My darling* from the dog;

---

* Literally, *My only one*, i. e., *My dear life*, my soul—Macbeth's "mine eternal jewel."

21 Save from the lion's mouth !—
    I made my prayer to Thee,
    And from the horns of th' unicorns
    THOU, LORD, HAST ANSWERED ME.

22 The agony is o'er,
    The triumph is complete :
    I to my brethren will declare
    Thy Name and praises sweet.*

---

23 Praise Him, all ye that fear
    Jehovah, the Most High—
    Ye Jacob's seed, ye Israel's,
    Fear Him and glorify !

24 For He did not despise,
    Abhor as others did ;
    But heard the Sufferer when he cried,
    E'en when His face seemed hid.

---

* One who appreciates the dramatic structure of many of the Psalms, will have no difficulty in ascribing the great difference of tone which characterizes different portions of the same psalm to a change of speakers. Take Psalm 69 for an example. The imprecatory language of verses 22-28 is so out of keeping with what precedes and follows that one is forced to refer it to another speaker. Coming from the mouth of a sympathizing and indignant spectator of the fiendish cruelty practised on patient innocence, all seems natural and proper. Such an one would answer exactly to the Chorus of the Greek Drama, offering his comment, favorable or otherwise, on what is passing. In the present Psalm, the anticipatory wail of the predicted Messiah, hanging on the Cross, reaches to verse 22. All that follows might properly proceed from the supposed Chorus representing the whole body of the faithful. See Milton's " Samson Agonistes " for an illustration of the office of the Chorus; also Shakespeare's " Henry V."

25 My praise shall be of Him ;
   I 'll in th' assembly great
Of those that fear Him, pay my vows,
   And myself consecrate.

26 The meek shall freely eat,
   He full supply will give :
Who seek the Lord they Him shall praise :
   'Your heart forever live !'

27 The farthest ends of earth
   Shall all return to Thee—
All kindreds of the nations shall
   Before Thee bow the knee.

28 For His the kingdom is ;
   His right it is to sit
Ruler among the nations, men
   To bless and benefit.

29 The opulent shall eat
   And worship ; and the poor,
That cannot keep his soul alive,
   Find his provision sure.

30 The unborn Him shall serve,
   And sire shall tell to son
How faithfully His promises
   He hath observed and done.

PSALM XXIII.

THE Lord my Shepherd is,
   He satisfies my needs;
In pastures green He makes me lie—
   By restful waters leads.

My sinking soul revives,
   When faint and spiritless;
For His Name's sake He guides my feet
   In paths of righteousness.

Though in the deep dark gorge
   I walk, I will not fear,
For through the death-shade black as night
   Thy crook and presence cheer.

Thou hast a table spread
   For me, in sight of foes;
My head anointed hast with oil,
   My cup of good o'erflows.

Goodness and mercy still
   Shall surely follow me,
And in Thy House* will I abide
   Forever, Lord, with Thee.

---

*If it be assumed that this was one of David's earlier compositions, as the Temple was not yet built, it follows, that by "the House of the Lord" in this place is meant no particular building—not the Tabernacle even—but that, in the estimation of the Psalmist, any place, mountain cave or bit of green sward, hallowed by the Divine Presence, is a veritable Bethel—House of God.

SECOND VERSION.

THE Lord is my Shepherd, I never shall want;
   Since He is my Keeper, no danger shall daunt;
He makes me lie down in green pastures, and leads
By the soft-sliding waters that gladden the meads.

He refreshes my soul; and in faithfulness sweet
Guides rightly my silly and ignorant feet:
Through the gloom of the glen I will walk without fear,
For my Shepherd is with me to lighten and cheer.

Thou prepar'st me a feast in the face of my foes,
My head Thou anointest, my cup overflows:
Surely goodness shall follow my steps all my days
And I'll dwell in Thy House, and my life spend in praise.

PSALM XXIV.

JEHOVAH'S right to all extends;
   He made, and all upholds as well—
  The earth with all it comprehends;
    The world and all that therein dwells—
2 He founded it upon the seas,
  And stablished it by firm decrees.

3 Who shall ascend into His Hill?
   Who stand within His Holy Place?
4 He with clean hands, pure heart and will,
   Who does not stoop to actions base;
  Who not deceitfully has sworn,
  But holds all lying arts in scorn.

5 He blessings shall from God receive—
    Dear pledges of His saving grace :
  The God of Truth will not deceive
    Those who sincerely seek His face—
6 The sons of Jacob who inquire,
  God's chosen, shall have their desire.

7 Lift up your heads, ye ancient gates !
    Ye everlasting doors, give way !
  For lo ! the King of Glory waits,
    And means to enter in to-day.
8 "Who is this King of Glory ? Who ? "
  Jehovah, mighty to subdue.

9 Lift up your heads, ye ancient gates !
    Ye everlasting doors, give way !
  For lo ! the King of Glory waits,
    And means to enter in to-day.
10 "Who is this King of Glory, then ? "
   The Lord of angels and of men.

PSALM XXV.

TO Thee I lift my soul—
    My God, I trust in Thee ;
  Let me not be ashamed, let not
    My foes exult o'er me.

3 Let none who on Thee wait
   In praying humbleness,
 Be e'er ashamed, but only those
   Who causelessly trangress.

4 Show me Thy paths, O Lord!
5   Instruct me in Thy way:
 Great God of my Salvation, I
   On Thee wait all the day.

6 Thy tender mercies, Lord,
   Have ever been of old:
7 Remember not my youthful sins
   And follies manifold.

8 The Lord I know is good
   And upright; He will teach
 Sinners, who seek the right to know,
   And guidance give to each;

9 The lowly and the meek
   Will lovingly direct:
10 Mercy and truth are unto such
   As His commands respect.

11 For Thy Name's sake, O Lord!
   Who only canst forgive,
 Pardon my guilt, for it is great,
   And let the culprit live.

12 What man doth fear the Lord ?
13   He, though of humble birth,
Shall dwell at ease, and his meek soul
  Inherit shall the earth.

14 The secret of the Lord
  With them that fear Him is ;
He will them show His covenant,
  And honor them as His.

15 Mine eyes are toward the Lord,
  In confidence that He
Will pluck my feet out of the net
  The fowler spread for me.

16 Have mercy on me, Lord,
  For desolate I grieve ;
17 My troubles are enlarged, do Thou
  My countless woes relieve,

18 And pardon all my sins ;
  Regard my sad estate ;
19 My foes are many, and they me
  With cruel hatred hate.

20 O keep my soul from shame ;
  I put my trust in Thee ;
21 Let my uprightness me preserve,
  And my integrity.

22 Since all who wait on Thee
    Thou holdest in esteem,
From all his troubles do Thou, Lord,
    Thine Israel redeem.

PSALM XXVI.

JUDGE me, O Lord! to Thee I dare
    In my integrity appeal:
I lay my inmost bosom bare,
    Attempting nothing to conceal.

In all uprightness I have walked,
    And have not wavered in my trust:
Bear witness if I've vainly talked,
    Have been injurious or unjust.

2 Examine me, O God! and try:
    I welcome so supreme a test
As the inspection of Thine eye,
    Searching the secrets of my breast.

3 Thy mercy is before mine eyes,
    And from Thy truth I have not strayed;
4 I have not sat with men of lies,
5   Nor friendships with dissemblers made.

6 I'll wash my hands in innocence,
    And so Thine altar will surround;
7 With love and thankfulness intense
    I will Thy wondrous works resound.

8 I love Thy Habitation, Lord !
  The Place where doth Thy Glory* dwell,
 Whence Thou dost saving help afford
  To Thine afflicted Israel.

9 Gather me not with men of blood ;
10   Mischief and bribes are in their hand :—
11 But as for me, I with the good
  Will walk uprightly in the Land.

 Redeem me, Lord, and show me grace,
  Confirm me in my righteousness !
12 My foot stands in an even place ;
  Thee in th' assemblies I will bless.

PSALM XXVII.

THE Lord my Saviour is, and Light ;
  Whom should I fear with Him to aid ?
 My life's stronghold and secret might ;—
  What cause have I to be afraid ?

2 When like some hungry beast of prey,
  My foes came on me to devour,
 They stumbled, fell—and snatched away
  I live unhurt until this hour.

3 Not though a host 'gainst me encamp,
  And war its ugly front uprear,
 Shall this my trust or courage damp,
  Or cowardize my heart with fear.

---

* The Shekinah.

4 One thing I greatly have desired,
   For which I will not cease to pray,
That I, from scenes of strife retired,
   Of battle fierce and bloody fray,

  In the Lord's House may dwell in peace
   All my life long, with ravished eyes
  His beauty to behold, nor cease
   To ask of Him and grow more wise.

5 In time of trouble, He'll me hide
   In His pavilion strong and safe;
He to a rock my feet shall guide
6   High o'er my foes that vainly chafe.

  I'll in His Tabernacle make
   Offerings of joy with trumpet sound;
  His praises loudly sing, and wake
   Melodious echoes all around.

---

7 Hear me, O Lord! When Thou didst deign,
8   Those words, "Seek ye My Face," to speak,
My grateful heart in contrite pain
   Replied, "Thy Face, Lord, will I seek."

9 Hide not Thy Face from me, I pray!
   Thou hast my help been in the past:
In anger turn me not away;
   Forsake me not, nor from Thee cast.

10 When of my parents I'm bereft
   Earth's holiest ties have sundered been,
   I know I have a Father left,
      Who will adopt and take me in.

11 Teach me Thy perfect way, O Lord!
      Because of foes that lie in wait;
12 From slanderers and others, guard,
      That breathe out cruelty and hate.

13 Unless I had believed to see
      Thy goodness, Lord, here verified,
   Sometime, somehow, it seems to me
      I must have fainted, must have died.

14 Wait on the Lord : Be strong, and let
      Thy heart take courage! Banish fear!
   No one defeat has suffered yet—
      Wait on the Lord : Be of good cheer!

PSALM XXVIII.

TO Thee, O Lord, I lift my cry—
   Be Thou, my Rock, not deaf to it,
Lest I become like them that die—
   Them that go down into the pit.

2 Now, while I on Thy footstool dwell,
   I raise my hands, my heart to Thee!
  Speak from Thy Holy Oracle,
   O be not silent, answer me!

3

3 Gather me not with those, who play
    Their cunning and deceitful parts!
Peaceful and kind the words they say,
    But mischief lurks within their hearts.

4 Render to them their just desert:
5   Because Thy works they disregard,
Break down and lay them in the dirt—
    Be utter ruin their reward.

6 Thrice blesséd be the Lord, for He
    Has silence broke, and answer given;
7 He is my Strength, He strengthens me,
    My Shield, my Helper, out of Heaven.

'Tis good to trust and wait I find;
    I trusted, and deliverance came;
Therefore will I with heart and mind,
    Rejoice in Him, and praise His Name.

8 He is His people's Strength; He is
    To His Anointed a Stronghold:
A shepherd's tenderness is His,
    He feeds His flock and guards the fold.

PSALM XXIX.

GIVE to the Lord, ye sons of might,
    Glory and strength—His throne address;
2 Him worship, clothed in robes of light,
    The beauty born of holiness.
Ye angel hosts on high proclaim
The dreadful honors of His Name.

3 His voice is on the billowy sea,
    Heard in the thunder of its waves,
4 Is full of power and majesty,
    Resounding through its countless caves,
  And, with its loud and deafening roar,
  It shakes and terrifies the shore.

5 Cedars of Lebanon it breaks;
6   They like a calf affrighted skip;
  It Lebanon and Hermon makes
    Like a young unicorn to trip;
8 The desert, Kadesh, quakes to hear;
9 And hinds untimely calve through fear.

7 His voice it cleaves the lightning's wing;
9   It strips and leaves the forest bare;
  And all Creation worshipping
    Saith, "Glory! glory!" everywhere:
10 He at the Flood and through all time
  Sits King upon His throne sublime.

PSALM XXX.

I WILL extol Thee and adore,
  For Thou hast raised me up once more;
And hast not chosen to fulfill,
The hope of those who wish me ill.

2 O Lord, my God, I Thee besought,
3 And Thou hast healed me: Thou hast brought
  Up from the underworld my soul—
  Saved from the grave and made me whole.

4 Sing to Jehovah, sound the fame
  Of His memorial Holy Name!
5 While that His anger is most brief,
  A sharp but momentary grief,

  His favor is a life time; pain
  And weeping may perchance remain
  O'er night, but when the morning breaks,
  The sleeping joy to praise awakes.

6 But foolishly, by pride misled,
  "I never shall be moved," I said—
7 "Thy favor, Lord, continued long,
  Has made my mountain to stand strong."

  When Thou Thy loving Face didst hide,
8 Then was I troubled, and I cried
9 To Thee, O Lord! and said: "What good
  Or profit is there in my blood?

  "When I go down into the pit,
  Shall the dust praise Thee? or shall it
10 Declare Thy truth?—Jehovah, hear,
  Pity and help, in love draw near!"

11 Thou hast (my penitence discerned)
  My mourning into dancing turned;
  My sackcloth loosed; and girded me
12 With joy—that I may sing to Thee.

PSALM XXXI.

IN Thee, O Lord, I put my trust—
    Let me not come to shame:
2 Haste to my help, deliver me,
    In Thy most righteous Name!

  Be Thou to me a rock of strength,
    Where I may safely bide:
3 And so Thou art; for Thy Name's sake
    Thou wilt me lead and guide.

4 Pluck from the net they 've hid for me,
    For Thou art my sure Friend;
5 Hast me redeemed—into Thy hand
    My spirit I commend.

6 Them that vain idols serve I hate;
    My soul on Thee relies,
7 I will be glad, for Thou hast seen
    My woes with pitying eyes;

8 And hast not me delivered up
    A prisoner to my foe;
  But set my feet in a large place,
    Left free to come and go.

---

9 Have mercy on me, Lord! mine eye
    With weeping wastes away;
  My powers of soul and body fail,
    And fall into decay.

10 For all my life with grief is spent ;
   With sighing all my years :
   By reason of my sins, I weep
   My strength away in tears.

11 Because of all my foes, reproach
   Me everywhere attends ;
   A scorn I to my neighbors am,
   A terror to my friends.

   They that did see me in the street
   Immediately fled :
12 I am forgotten, out of mind,
   Like one already dead.

13 I heard the many me traduce—
   The envious sons of strife—
   While they took counsel, and devised
   To take away my life.

14 But in the Lord I trusted still :
   I said : " Thou art my God ;
15 My times are in Thy hand, I wait
   For Thy delivering rod."

16 Upon me cause Thy Face to shine ;
   Save, for Thy mercies' sake :
17 Let me not be ashamed, O Lord !
   But so the wicked make,

Let them in Sheol silent be ;
18 Let lying lips be dumb,
From which proud words and insolent
Now 'gainst the righteous come.

---

19 How great Thy goodness treasured up,
Ne'er told by tongue or pen,
For those who fear and trust in Thee
Before the sons of men !

20 Thou in Thy presence wilt them hide,
From plotters 'gainst their life ;
In Thy pavilion them conceal,
Safe from the tongues of strife.

21 O blessed be the Lord, for He
Strange kindness me hath shown,
In a strong city, fenced with walls,
That could not be o'erthrown.

22 In my alarm and haste, I said :
" I am cut off," but no—
For when I cried for help, Thou didst
The needed help bestow.

23 O love the Lord, all ye His saints ;
The proud He will reward :
24 Be strong, take courage, O all ye,
Whose hope is in the Lord !

PSALM XXXII.

BLEST is the man, who stands forgiven
  Of trespasses and debts;
To whom the Lord imputes not guilt,
  But cancels and forgets.

2 Whose penitence is found sincere;
  Whose spirit knows no guile;
Whose earthly pilgrimage is cheered
  By God's approving smile.

3 When I kept silence I waxed old,
  Through moaning all day long;
4 Thy hand was heavy day and night,
  For unacknowledged wrong.

The moisture of my fevered frame
  Was changed to summer drought;
I felt the sting of conscious guilt,
  But could not pluck it out.

5 Acknowledged I my sin to Thee,
  With sense of what was fit;
I said, I will confess my fault,
  And Thou forgavest it.

6 For this let every godly one
  To Thee in prayer abound
In an accepted time, when Thou
  May'st certainly be found.

They surely shall not reach to him,
    When whelming waters rave ;
When danger 's near, Thou 'rt nearer yet,
    And powerful to save.

7 Thou art for me a Hiding Place
    In trouble, Thou wilt make
Songs of divine deliverance
    On every side to break.

---

8 I will instruct Thee in the way,
    Thy duty 't is to go—
With mine eye on Thee, counsel thee
    What paths to tread below.

9 Be not as horse or mule that must,
    Irrational and dumb,
With bit and bridle be held firm,
    To make them stay or come :

10 The wicked many sorrows have ;
    But whoso trusts the Lord,
Mercy shall compass him about
    And grace be on him poured.

11 Exult, ye righteous, and rejoice ;
    In praise bear each his part ;
Ring out your gladness, O all ye
    Who upright are in heart !

PSALM XXXIII.

REJOICE, ye righteous, in the Lord,
    For praise and thanks the upright suit;
2 Now test the sweetness of each chord
    Of holy harp and ten-stringed lute—
3 Awake new ecstasies and joys;
    Play skillfully with a loud noise!

4 Sing how Jehovah's word is right—
    The awful rule of rectitude:
    His works of mercy and of might,
    How faithfully He has pursued:
5 How loves He righteousness; how earth
    He fills with melody and mirth!

6 Say, By His word the heavens were made,
    And their unreckonable hosts:
7 He garnered seas, their depths uplaid
    In magazines shut in by coasts:
    He bound the whole by chains of law—
8 Let the earth fear and stand in awe.

9 All things that are, in Him begun—
    By Him created in the past!
    HE spake the word, and it was done;
    Commanded, and the world stood fast.
    On high He sits, serene and calm,
    Holding creation in His palm.

10 The counsels of the nations He
    Makes void, their thoughts of none effect;
11 His counsels stand eternally,
    Impaired by time in no respect.
12 Happy the nation, happiest known,
    Whose God Jehovah is alone.

13 The Lord from heaven at once surveys
    The myriads of human birth;
14 From His high throne directs His gaze
    On all th' inhabitants of earth:
15 He fashioned all their hearts, and knows
    Who are His friends and who His foes.

16 Not by the number of his host
    Is the king saved, and victory gained;
  Not by his might, the warrior's boast,
    Is his deliverance obtained.
17 The war-horse, when it has to cope
  With mightier strength, is a vain hope.

18 Jehovah watches from above
    The trembling footsteps of the just:
19 From famine, and from death, in love,
    Preserves all those who in Him trust.
20 To us, O Lord! our Help! our Shield!
  Be now Thy saving power revealed!

21 Our heart in Thee shall happy rest,
    Because we 've trusted in Thy Name;

Thy faithfulness 't is sweet to test—
Thou Who forever art the same.
22 Thy mercy, Lord, upon us be,
According as we hope in Thee.

PSALM XXXIV.

I WILL bless the Lord, and raise
  Ceaseless canticles of praise;
From full fountains running o'er,
I perpetual thanks will pour.

2 I will praise Him when I'm glad;
I will praise Him when I'm sad;
While my eyes with tears are dim,
I will make my boast of Him.

3 Magnify the Lord with me;
Let His Name exalted be:
4 When I seek the Lord, He hears
And delivers from my fears.

5 They who look to Him, their gloom
He shall scatter and illume:
Whoso call upon His Name,
They shall never blush for shame.

6 To the poor man in his grief,
Brings He succor and relief:
7 And His angel camps about
All the pious and devout.

8 Taste and see the Lord is good :
'T is a truth not understood,
They alone are truly blest
Who upon His bosom rest.

9 Fear the Lord all ye His saints ;
Wants He 'll banish and complaints—
10 Though young lions suffer lack,
He 'll no good from you keep back.

11 Come, ye children, now draw near,
Hear me teach Jehovah's fear:
12 Would ye walk in pleasant ways,
See long life and happy days,

13 Keep your tongue from slanders vile,
And your lips from speaking guile ;
14 Practice good, no evil do ;
Seek ye peace and it pursue.

15 Turns the Lord approving eyes
On the good, He hears their cries ;
16 But His face is turned away
From the wicked, them to slay.

17 To the broken-hearted, He,
Dweller in eternity,
18 Stoops contrition's sigh to hear,
And to wipe the bitter tear.

19 Many are the good man's woes,
    But they spoil not his repose :
20 Of his bones God keeps each one,
    And of all there's broken none.

21 Evil shall the wicked slay—
    Doomed the penalty to pay :
22 They, who in Jehovah trust,
    Shall accounted be as just.

PSALM XXXV.

STRIVE Thou with those who strive with me ;
    Fight Thou 'gainst those who 'gainst me fight ;
2 Grasp shield and buckler ; And, O be,
    Jehovah, helper of my right !
3 Draw out the spear, and block their way ;
    And, "I will save thee," to me say.

4 Confound and put to shame all those,
    Who seek my life, my hurt contrive ;
    Turn Thou them back ; and make my foes
5   Like chaff that storm-winds fiercely drive :
6 Let, through a dark and slippery place,
    The Angel of the Lord them chase.

7 For without cause, for me a snare
    They hid, and digged for me a pit ;
8 As for their trap, all unaware
9   May they themselves fall into it.
10 "Who is like Thee," I then shall say,
    "Who spoils the spoiler of his prey ?"

11 Malicious witnesses arise ;
  They ask me things I do not know ;
12 They ill for good 'gainst me devise ;
  Bereave, and plunge my soul in woe.
13 Whereas, when they were sick, I wore
  Sackcloth, kept fast, watched, prayed, wept sore.

14 As to a cherished friend or brother
    I bore myself, I to him clung ;
  I mourned as for a dying mother ;
15   But at my halting, their sharp tongue
  They did like sword 'gainst me unsheath—
16 They gnashed upon me with their teeth.

17 How long, O Lord, wilt Thou look on ?
    Restore destructions ! Let my life
  From the young lion's jaws be won—
    The purposed prey of men of strife :
18 In the great congregation I
  Will then Thy goodness magnify.

———

19 Let not them, wrongfully my foes,
    Rejoice o'er me ; permit not them,
20 Who without cause hate and oppose,
    To sneer, wink with the eye, contemn,
21 And with wide mouth exclaim, "Ha ! ha !
  We'd have it so, we 're glad we saw."

22 Lord ! Thou hast seen it—Be not far ;
23   Wake to the justice of my cause :

24 Judge me, judge them, who guilty are,
   According to Thy righteous law.
25 Let them not say with humor grim,
   "Ha! ha! we now have swallowed him."

26 May those who at my hurt rejoice,
   Confounded and dishonored lie,
   My foes, who with united voice
   Themselves against me magnify.
27 Friends of my right, let them in song,
   Sing Thy glad praises all day long!

PSALM XXXVI.

WICKEDNESS within the heart
   Of the sinner whispers lies,
Drawn to act the atheist's part,
   To God's fear he shuts his eyes;—

2 Duped by that false oracle,
   By self-flatteries within—
Thinks that none will know or tell
   Th' odious secret of his sin.

3 False his words are; to be wise,
   And do good he has left off:
4 Plans in bed iniquity; .
   His chief business is to scoff.

5 Lord, Thy truth and goodness strike
   Highest reaches of the sky;
6 And Thy righteousness is like
   Thy great mountains lifted high :

  And Thy judgments are a deep,
    Deeper than the deepest sea :
  Man and beast, Thou, Lord, dost keep—
    All would perish without Thee.

7 Precious is Thy love and dear;
   Safe the shelter of Thy wing;
8 Great abundance of good cheer
   Thou wilt to Thy children bring :

  Thou wilt make them drink their fill
    From Thine Eden river bright :
9 With Thee is life's fountain still,
    In Thy light shall we see light.

10 Let Thy goodness bide and stay :
11   Let not foot of pride o'ertake :
   Let no hand drive me away :
12   They shall fall who Thee forsake.

PSALM XXXVII.*

A T evil-doers do not fret;
 Let their success not thee disturb—
2 They soon like grass will be cut down,
 And withered be like the green herb!

3 But in Jehovah trust; do good;
 Dwell in the land and safely feed:
4 And in the Lord delight thyself,
 And He 'll supply thy every need.

5 Commit thy way unto the Lord:
 Confide in Him to make all right.
6 He will bring forth thy righteousness,
 And judgment as the noonday light.

7 Depend upon the Lord, and wait;
 Fret not thyself at other's gain:
8 From anger cease, and wrath forsake—
 It tends to crime, is worse than vain.

9 Evil who sow, shall evil reap;
 But those who wait, shall yet possess.
10 The wicked soon shall be no more,—
 His mansion be left tenantless.

---

* This Psalm belongs to the acrostic or alphabetic class, in which the initial letters of the Hebrew alphabet, in their regular order, are the initial letters of the successive lines or stanzas of the poem. They are seven in number, viz.: Psalms 25, 34, 37, 111, 112, 119, 145. The aphoristic character is common to them all. Made up of practical precepts to be learned by heart, it is probable that the alphabetic arrangement was meant to serve as a mnemonic device to assist in remembering them. In the present case the English alphabet has been substituted for the Hebrew.

11 Favored of God are all the meek,
　　The meek inherit shall the earth—
　Abundance shall they have of peace,
　　In testimony of their worth.

12 Gins for the good the wicked lays,
　　He gnashes on him with his teeth.
13 　The Lord shall laugh at him ; He sees
　　Destruction moving from beneath.

14 Hands of the wicked draw the sword,
　　They bend the bow to slay the upright—
15 　Their sword shall enter their own hearts ;
　　Their bow shall broken be outright.

16 In little has the righteous more,
　　Than many wicked have in much :
17 　The arms of these shall shattered be,
　　But God lets none the righteous touch.

18 Knows God the days of the upright ;
　　Their heritage shall aye endure ;
19 　They shall at no time come to shame ;
　　Their bread in famine shall be sure.

20 Let all the wicked know, that theirs
　　Is the brief glory of the meads :
　Like smoke it vanishes away,
　　The final fate of fairest weeds,

21 Money they borrow and pay not;
   The righteous favor show, and give:
22 Those whom God blesses, title gain
   To vast estates, and long shall live.

23 Need is our steps should ordered be
   By God, who therein takes delight;
24 For though we fall, we'll rise again,
   By help of His upholding might.

25 On the Lord's faithfulness rely:
   For I've been young and now am old,
   Yet have I seen forsaken none
   Who trusted God, and kept fast hold.

26 Practice the precepts thou hast learned:
   Keep God's pure law thine eyes before:
   Depart from evil and do good:
   And so abide forevermore.

28 Quite sure it is He judgment loves;
   And He will not His saints forsake:—
   They are preserved for aye; but He
   An end will of the wicked make.

29 Revolves the righteous in his heart
30   The words of wisdom he would speak;
31 His steps they waver not, because
   God's law makes steadfast what is weak.

32 Sly secret watch the wicked keeps—
    Lying in wait just blood to spill:
33   God will explode a sentence given,
    Where Hate sits judge and thirsts to kill.

34 Thou on Jehovah wait; stand fast!
    He'll raise thee to possess the land:
    And when the wicked is cut off,
    Thou shall it see and understand.

35 Under a golden canopy
    I saw a wicked man and proud,
    Having great power unjustly got,
    Claiming base worship from the crowd,

36 Vain glorious, self-deified,
    Spreading himself like a green tree
    In its own soil. I passed again,
    And he was not—gone utterly.

37 Watch thou the perfect man, behold
    The upright, for his end is peace:
38   As for transgressors they shall be
    Destroyed together, and shall cease.

39 'Xult—salvation's of the Lord;
    In time of trouble your Stronghold,
40 Your Help and your Deliverer
    From the ungodly, as of old.

PSALM XXXVIII.

SPARE me! howe'er deserved,
　　My punishment curtail:
Let Thy abundant mercy, Lord,
　　O'er wrath provoked prevail.

2 Thine arrows are sunk deep;
　　There's nothing in me whole;
3 There is no soundness in my flesh,
　　No comfort in my soul.

4 I sink, weighed down by sins
　　That heavier are than lead,
In whelming waters whose loud waves
　　Are roaring o'er my head.

5 My stripes are festering wounds;
6 　My agony is great;
I with unceasing tears bewail
　　My sorrowful estate:

7 There's burning in my loins;
8 　I am benumbed and bruised;
I cry out from disquietude
　　That's everywhere diffused.

9 My longing is not hid;
　　To Thee each sigh and groan,
10 My fluttering heart, my failing eyes,
　　My feebleness, are known.

11 My lovers and my friends,
   My kinsmen stand aloof;
12 My foes weave hateful calumnies,
   Most false in warp and woof.

13 But I've been deaf and dumb,
14   Like one that did not hear;
15 For Thee I waited, O my God!
   My character to clear.

16 They will, I said, exult,
     If I commit a fault—
   If slips my foot, and well I know
17   I ready am to halt.

18 My grief I kept in mind—
     How guilty I have been;
   I will my guiltiness declare,
     Be sorry for my sin.

19 But many are my foes,
     They deadly are and strong;
20 Evil for good they render me,
     For kindness do me wrong.

21 Forsake me not, O Lord!
     Be never far away;
22 Make haste to help me, O my God!
     Thy saving power display.

PSALM XXXIX.

I SAID, I will take heed, that I
    Offend not with my tongue ;
My mouth with bridle keep, while I
    The wicked am among.

2 And I was dumb, I held my peace,
    I uttered not a word,
Abstained from even proper speech—
    Then was my sorrow stirred ;

3 My heart was hot within ; the fire
    While I was musing, burned ;
Then spake I with my tongue once more
    Of what me most concerned.

4 Make me to know my end, O Lord !
    The measure of my days ;
That I may know how frail I am,
    How fatal my delays.

5 Behold my days as handbreadths are,
    So brief are they and few ;
My life is naught—a bubble I
    And bubbles I pursue.

6 Man at his best, when standing firm,
    In truth is but a breath ;
He heaps up gold with restless toil
    For unknown heirs at death.

7 And now, what wait I for, O Lord?
   My hope is all in Thee;
8 O make me not the sceptic's scorn;
   From my transgressions free.

9 Because Thou didst it, I was dumb,
   I opened not my mouth:
10 Remove Thy stroke away from me,
    That parches likes a drouth.

11 When Thou with just rebukes dost man
    For his misdeeds correct;
    Thou spoil'st his beauty as a moth,
    And turn'st away respect.

12 Hear Thou my prayer for help, O God!
    Reply to tears I pour:
13 Let me recover strength*, ere I
    Go hence and be no more!

PSALM XL.

I WAITED for the Lord till He
   His answer did no more delay;
2 With a strong arm He lifted me
   From darksome pit and miry clay,
  And placed my feet on rocky ground,
  And made my joy and peace abound.

---

* *Or*, O let me smile again,

3 He gave me a new song to sing,
   And His great goodness was my theme;
I made the hills and valleys ring,
   For O my rapture was supreme!
Many shall see and fear and trust,
Happy is he whom lies disgust.

5 Many the wonders Thou hast wrought,
   O Lord my God, on our account:
Tried I to tell each gracious thought,
   I could not to the number mount.
O Thou with whom none can compare,
How can I speak Thee or declare?

6 Since sacrifice and offering Thou
   Hast no delight in any more,
But only in obedience now,
   Thou didst mine ears for service bore—
Then said I, "Lo, I come Thy will,
My God, completely to fulfill."

9 To preach glad news of righteousness,
   Thou knowest, Lord, I've not refrained;
Mid gathered Israel's mighty press,
   My ardent lips I've not restrained,
10 From publishing and making known
The truth and mercy of Thy throne.

---

11 Withhold not Thy compassions, let
   Thy love and truth continued be:

12 For countless ills have me beset,
    My sins have overtaken me—
So many are they, shame and dread
Forbid that I should lift my head.

13 Make haste to answer me, O Lord!
14   Let those, who would my soul destroy,
    Confusion have for their reward,
      And those who in my hurt would joy.
15 Let them therefore be desolate,
Who say Aha! in scorn and hate.

16 Make glad all who in Thee confide;
    Let such as Thy salvation prize,
Repeat: "The Lord be magnified!"
17   Though poor, Thou dost not me despise;
Thou art my Help—deliv'rance bring,
Make, O my God, no tarrying!

PSALM XLI.

HAPPY is he whose heart unlocks
    And swings a hospitable door,
Whene'er the hand of pity knocks,
    And claims admittance for the poor:
Who lends to grief a willing ear,
And sheds the sympathizing tear:

2 The Lord will in the evil day
    Deliver such, and keep alive;
He'll prosper him and turn away
    The ruin that his foes contrive:

3 Stretched on his couch will stay his head,
   And in his sickness make his bed.

4 Have mercy on me, Lord, I said,
    Heal Thou my soul, for I have sinned :
5 My foes speak evil, wish me dead :
6   Visits he me ? My ears are dinned
  With falsehood. He employs his wit
    To frame a lie, then blazons it.

7 Gather in knots all who me hate ;
    Malicious whispers go around ;
  They feign much grief, calumniate,
    And try which can the deepest wound :
8 There clings, say they, some evil thing
  To him that will to death soon bring.

9 My trusted own familiar friend,*
    Who ate my bread, has lifted up
  His heel against me—to same end
    Held to my lips a poisoned cup :
  In secret played a traitor's part,
  With stabs directed at my heart.

10 Be gracious, Lord, and me restore,
    That I may properly requite ;
11 Because my foe's short triumph 's o'er,
    I know Thou dost in me delight,
12 In my integrity dost place
  Me evermore before Thy face.

* Ahithophel.

13 O blessed and thrice blessed be,
    Jehovah, God of Israel !
  Whose dwelling is eternity,
    Whose being is perpetual—
  From everlasting it begun—
  To everlasting it will run.
                    Amen and Amen.

The supposition, that Psalms 38, 39, 41 and 55 were composed while David was weighed down by the debilitating languors of a protracted bodily illness, aggravated by cruel rumors of the unnatural conduct of his son Absalom, and the secret or open defection and treachery of some of his most trusted counsellors (Ahithophel, in particular), is favored not only by direct hints and allusions, but by the help it affords in explaining some things otherwise unaccountable—for example, the supineness and slackened vigor which allowed the conspiracy to ripen without any steps being taken to defeat it. The King's inability, moreover, from this cause, to perform the duties of his office would naturally give rise to those postponements and delays in the administration of justice and the hearing of causes, which Absalom so adroitly turned to his own advantage in breeding disaffection, and stealing the hearts of the people (2 Sam. 15: 4-6) by an ostentatious forwardness and pretended zeal for their welfare.

David's sin in the matter of Uriah was ever before him (Ps. 51: 3) and darkened the whole of his subsequent life. If sin be, as etymologically defined, "a missing of the mark," it was never more strikingly verified than in his case. He was soon made aware that he had committed not only a crime but a blunder. Though forgiven, he carried a dull ache in his heart's core, that never left him. His heart oft failed him; he was degraded in his own eyes; he was so ashamed that he was not able to look up; his iniquities had laid hold of him (Ps. 40: 12) and would not let go. Ever after his fall, all his adverse fortune he never doubted was a chastisement for that sin—a buffet (Ps. 39 : 10) of the Divine Hand. Again and again he refers to it. It is an interesting psychological study to note how the recollection of his great fault affected him. He who had said " I will walk within my house with a perfect heart" (Ps. 102 : 2) had been guilty of treachery, adultery and murder. O the shame of it ! During all the miserable months which passed prior to Nathan's visit he penned no psalms nor sung any. His harp was silent. The Nemesis of a troubled conscience kept his eyes waking. He speaks of his "roaring all the day long." The anguish of his mind fevered his body. Then came confession. Both (Ps. 51 and 32) are saturated with the tears of penitence and a broken heart. But the sickness, noted in Psalm 41, is evidently of a more chronic kind, in which figure the plotters concerned in the Absalom rebellion. Compare Ps. 55.

BOOK II.

PSALMS XLII AND XLIII.*

As the flying hart, pursued,
    Pants for streamlets running free,
So in this lone solitude
    Pants my soul, O God, for Thee—

2 Thirsts for Thee, the Living God:
    When before Thee shall I come?
3 Tears have been my daily food,
    While they asked and I was dumb,

"Where is now Thy God? O where?"
4   I recall, how with the throng,
While thanksgivings shook the air,
    To Thy House I passed along.

Dear to memory those days,
    When dense crowds went up to pray;
And with voice of joy and praise
    In Thy Courts kept holy day.

---

*These two Psalms, which are properly one, are strophic in form, being divided into three parts by a refrain. David, a discrowned fugitive, has reached Mahanaim, or is on his way thither. The Psalm has for its *entourage*, frame, or setting, the Jordan with its cataracts; its mountain affluent, the Jabbok, visited by the hunted hart; and Mt. Hermon with its three summits. He laments his exclusion from the Sanctuary at Jerusalem. See 2 Samuel 15:25.

5 Why art thou cast down, my soul?
   Why this tossing, sick unrest?
  Hope in God, and Him extol,
   Who the health is of thy breast.

6 O my God! I, sad and ill,
   From the land of Jordan cry:
  Hermon's heights and Mizar's hill
   Refuge for the time supply.

7 Musing on the farther shore,
   On successful treason's acts,
  In full hearing of the roar
   Of the mighty cataracts,

  Bounds no more my spirit keeps,
   Voicing deeps assume control,
  All Thy waves and billows sweep
   Over my astonished soul.

8 Yet the Lord will be, I know,
   Gracious as He was of yore;
  Will His loving-kindness show,
   And will former songs restore.

9 I will say, My God! My Rock!
   Why hast Thou forgotten me?
10 Why do I endure the mock
   Of th' insulting enemy?

11 Why art thou cast down, my soul?
  Why this tossing, sick unrest?
 Hope in God, and Him extol,
  Who the health is of thy breast.

---

1 Judge me, Lord! defend my right,
  'Gainst a nation in revolt;
 From chief traitor* urging fight,
  Rescue, and repel assault.

2 Thou who art my Strength, O why
  Dost Thou cast me off and spurn?
 Why, oppressed by foes, go I
  Mourning, waiting Thy return?

3 Send out now Thy light and truth!
  They shall guide me, they shall bring
 To Thy Holy Hill, in sooth,
  Where I'll lay thank-offering

4 On Thine altar. For relief
  From my tribulation sharp,
 For great joy succeeding grief,
  I will praise Thee on the harp.

5 Why art thou cast down, my soul?
  Why this tossing, sick unrest?
 Hope in God, and Him extol
  Who the health is of thy breast.

* Ahithophel?

PSALM XLIV.

O GOD ! we with our ears have heard,
  Our fathers have us told,
What work Thou wroughtest in their days
  The famous days of old.

2 Thou didst the heathen dispossess,
    And plantedst them therein :
3 They by the sword gat not the Land,
    Nor by their arm did win ;

  But Thou, by Thy right hand and arm,
    Didst mightily befriend ;
  Their conquests multiply, their bounds
    On every side extend.

4 Thou art my King : Do Thou, O God,
    Deliverance command
  Once more for Jacob ; yet once more
    Display Thy helping hand.

5 Through Thee we will push down our foes,
    Trample and put to shame ;
6 For I 'll not trust in bow or sword ;
7   But only in Thy Name.

  Thou hast our adversaries quelled,
    And chased their flying ranks :
8 In Thee we made all day our boast,
    To Thee will still give thanks.

9 But now Thou hast us quite cut off,
   And to dishonor brought :
  Thou hast not gone forth with our hosts,
   Nor on our side hast fought :

10 And they who hate have us for spoil ;
   We at their feet are flung :
11 Thou givest us as sheep for food,
   And scatterest them among.

12 Thy people Thou dost sell for naught ;
13   We 're sneered at without rest ;
14 Among the nations a by-word,
   The Gentiles' constant jest.

15 I have all day before my eyes
   These tokens of disgrace ;
16 The shame of their loud blasphemies
   Calls blushes to my face.

17 All this has come upon us, Lord !
   But we 've not Thee forgot ;
18 Nor false been to Thy covenant ;
   From Thee departed not :

19 Though Thou hast crushed us in the place
   Of jackals howling near ;
  Hast shrouded us with shades of night,
   And blackest glooms of fear.

20 If we've the Name of God forgot,
   And played a treacherous part;
21 Shall God not search this out? He knows
   The secrets of the heart.

22 We're all day long for Thy sake slain;
   Accounted are as sheep
  Designed for slaughter, each in turn,
   Our life is held so cheap.

23 Awake: why sleepest Thou, O Lord?
   Arise for our relief:
24 Why hidest Thou Thy face from us,
   Forgetful of our grief?

25 For to the dust are we bowed down,
   We cleave unto the clod—
26 Rise for our help, redeem us for
   Thy mercies' sake, O God!

PSALM XLV.

FROM my heart's fountain, my great theme
   Wells up, an overflowing stream;
Because my words concern the King,
Uprushing, copious, they spring:
My tongue possesses a new gift,
The ready writer's pen less swift.

2 Fair, fair art Thou, O fairer far
  Than fairest of earth's children are:
  What grace into Thy lips is poured!
  What hives of sweetness there are stored!
  Therefore has God pronounced Thee blest—
  Th' Eternal Darling of His breast.

3 Gird Thou Thy sword upon Thy thigh,
4 O Mighty One, for triumphs high:
  In glory and in majesty
  Ascend Thy car, ride prosperously:
  Because of meekness, truth and right,
  Thy trained hand terribly shall smite.

5 Sharp are Thine arrows in Thy foes,
  Whereby the people that oppose
  Fall under Thee: Thy work pursue,
  Till Thou all nations shalt subdue.
6 Thy throne, O God, forever stands—
  Thy righteous sceptre sways all lands.

7 Thou righteousness lov'st evermore,
  And hatest wickedness—therefore,
  Hath God, Thy God, anointed Thee
  With oil of gladness plenteously
  Above Thy fellows.   When astir,
8 All Thy rich garments smell of myrrh,

  Of aloes, cassia, fragrant gums—
  While, ever and anon, there comes

Out of the ivory palaces
The noise of instruments to please—
The mighty melody of strings,
That lifts the soul on heavenly wings.

9 Daughters of kings are with Thee seen :
On Thy right hand there stands the Queen,
In gold of Ophir : Daughter, hear !
10 Forget thy father's house once dear ;
11 So shall the King thy beauty prize :
For He 's thy Lord, lift reverent eyes !

His beauty makes thy beauty dim ;
But thou art fair since fair to Him :
The sweet reflections of His face
Give majesty to thine and grace—
Thou art a portion of His state,
So that His greatness makes thee great.

12 Therefore proud Tyre, will, bowing low,
On thee rich nuptial gifts bestow ;
Th' opulent will thee entreat,
And sue for favors at thy feet :
Honors flow in from every side,
Such as befit a royal bride.

13 Lo, the king's daughter sits admired
In her apartments : all attired
In gorgeous dress inwrought with gold—
Embroidered work fair to behold—
14 She shall be led in to the King ;
15 Attendant virgins shall her bring.

16 Thou in Thy fathers' stead shalt see
   Thy sons, a royal progeny,
   Whom Thou, in view of their high birth,
   Shalt princes make in all the earth.
17 Thy Name shall still remembered be,
   And praise forever rise to Thee.

PSALM XLVI.

GOD is our Refuge and our Rock,
   Our Help in tribulation—
2 Therefore we will not fear the shock
   That moves the world's foundation.
         Let mountains be
         Sunk in the sea;
3   Its waters roar
         And shake the shore—
   Our hearts shall ne'er be shaken.

4 There is a river, whose pure streams
   Make glad the Holy City;
   Hard by the Hill it glides and gleams,
   Where dwells the God of Pity.
5   Where God abides
         No danger hides;
         Seems He withdrawn,
         At break of dawn,
   His help will be extended.

6 The nations raged, the kingdoms were
    In turmoil and commotion ;
  He spake, earth melted ; ceased the stir
    And madness of the ocean.
7   The Lord of hosts
        Defends our coasts ;
        In perils high
        To Him we fly,
  And all the peril passes.

8 Come, see Jehovah's works of peace—
    Who wrought earth's desolations,
9 Now causing wars and strifes to cease
    Among all tribes and nations :
        He breaks the bow,
        The spear also ;
        The chariot burns ;
        To ashes turns
  The engines of destruction.

10 Be still, and know that I am God !
    My name shall be exalted—
  I'll stretch my peace-restoring rod
    O'er nations that revolted.
11   The Lord of hosts
        Defends our coasts ;
        In perils high,
        To Him we fly,
  And all the peril passes.

PSALM XLVII.

O ALL ye peoples, clap your hands :
    Shout unto God, the Lord Most High ;
2 Who is the Monarch of all lands,
    Whose dreadful sceptre rules the sky !

3 He nations under us subdues ;
    Puts hostile kingdoms 'neath our feet :
4 Our heritage He deigns to choose—
    The pride of Jacob makes His seat.

5 God has gone up with shouts—the Lord
    With blare of trumpets echoing—
6 Strike harps of praise ; instruct each chord
    To testify God is our King.

7 Sing praise to God with harpings loud !
8   He o'er the nations reigns alone—
In unshared rule, above the proud,
    He sits upon His holy throne.

9 Princes of peoples hither throng,
    People of Abrah'm's God to be :
The shields of earth to God belong—
    Exalted high o'er all is He.

PSALM XLVIII.

GOD is great, and only great;
   Be His praise proportionate!
In the City of our God,
In the Place of His abode,
In the Mount of Holiness,
Magnify His Name and bless!

2 Rare and beautiful for site,
  Earth's chief wonder and delight
3 Is Mount Zion: God is known
  For a refuge there alone:
  City, for defence renowned,
  Castles, gates, and walls around.

4 Kings, assembled, on her gazed,
5 Hastened then away amazed.
6 By dismay and grief o'erta'en,
  Like a travailing woman's pain;
7 Like the ships of Tarshish broke
  By the east-wind's dreadful stroke.

8 As we 've heard, so we have seen,
  In Jehovah's City clean,
  By His presence holy made—
  Its foundations by Him laid
  On the everlasting flint,
  Which no violence can dint.

9 In Thy Temple, Lord, oft sought,
   On Thy kindness we have thought.
10 To the earth's remotest ends
   Praise of Thy great Name extends.
11 Let the City of Thy choice
   In Thy righteousness rejoice!

12 Compass Zion, she is ours;
   Walk about her; count her towers;
13 Mark her bulwarks; note ye well
   All her palaces, to tell
14 To your sons her strength and pride:
   God till death will be our Guide.

PSALM XLIX.

ALL men, where'er ye dwell, give ear—
   Both high and low, both rich and poor;
3 While I upon my harp make clear
4   Dark truths, discredited but sure:

5 In evil days, why should I dread
   Crafty supplanters of my right?
6 Who, glorying in their wealth, are led
   To trust in gold's imagined might.

7 No one his brother can redeem,
   A ransom give to God for him;
   When death arrests life's flowing stream,
   And rigid grow each joint and limb:

8 When strikes the hour, a moment more
   Too costly is for him to buy ;
9 However great his golden store,
   Though all were his beneath the sky.

10 Yea, he shall see it ; wise men die—
   The fool, the brutish too, bereft
  Of brief pre-eminence and rule,
   The wealth they prize to others left.

11 Their inward thought is, that their fame
   And houses will forever last :
  They call their lands by their own name
   To tell their greatness in the past.

12 But man in honor does not stay ;
   He's like the beasts that perish all ;
13 Though men approve their foolish way,
   And their vain sayings wisdom call.

14 They are like sheep the shepherd, Death,
   Gathers in Sheol's gloomy fold,
  Found in the morning without breath ;
   While live th' upright strong and bold.

  Sheol their beauty shall devour,
   And of their frame shall nothing leave :
15 But God my soul shall from hell's power
   Deliver, and shall me receive.

16 Fear not, should chance on one convey
   Riches and honors without end;
17 He dying carries naught away,
   No honors after him descend.

18 Though while he lived he blessed his soul,
   And though success men glorify;
19 Yet shall he perish as a whole,
   And in perpetual darkness lie.

20 Man that is high in honor, yet
   Wisdom to learn no time allots,
  Is like (his thoughts on vain things set)
   The beast that perishes and rots.

PSALM L.

THE Mighty God, the Lord of All,
   The earth from east to west doth call:
2 From Zion (His most Holy Shrine,
  Perfect in beauty) God doth shine.

3 Be sure, that when our God shall come,
  His holy lips will not be dumb:
  A fire before Him shall devour;
  Round and above black tempests lower.

4 He both the heavens and earth will cite
  To witness that He judges right:
5 "Let all My saints assembled be
   That made a covenant with Me."

6 The heavens declare His righteousness,
  And sinful earth the same confess:
  For God Himself is Judge, and He
  Is perfect truth and equity.

7 "Hear, Israel, I thee arraign;
  Will speak against Thee, and complain,
  I that am God, Thy God—draw nigh,
8 Not for thy sacrifices, I

  "Will blame thee: thy burnt offering
  Is frequent and most wearying.
9 No bullock I from thee require;
  No he-goats from thy folds desire:

10 "Each beast is mine the forest fills;
   The cattle on a thousand hills;
11 Birds of the mountains, one and all,
   Beasts of the fields are at my call.

12 "If hungry, I'd not ask for thine;
   The fulness of the world is Mine.
13 Think ye on flesh of bulls I feed?
   That blood of goats for drink I need!

14 "Offer to God thanksgiving; pay
   Thy righteous vows; and to Me pray
15 In trouble, and I'll answer thee;
   And thou with praise shalt honor Me.

16 "But God saith to the wicked: What
Hast thou to do, thy right whence got
My statutes to declare, to take
17 Into thy mouth laws thou dost break?

18 "No vile companionship thee grieves;
Thy friends adulterers are and thieves:
19 Assassin thou, false to each trust,
20 That dost behind thy brother thrust.

21 "Meanwhile, because I silence kept,
Thou vainly thoughtest justice slept;
But all thy sins, stript of disguise,
I will array before thine eyes.

22 "O ye, that God forget, attend!
Lest I in pieces you shall rend.
23 To him who orders well his way
I My salvation will display."

PSALM LI.

HAVE pity on me, Lord!
Withhold forgiveness not;
According to Thy mercy spare,
And my trangressions blot.

2 O wash me from my guilt,
And make me clean within:
3 For my trangressions I confess,
Before me is my sin.

4 Against Thee only, I
    This evil did commit;
  That so thou may'st be justified
    When I'm condemned for it.

5 Lo, in iniquity
    I shapen was and born—
  In sin my mother me conceived,
    And I'm a wretch forlorn.

6 Behold, Thou hast desired
    Truth in the inward part:
  With wisdom, secret and sincere,
    Acquaint my darkened heart.

7 Purge me with hyssop, I
    Shall then true cleansing know:
  Me in Thy laver wash, and I
    Shall whiter be than snow.

8 Make me the music hear
    And gladness of Thy voice;
  That so the bones which justly Thou
    Hast broken may rejoice.

9 My wickedness wipe out;
    Thy face hide from my sin;
  A clean heart me create; renew
    A spirit right within.

11 O cast me not away
    From Thy dear presence; take
 Thy Holy Spirit not from me,
    Nor wholly me forsake.

12 Restore to me the joy
    Of Thy salvation, Lord!
 With a free spirit me uphold,
13   Then I will teach Thy word,

 And other sinners shall
    Converted be to Thee:
14 O God of my salvation, from
    Blood-guiltiness me free.

15 My tongue shall sing aloud
    Then of Thy righteousness:
 Lord, open Thou my lips, and I
    Will praise to Thee address.

16 For not in sacrifice,
    Nor in burnt-offering
 Delightest Thou, else I would these
    Unto Thine altar bring.

17 A broken spirit is
    God's only sacrifice;
 A broken and a contrite heart
    Thou, Lord, wilt not despise.

18 In Thy good pleasure, Lord!
    Do good to Zion; build
    The ramparts of Jerusalem;
19   Then bullocks shall be killed.

SECOND VERSION.—*Paraphrase.*

HAVE mercy, my offended God;
    According to Thy goodness, spare!
Let not the judgment of Thy rod
    Sink me still deeper in despair!

O hear, and my transgressions blot:
    Save me from my enormous guilt:
2 Wash from my soul each leprous spot,
    For Thou canst cleanse me if Thou wilt.

3 My sins are mountainous, they climb
    The heights of air and reach the skies;
The ghastly horror of my crime
    Is night and day before my eyes.

4 'Gainst Thee this odious deed was done;
    I struck my Maker in the face;
No wonder blushed th' astonished sun,
    And earth saw shuddering the disgrace.

Were not Thy mercies as the sand,
    I do not know that I would dare
Thus lift to Thee these bloody hands,
    In agonizing act of prayer.

5

> Though well, I know, there cries to Thee
>   The crimson of th' accusing sod,
> 14 Hide not Thy face, deliver me
>   From my blood-guiltiness, O God!
>
> 16 Burnt offerings and sacrifice,
>   Didst Thou desire, I would impart:
> 17 One off'ring Thou wilt not despise—
>   A broken and a contrite heart.
>
> 10 Create in me a heart that's pure;
>   Renew, transform, and make me o'er;
>   Not otherwise can I be sure,
>   I will not stumble as before.
>
> By Thy free Spirit me uphold;
>   For I am weak and sick and sad;
> 12 Forgive, and love me as of old,
>   And give me back the peace I had.
>
> 13 Then to transgressors I will teach,
>   How there are none so far from Thee,
>   But Thy salvation can them reach,
>   For, lo, it did extend to me.

PSALM LII.

SONNET.

> WHY boastest thou thyself in mischief, mighty man?
>   The mercy of th' Almighty never fails;
> 2 Thy tongue, like a sharp razor, wickedness doth plan,
>   Working deceitfully, inventing tales.

3 Thou lovest evil more than good ; and lies
4   Far more than truth, O thou deceitful tongue!
5 He shall destroy thee, fatal man, likewise.
   He shall lay hold of thee ; thou shalt be flung
  Out of thy tent ; He 'll thee uproot at length :
6   Good men shall laugh at thee, and say,
7 "Lo, this is he that made not God his strength,
   Making th' abundance of his wealth his stay."
8 But I am like an olive tree, forever seen
9 In the Lord's house still flourishing and green.

PSALM LIII.

THERE is no God"—the fool hath said,
   His heart dictating to his head,
To every noble feeling dead.

   Corrupt are they, from sun to sun
   They foul iniquity have done,
   None doeth good, not one, not one.

2 The Lord looked down from heaven to see
  Who understood, who bowed the knee :
  Complete is the apostasy ;

3 All are gone back, all filthy found,
  All vilest infamies abound,
  No one does good above the ground.

4 Are evil-doers mad, who eat
My people up as they do meat,
And think they need not God entreat?

5 Where no fear was, great fear arose:
The bones of the besieging foes
God scattered—for despised were those.

6 O that from Zion might proceed
Salvations great for Israel's need—
Jacob made glad, from bondage freed.

PSALM LIV.

PRESERVE me by Thy Name, O God!
    Thy Name is my Strong Tower;
2 Defend me by Thy might against
    The cruelty of Power.

3 For strangers have against me risen,
    The violent have sought
To take away my life—they have
    Of God nor fear nor thought.

4 God is my Helper, and He yet
    My life upholds; and will
5 Return the evil of my foes
    By killing them who kill.

6 I, with a free-will offering,
   Will sacrifice to Thee;
7 Will praise Thy Name, for praise is good,
   For Thou hast rescued me.

PSALM LV.

GIVE ear unto my prayer, O God!
   Attend and answer me:
2 I'm tost in my lament, and moan
   Like an unquiet sea;

3 Because my foes iniquity
   On me precipitate—
   Revile, oppress, and persecute
   In anger and in hate.

4 My heart is pained within me, I
   With mortal terrors quake:
5 Trembling and fear lay hold, great waves
   Of horror o'er me break.

6 O that I wings had like a dove,
   Then would I fly away
7 And be at rest: would wander off
   And in the desert stay.

8 I would me to some shelter haste,
   Where safety can be found;
   Out of the reach of stormy wind,
   And tempest howling round.

9 Destroy, O Lord, divide their tongues;*
    Confound their counsels; thwart
The wiley chief's state policies,
    And his consummate art.

10 For I have in the City seen
    The circulating life—
The daily movements on the walls,
    Significant of strife.

11 All forms of wickedness are there,
    Oppressions and deceits;
Corruption's in her market-place,
    And fraud in all her streets.

12 I could have borne it, had it been
    A foe the evil did,
One hating me, for then I would
    From him myself have hid.

13 But it was thou, mine equal held,
    My most familiar friend—
14 Together we sweet counsel took;
    And we were wont to wend

Our way together to God's House,
    With all the festal throng:
I knew not then thy perfidy
    Would work me shame and wrong.

---

* Absalom had been hatching treason during four years. Practically the City was now in his hands. David's fondness for his son, even after the discovery, would lead him to temporize. Ahithophel's defection was a serious blow.

15 Let sudden death upon them come ;
　　Earth swallow them alive ;
　For all the seeds of wickedness
　　Within them lodge and thrive.

---

16 But I will call on God ; the Lord
　　Will save me from His throne :
17 Evening and morning and at noon
　　I will complain and moan.

18 He hath redeemed my soul in peace,
　　For me deliverance wrought ;
　Of doubtful battle turned the scale,
　　For many 'gainst me fought.

19 God shall yet hear and answer them ;
　　He Judge sits from of old :
　Having no changes, and no fear,
　　They 've grown in sinning bold :

20 He has dealt treacherously, broke faith—
　　Butter and oil his words,
21 All smooth and soft, but meaning war,
　　The conflict of drawn swords.

22 Thy burden cast upon the Lord,
　　And He will thee sustain.
　The righteous man shall ne'er be moved
　　But stablished shall remain,

23 While bloody and deceitful men
    Shall not live half their days,
  Plunged by Thy hand into th' abyss—
    I'll trust in Thee always.

PSALM LVI.

BE merciful, O God, to me,
    For man would me devour:
2 I am hard pressed, for many join
    To get me in their power.

3 What time I am afraid, I then
    Will put my trust in Thee;
4 And, reassured, I'll cease to fear
    What flesh can do to me.

5 All the day long they wrest my words,
    Their thoughts are full of hate;
6 Gathered in bands they mark my steps,
    In ambush for me wait.

7 Would-be supplanters of my right,
    Do thou upon them frown:
  Prevent iniquitous escape,
    And cast the peoples down.

8 Thou counted hast my wandering steps,
    Now on my sorrows look;
  Into Thy bottle put my tears—
    Are they not in Thy book?

9 Then shall mine enemies turn back,
    When I to God have cried ;
  And this I say because I know
    That He is on my side.

  In God I'll trust ; Jehovah's word,
10   Theme of my praise shall be ;
11 Because I've trusted, I'll not fear
    What man can do to me.

12 Thy vows upon me are, O God !
    Thank-offerings I will pay :
13 To Thee I owe it that I still
    Enjoy the light of day.

PSALM LVII.

BE merciful to me, O God !
  Where Thy great wings their shadow cast,
There shalt my place of refuge be,
  Till these calamities are past.

2 I'll cry to God, the Mighty One,
  Whose love ne'er stops short of its end—
Completing what it has begun—
3   And He from heaven shall swiftly send

Mercy and Truth, celestial powers,
  From His right hand my life to save,
To quell the monster that devours,
  And snatch me from a cruel grave.

4 My soul fierce lions is among;
    I must lie down, distraught with fears,
  Midst fiery ones—a sword their tongue,
    Arrows their teeth and pointed spears.

5 Be Thou exalted, God Most High,
    Above all praise, all thought above,
  Above the earth, above the sky,
    High seated on Thy Throne of Love!

6 They for my steps prepared a net;
    They bowed my soul, they dug a pit—
  The trap which they for me had set
    They fell into the midst of it.

7 My heart is fixed, my heart is fixed,
    I will, O God, Thy praises sing:
8 Awake, my tongue! With voice be mixed,
    O harp and lyre, your every string.

9 I'll wake the dawn! I'll celebrate
    Thy praise among the nations, Lord!
10 For high Thy mercy is and great,
    And true and faithful is Thy word.

11 Be Thou exalted, God Most High,
    Above all praise, all thought above,
  Above the earth, above the sky,
    High seated on Thy Throne of Love!

PSALM LVIII.

How is it, judges, ye sit dumb,
When crime and wrong before you come—
  Silent what time ye ought to speak?
2 Who equity and right betray,
Work wickedness, corruptly weigh
  Out violence unto the weak.

3 Men from the womb devoid of worth,
Habitual liars from their birth,
  With serpent's deadly poison filled:
4 Like adder deaf that stops her ear,
5 And will the charmer's voice not hear,
  Howe'er the charmer may be skilled.

6 Lord! crush their teeth; the grinders break
Of the young lions; and them make
7   Like water hurrying fast away:
Like arrow snapped upon the bow,
8 Like snails dissolving as they go,
  Abortions that ne'er saw the day.

9 Before your pots can feel the thorn,
On swiftest whirlwind shall be borne
  The burning and the green alike:
10 The righteous shall rejoice, when he
God's holy arm revealed shall see,
  Audacious wickedness to strike.

11 Seeing His judgments, men will say:
"There is full recompense and pay,
  For men of piety and worth—
He blesses them, and calls them His,
Whereby it is made plain, there is
  A God that judges in the earth."

PSALM LIX.

DELIVER me from those,
    O God, who are my foes;
2 Above their utmost reach set me on high!
    Save me from men of blood,
    The banded foes of good,
3 Strong ones who for my life in ambush lie!

    It is not for my fault
4   They run, prepare assault:
Awake to meet me, Lord, their malice see!
5   O Thou Unspeakable!
        Thou God of Israel!
The heathen smite, spare none who traitors be.

6   At evening they return,
        Of me they nothing learn;
They howl like dogs, and round the city go;
7   They belch out evil words,
        That cutting are as swords,
"For who doth hear?" they say, "and who doth know?"

8	But Thou shalt laugh at them ;
	Shalt mock them and contemn :
9	I'll wait on Thee, O Thou who art my Strength !
	For Thou art my High Place,
10	Wilt meet me, God of Grace,
	And give me triumph o'er my foes at length.

11   Lord ! slay them not ; lest yet
              My people should forget,
    Scatter and bring them down, O Lord, our Shield !
12   Whose mouth, whose lips are sin :
              Let them be taken in
    Their pride, and for their blasphemies revealed.

13   Thine anger on them pour,
              Consume till they 're no more ;
    And let them know that God in Israel rules :
              Let the report go forth
              To east, west, south and north,
    For warning to all atheists and fools.

14   They will return at eve ;
              Sullen and snarling, grieve ;
    Howl like a dog, and go the city round :
15   They'll wander all the night,
              Until the morning light,
    Wolfish and lean in quest of prey not found.

16   But I'll the morning crowd
              With anthems sweet and loud,

In praise of Thy dear might and faithfulness :
17   For Thou in danger's hour
        Hast still been my High Tower,
A Refuge in the day of my distress.

PSALM LX.

THOU, God, hast cast us off ;
    Thou hast us broken down ;
Thou hast been angry—from Thy face
    O drive away Thy frown !

2 Thou shaken hast the land ;
    Hast it with earthquakes rent ;
Great breaches made, it trembles still
    With dread astonishment.

3 Thou hast Thy people showed
    O many a hard thing !
Hast for our sins made us to drink
    The wine of staggering.

4 To them who fear Thee, yet
    Thou hast a banner given,
That it may be, because of truth,
    Displayed in sight of heaven.

5 That Thy belovéd ones
    May be delivered, save
With thy right hand, and o'er us let
    Victorious ensigns wave.

6 God in His holiness
    Has spoken—I, therefore,
  Will triumph in the confidence
    He will the lost restore:

  Then the reconquered Land
    I will again divide—
  Shechem and Succoth*—and mete out
    His part to every Tribe.

7 Mine's Gilead; and mine's
    Manassah's either half;
  My head's defence is Ephraim;
    Judah's my royal staff;

8 Moab my washpot is,
    Wherein I'll wash my feet;
  O'er Edom will extend my sway;
    Philistia will unseat.

9 Who will me bring into
    Edom's fenced capital?
  Surmount its muniment of rocks
    Impregnable high wall?

10 Thou who didst cast us off,
    Wilt Thou Thyself not lead?
  Wilt Thou not go forth with our hosts,
    And help us in our need?

* Representing the two great divisions of the Country, east and west of the Jordan, where Jacob pitched his tent on his return from exile.

11 Give us Thy help! In vain
   We on man's help repose :
Through God we shall do valiantly,
   For He'll tread down our foes.

PSALM LXI.

HEAR Thou, O God, my cry;
   A mourning exile, I
From Zion weeping pass and its encircling hills—
   Beyond the bounding blue
   That terminates the view
To where a prospect strange a new horizon fills.

2   From thence I to Thee call
    Who art my all in all—
Homesick, o'erwhelmed, and faint at heart—and
   Thou'll me lead
       To craggy rock and high,
       Up towering toward the sky,
3 Too high for foes to reach—sure refuge in my need.

4   To dwell I were content
       Aye in Thy Holy Tent;
Kept safe beneath the shade and shelter of Thy wings:
5   For Thou, O God, hast heard
       My vows, and pledged Thy word
To pass the heritage to my descendant kings.

6 The King's life, hale and strong,
      To ages Thou 'lt prolong :
7 He before God shall sit enthroned forevermore,
      Mercy and Truth shall be
      For his security—
8 So will I to Thy Name eternal praises pour.

PSALM LXII.

MY soul is silent unto God,
      My Rock is only* He,
  2 My sole Salvation and High Tower—
      I shall not shaken be.

  3 How long will ye set on a man,
      All banded him to slay,
    Like bowing wall or tottering fence,
      Which yet does not give way?

  4 Only from his imperial seat
      To thrust him down they plan;
    Delight in lies, bless with their mouth,
      But inwardly him ban.

  5 Only in God confide, my soul!
      On Him my hope I base—
  6 He only is my Rock, my Rest,
      Salvation and High Place.

---

* The repetition of the word " only " is characteristic of this Psalm.

7 My honor and salvation rest
    On God ; I firm shall stand—
  Rock of my Strength, my Refuge, He
    Guards me on every hand.

8 Ye people, put your trust in Him,
    At all times, and ye thus
  Will have sure proof how only God
    A Refuge is to us.

9 Only a breath are men, both those
    Of low and high degree ;
  Empty and false, they are when weighed
    Lighter than vanity.

10 Trust in oppression not ; nor grow
    In robbery vain ; nor let,
  In case your wealth and power increase,
    Your heart thereon be set.

11 Once has God said, twice have I heard ;
    All power to Him pertains,
12 And mercy too, and He to each,
    Right recompense ordains.

PSALM LXIII.

O GOD, my God Thou art
    I dare to call Thee mine :
  My thirsty soul and longing heart
    For Thy sweet presence pine.

Here in a land of drought,
   Where all the brooks are dry,
Methinks I perish must, without
   Some token Thou art nigh.

2 Grant, Lord, that I may now
   Thy power and glory see,
As in the Sanctuary Thou
   Hast shown them unto me.

3 Better than life Thy love :
   I'll bless Thee all my days :
Will in Thy Name to Thee above
   Lift up my hands in praise.

  My hungry soul shall feed
4   On viands rich and choice,
5 And—satisfied my every need—
   I will in Thee rejoice.

6 Upon my bed at night,
   Will meditate on Thee ;
Recall the mercies of the light—
   Thy goodness unto me.

7 Rejoicing in the shade
   Of Thy protecting wing :
8 My eager soul shall not be stayed,
   On Thee hard following.

9 But those who would me kill
10   Shall by the sword of power
  Be slain, and howling jackals will
    Their carcasses devour.

11 In God I will rejoice,
   Their boast who by Him swear:
  Stopped is the mouth, stilled is the voice
    Of them that lies declare.

PSALM LXIV.

O GOD! hear my complaint and prayer,
   And make my threatened life Thy care:
2 O hide me from the secret league,
  The wicked masters of intrigue,
  Who whisper first, then speak aloud
  Their treason to the noisy crowd.

3 Their tongue they sharpen as a sword;
  Their arrow fit (a bitter word)
4 To shoot—naught fearing—th' upright,
  Shoot suddenly, concealed from sight.
5 They strengthen their malicious plot;
  Lay snares, quite sure they seen are not.

6 Fine villainies, far-sought and nice,
  They count an exquisite device:
  "All things are ready now and ripe,
  We have him," say they, "in our gripe."
7 But God has with a surer aim
  Shot them—the shooter made the game.

8 Smitten they stumble; they are stung
   With their own sharp envenomed tongue.
9 They flee away, and every one
   That sees, admires what God has done.
10 The righteous in the Lord shall trust;
   In Him shall triumph all the just.

PSALM LXV.

PERPETUAL worship for Thee waits
   Within hushed Zion's Temple-gates—
A prayerful silence, Lord! and then
Breaks forth the uttered praise of men;
Who hither come, before Thee bow,
And punctually pay their vow.

2 O Thou who hearest prayer, to Thee
   Must all flesh come, who blest would be;
3 Conscious iniquities assail,
   But our transgressions Thou wilt veil,
   Heal our backslidings when we stray,
   And purge our many sins away.

4 Happy the man whom Thou even here
   Shalt choose, and to Thyself bring near;
   That in Thy House he may abide,
   And with its good be satisfied;
   May in Thy Holy Temple rest
   A permanent and honored guest.

5 By fearful things in righteousness—
　Mercies and judgments numberless—
　O God of our salvation, Thou
　Wilt answer us: Be gracious now!
　Ends of the earth confide in Thee,
　And dwellers on the far-off sea.

6 Girded with might, Thou dost set fast
　By Thy great strength the mountains vast:
7 Dost roaring seas hush at Thy will,
　And tumult of the peoples still:
8 Dwellers on farthest shores are made
　By tokens of Thy power afraid.

　Thou makest with rich purple clad
　Th' outgoings of the morning glad;
　With golden splendors renderest gay
　The footsteps of departing day,
　Like bird with outspread gorgeous wing,
　The bards of morn and evening sing.

9 Thou floodest all the fields, by which
　The earth Thou greatly dost enrich:
　Fed by th' unfailing streams of God,
　With mighty marvels teems the sod—
10 Its furrows drenched, made soft with showers,
　How spring the grain, the grass, the flowers!

11 With goodness Thou hast crowned the year;
　Where Thy feet pass fair sights appear—

12 The wilderness fat pastures yields,
13 Joy girds the hills, flocks clothe the fields,
   Grain all the valleys covering—
   They shout for joy, they also sing.

PSALM LXVI.

SHOUT unto God, all lands,
   His majesty proclaim!
2 Ascribe to Him the honor due,
   And glorify His Name!

3 How fearful are Thine acts:
   Through knowledge of Thy power,
   Thine enemies submission feign,
   And at Thy footstool cower.

4 All lands shall worship Thee,
   The Universal Lord—
   They shall sing praises to Thy Name
   On harp and decachord.

5 Come, see what He has done!
   The dreadful power of God—
6 He turned the sea into dry land,
   They Jordan crossed dry shod:

   Then we rejoiced in Him.
7   He rules on high and here,
   His eyes keep watch the nations o'er—
   Let the rebellious fear:

8 Ye nations, bless our God!
    Be praise to Him preferred,
9 Who holds our soul in life, nor lets
    Our firm-set foot be stirred.

10 For Thou hast proved us, Lord!
    Tried us as silver's tried;
11 Brought us within the hunter's net,
    Our loins with burdens plied.

12 Hast suffered men to ride
    Triumphant o'er our head:
  Through fire and flood we went, but Thou
    To a rich place hast led.

13 I with burnt offerings
    Into Thy House will come:
14 Of vows I made in my distress,
    Will pay the perfect sum.

15 I will burnt offerings
    Of fatlings bring to Thee;
  Incense of rams, bulls and he-goats
    Shall my oblation be.

16 Come, hear, and I'll declare,
    All ye that fear the Lord,
  That which He for my soul has done,
    The favor on me poured.

17 I said—what time I cried,
　　And offered praise sincere—
18 If in my heart I sin regard
　　I know He will not hear.

19 But, verily, God heard :
　　His Name thrice blessèd be,
20 Who hath not turned away my prayer,
　　His mercy kept from me.

PSALM LXVII.

BE merciful and bless,
　　Eternal God of grace !
Upon us let the brightness fall
　　And gladness of Thy Face.

2 That Thy most blessèd way
　　May on the earth be known ;
Thy saving power and goodness be
　　Among all nations shown.

3 Let peoples of all lands
　　In praise find sweet employ ;
4 The various nations one and all
　　Be glad and sing for joy !

　For Thou with equity
　　Shalt judge them from above ;
　And they shall see stretched over them
　　The sceptre of Thy love.

5 Let Thee the peoples thank,
6   For bounties of the year;
7 Let the extremities of earth
     Be made to learn thy fear.

PSALM LXVIII.*

GOD shall arise and scatter them,
    And push His flying foes:
As smoke is driven, Thou wilt them drive;
    As melts away and goes
Th' unstable wax before the fire,
So pass the wicked in Thine ire.

3 They perish; but the righteous shall
     Exceedingly rejoice.
4 Sing ye to God, sing to His Name
     With harp and lute and voice!
  Cast up, prepare a way for Him,
  Who rides upon the Cherubim!

---

* This magnificent Battle Hymn, or Triumphal Song, composed in celebration of some recent victory or success achieved through Divine Help, is made commemorative of gracious interventions and deliverances in the past, outlining the history of Israel from the exodus to the full establishment of the monarchy on Zion. Jehovah is described (v. 4) as "riding *through the deserts*" [not "*upon the heavens*" as the Common Version has it] in the manner of a king marching at the head of his army. Special reference is made (vs. 7-10) to the journeying through the Wilderness, where the "Cloud," otherwise, "the Glory of the Lord," the visible manifestation of the Divine Presence accompanying the Ark with its symbolic Cherubim, was the signal to all the people to move forward or to halt. If by Cherubim be understood Nature (as argued in Note, p. 27); and by God's enthronement above them, the subjection of all things to Him, we see how it belongs, not only to poetic but intrinsic fitness, that the announcement of any special Appearance of the great Lord of All should be attended with extraordinary natural phenomena—such as thunderings and lightnings and earthquakes, testifying to a mighty, trembling, and adoring awe. We think, moreover, that

Not up the skyey steeps, star-paved,
　His sacred car He guides;
Not o'er the ample plains of heaven—
　He through the desert rides
By His Name Jah : Unto Him sing,
Who leads you in your journeying.

5 God in His Sanctuary is,
　The widow's Judge and Friend ;
A Father of the fatherless
　To care for and defend :
6 No more the solitary roam,
He gives fixed dwellings and a home.

The sons of bondage He brings forth,
　And blesses with full hand :
But the rebellious and perverse
　Inhabit a parched land—
The prisoner, who hugs his chains,
In bondage rightfully remains.

Verse 17 admits of being construed in the same sense. It is there said, "The chariots of God are myriad-fold, thousand upon thousands; the Lord is among them—Sinai in the Sanctuary," meaning that the vehicles of Divine Power as found in Nature defy enumeration ; that God is a God of law: that the Ark of the Covenant, containing the Decalogue, having the Mercy-Seat above, is significant of the fact that even mercy rests on law, or, as it is poetically expressed, "Sinai is in the Sanctuary." While the close conjunction of the Cherubim, so close as to form a part of it (*i. e.*, the Mercy-Seat), is fitted to suggest that the God of Nature is likewise the God of Grace.

The true reading of Verse 5 is, "The Lord gives the word: the women that publish the glad tidings [of victory] are a mighty host," as in Ex. 15 : 29 ; 2 Sam. 18 : 16. The accepted reading of Verse 12 is, "Will ye lie among the sheep-folds—as the wings of a dove covered with silver and her pinions with yellow gold ?"— the allusion being to Judges 5 : 16, where Deborah in her song rebukes the recreancy of Reuben, who luxuriated in the selfish indulgence of a soft pastoral repose, unsoiled with the dust of conflict, while others, like Zebulun and Naphtali were

7 O God! when through the wilderness
    Their march Thy people made,
8 Earth trembled, and the heavens dropped rain,
    And Sinai was afraid:
  All Nature knew Thy presence well—
  The mighty God of Israel!

9 Thou didst, O God, Thy heritage
    Refresh with plenteous rain;
  Didst visit it when it was faint,
    And make it strong again:
10 Thy flock therein was made to bide;
  And for the poor Thou didst provide.

11 God gives the word, the battle won,
    Women, a mighty throng,
  Triumphing, publish the good news,
    With timbrel, dance and song.
12 The kings of armies flee, they flee,
  Rich spoils rewarding victory.

13 Will ye among the sheepfolds lie
    In pastoral repose—
  Like bright-winged dove in her soft nest,
    Not helping 'gainst God's foes—
14 What time He puts leagued kings to flight
  On Zalmon, made with bones snow-white?

jeoparding their lives unto the death in the high places of the field." Verses 11-14 belong apparently to the period of the Judges; verses 15-19 to the establishment of the monarchy and the national worship on Mt. Zion; verses 24-27 describe the triumphal procession; verses 28-31 point to the universal conquest yet to come. In the concluding verses (vs. 32-35) all nations are called on to unite in praise to the God of Israel.

15 Mountain of Bashan, mountain high,
    Proud peak and pinnacle!
16 Why look askance ye at the Mount
    Where God vouchsafes to dwell?
  If height is less, by easier road
  We climb the Hill of His Abode.

17 Zion is strong, God in her midst:
    His chariots of war
  Thousands on thousands, myriads
    Incalculable, are;
  Approach that Sacred Place with awe,
  Where God of Sinai guards His Law.

18 Thou hast ascended, Lord, on high,
    The captured captive led;
  For distribution gifts received—
    The conquest perfected.
  Preserve, while men Thy triumphs hymn,
  Thy place between the Cherubim.

19 Blesséd be God who daily bears
    The burden on us laid—
20 Ev'n God, who our salvation is,
    Our ever-present aid;
  We to Jehovah owe our breath,
  And manifold escapes from death.

21 But God will crush the head of foes;
    In vain the wicked flee:
22 He said: "From Bashan I'll bring back
    From depths ev'n of the sea,

    The fugitives o'er Jordan's flood,
23 That thou may'st dip thy foot in blood."

24 They Thy triumphal goings saw;
    Thy goings, God our King!
    Thine entrance in the Holy Place;
25   While those engaged to sing,
    Went foremost praising; harpers then;
    Maids beating timbrels; marching men.

26 In companies they bless the Lord,
    Tribes that from Israel spring:
27 There, is the ruler Benjamin;
    There, Judah's following;
    There, banners of the princes fly
    Of Zebulon and Naphtali.

28 That we be strong is God's command—
    Strengthen what thou hast wrought.
29 To Thee, Lord, at Jerusalem,
    Shall gifts of kings be brought.
30 Egypt rebuke, and scatter far
    The peoples that delight in war.

31 Princes shall out of Egypt come;
    And Ethiopia soon
    Shall stretch out eager hands to God,
    And His high praises tune.
32 Kingdoms of earth! praise Him who rides
33 On whirling spheres, and planets guides!

34 Ascribe ye strength to God, your Strength!
   His majesty He shrouds—
   But high o'er Israel spreads His wings,
   And thunders in the clouds.
35 Out of Thy holy places, Lord,
   The strength Thy people need, afford.

PSALM LXIX.

SUCCOR, O God! and save
   From drowning waters deep!
2 I sink in mire of the abyss,
   Great billows o'er me sweep.

3 With calling I am tired,
   My throat is parched and dry;
   Mine eyes are wasted and worn out,
   While I wait Thy reply.

4 O numberless are those
   Who hate me without cause;
   They mighty are to cut me off,
   Despisers of Thy laws.

5 My foolishness and sin
   Not hidden are from Thee:
6 Let them not, Lord! who on Thee wait
   Be made ashamed through me.

7 I for Thy sake have borne
    Reviling and disgrace;
8 A stranger to my brethren been,
    An alien to my race.

9 Because zeal for Thy House
    Within me quenchless burned,
Those, who reproached Thee, have on me
    Their sharp reproaches turned.

10 I wept and fasted, they
    Stood ready to contemn;
I put on sackcloth, I became
    A proverb unto them.

12 I am their public talk;
    Drunkards make me their song;
13 But, Lord, my prayer is unto Thee,
    Delay not answer long.

14 Out of the mire me raise,
    The waters of my foes;
15 Let not the deep me swallow up,
    The pit's mouth on me close.

16 Hear, Lord, and answer me,
    For Thy abundant grace;
In Thy compassion turn to me
17   And do not hide Thy face,

For I am in distress;
  Make haste me, Lord, to hear:
18 Draw nigh my soul to ransom it:
  Because my foes are near.

19 Thou knowest my reproach,
  My shame and my despite,
Mine adversaries one and all
  Are ever in Thy sight.

20 Reproach has broke my heart;
  I 'm full of heaviness;
I looked for some to pity me,
  But all were pitiless.

There comforters were none;
  All men from me did shrink;
21 They gave me also gall for meat,
  Me vinegar to drink.

THE CHORUS SPEAKS:*

22 Their table make a snare;
  Their confidence a trap;
23 Darken their eyes; make their loins shake;
  Their strength and vigor sap!

---

*That Verses 22-28 are the utterances of another speaker, may, we think, be confidently asserted. For why should the dramatic character, so freely accorded to other Psalms, be denied to this, where it is most needed? Assume the existence of two speakers and all is clear. The words spoken no longer are an offense. Instead of being painfully discordant with all that precedes and follows, they are seen to possess a dramatic propriety of the highest order, heightening immensely the tragic interest of the whole composition. For they are exactly the words

24 On them Thine anger pour;
25   Make their house desolate;
Let none dwell in their tents—because
26   They persecute and hate

Him, Thou hast smitten sore:
His woes they tell with zest;
Pain of his wounds they make the theme
Of coarse unfeeling jest.

27 Add sin to sin, heap guilt!
Let them not pardoned be!
28 But blotted from the book of life—
Condemned by just decree.

---

which the sympathetic reader is burning to say. They are the mildest possible expression of an irrepressible indignation which must fill every virtuous heart let the condemnation concern whom it will. It matters little who the second speaker may be supposed to represent—whether it be Justice personified; or some horrified spectator, say James or John, who on one occasion were ready to cal down fire from heaven on the perpetrators of a slight affront put upon their Master. Or was it the weeping daughters of Jerusalem that performed the office of Chorus as described in Note to Psalm 22, page 39? For the sake of the argument, let us suppose the first speaker—a meek Sufferer—to be the Christ that was to come. We listen to His prolonged wail: how He was hated without cause; how He was despised and rejected of men; became a stranger and an alien to His own countrymen who refused to receive Him; was made a terror to His friends; was forsaken and disowned by His disciples; how reproach broke His most loving heart; how, hanging on the cross, vinegar mixed with gall was given Him to drink. Everybody must be struck with the strict correspondence between this recital and what actually took place. But Christ prayed for *forgiveness*. To suppose He imprecated *vengeance* is to contradict the verity of Scripture. The thing is impossible. While Christ quotes and appropriates parts of this Psalm to Himself, the reader is sure that verses 5, 6 do not belong to Him. May it not be that when "holy men spake as they were moved by the Holy Ghost," the prophetic utterance was sometimes designedly mixed up with the human and personal, but in a way to be easily distinguished?

29 I'm poor and sorrowful—
    Lord! set me safe on high,
30 And I will praise Thy Name in song,
    Thank Thee and magnify;

31 And it shall please Thee more,
    These loud resounding proofs,
Than offered ox or bullock slain
    With horns and cloven hoofs.

32 The meek have seen with joy
    A high deliverance wrought:
Seekers of God! be cheered, for you
    Shall have th' assistance sought.

33 The Lord the needy hears,
    The prisoners as well:
34 Let heaven and earth Him praise, the seas
    And all that therein dwell.

35 For God will Zion save;
    And Judah's cities build—
36 The Land by His true servants shall
    Be occupied and tilled.

PSALM LXX.*

DELIVER me, O God!
    Lord, to my help make haste;
2 Let them who seek my life be shamed,
    Confounded and disgraced.

---

* This Psalm is a repetition of Psalm xl. 13-17.

3 Let them be backward turned ;
    Be to dishonor brought ;
  Turned back for a reward of shame,
    That say, Aha ! for naught.

4 Let all those that Thee seek,
    With joy in Thee abide !
  Let such as Thy salvation love,
    Say, "God be magnified !"

5 Needy and poor am I,
    O Lord, do not delay ;
  My Help and my Deliverer,
    Make haste to come this way !

PSALM LXXI.

I PUT my trust, Lord ! in Thy Name :
  O let me never come to shame !
2 Promised deliverance I crave,
  Incline Thine ear to me, and save !
3 A Rock of Habitation be,
  Where I may come continually !

Since Thou my rescue hast decreed—
My Cliff, My Fort, in time of need—
4 Now my deliverance command
  Out of the wicked's cruel hand !
5 Thou art my Hope, my Trust—Thy truth,
  Have I relied on from my youth.

6 Yea, from the womb have leaned on Thee;
Thou art my praise continually;
Many me as a wonder rate,
7 But Thou 'rt my Refuge, strong and great;
8 I, all the day, will sing Thy praise,
And to the stars Thy glory raise.

9 Cast me not off in my old age:
When failing powers my end presage,
10 Do not forsake me: but disclose
How false is the pretence of foes,
11 Who say—their malice peeping through—
"There's none to rescue, take! pursue!"

12 Haste to my help! O be not far!
13 Confound, consume all those who are
Foes of my life. Lay in the dirt
The evil men that seek my hurt.
14 But I 'll still hope, and thanks will pour,
And love and praise Thee more and more.

15 My mouth shall tell Thy righteous acts;
And all the day rehearse the facts
16 Of Thy salvation—mighty deeds
Which all arithmetic exceeds—
I will Thy righteousness make known
And speak of it, and it alone.

17 Lord! from my youth Thou hast me taught
To sing the wonders Thou hast wrought.

18 Forsake me not, now I am old—
   I would Thy saving power unfold
   To every one that is to come,
   Ere yet my mouth and lips are dumb.

19 Who is like Thee, so great, so high,
   Whose righteousness surmounts the sky?
20 Thou, who hast showed me troubles sore,
   Shalt quicken and again restore;
21 My greatness shalt make greater still,
   And me with every comfort fill.

22 With psaltery and harp and voice
23 I 'll sing Thy praises and rejoice!
24 Thy truth and faithfulness will tell,
   O Holy One of Israel!
   Thy righteousness shall all day long
   Be the sweet subject of my song.

PSALM LXXII.

O GOD! Supremest Source
    Of government below:
  Thy judgments and Thy righteousness
    Upon the King bestow.

2 Then he upon the earth,
    Thy deputy, shall reign;
  With rectitude Thy people judge,
    And equity maintain.

3 The mountains and the hills
    Shall yield the people peace,
4 Beneath his just and gentle sway,
    Shall all oppression cease.

5 While sun and moon endure,
      And night succeeds to day,
   Throughout all generations, men
      Shall fear him and obey.

6 He shall come down like rain,
      As earth-refreshing showers
   On new-mown meadows, made to smile
      With springing grass and flowers.

7 The righteous in his days
      Shall flourish and prevail;
   And peace shall everywhere abound,
      Until the moon shall fail.

8 His empire shall extend,
      Likewise, the wide world o'er,
   From sea to sea—Euphrates' banks
      To earth's remotest shore.

9 The dwellers in the wild
      Shall crouch and kiss his feet;
   His enemies shall lick the dust;
10   The kings bring presents meet,

      From Tarshish and the Isles;
        Sheba and Seba—yea,
11 All kings before him shall bow down,
      All nations homage pay.

12 He shall the needy save,
13   The poor too when he cries;
14 The lives of all his subjects shall
      Be precious in his eyes.

15 And he shall live; to him
      Shall Sheba's gold be given;
   And ceaseless prayer for him be made,
      With daily thanks to heaven.

16 From handful of seed-corn
        On top of mountains sown—
   Vast fruit shall shake, great harvests wave
      Like Lebanon wind-blown.

   Jerusalem shall bloom,
      New cities shall have birth;
   They flourish shall like the green herb
      That beautifies the earth.

17 While shines the sun, shall last
      His undecaying fame:
   Men everywhere be blest in him
      All nations bless his name.

18 The Lord God blesséd be,
    The God of Israel !
  Who only doeth wondrous things,
    And doeth all things well ;

19 And be His glorious Name
    Blesséd forevermore ;
  The earth be with His glory filled,
    And all men Him adore.

                    Amen and Amen.

The prayers of David the Son of Jesse are ended.*

---

* How this line of prose came to be inserted in this place we have no certain means of knowing. We know that the Psalms that precede are not all by David; and that, among those that follow, there are several undoubtedly his, being expressly attributed to him.

BOOK III.

PSALM LXXIII.

M Y tongue was loosed, I broke the spell,
    I sternly bade the fiend depart:
Sure God *is* good to Israel,
    To Him *is* dear the pure in heart.

2 But as for me, my tempted feet
    Were almost gone, by folly tripped:
My steps, perplexed by vain deceit,
    In slippery paths had well-nigh slipped.

3 For I was envious of the proud,
    Seeing th' abundance of their wealth;
4 The easier death to them allowed,
    Their full-fed happiness and health.

5 Because not plagued as others are,
6   Disdain they as a necklace wear;
7 From common men they stand afar:
    Oily and round, with haughty air,

8 They from on high oppression speak;
 9   They in the heavens their mouth have set;
      Their tongue walks through the earth; the weak
      They trample down without regret:

10 Therefore His people, tossed with doubt,
      Sorely perplexed, are made to drain
   Waters of a full cup, wrung out
      With agonies of heart and brain.

11 They 're moved to say : " How does God know ?
      Knowledge is there in the Most High ?
12 The wicked prosper here below,
      'T is vain to ask the reason why :

13 " 'T is all in vain I've cleansed my heart;
      In innocence have washed my hands;
14 My chastisements do not depart;
      My daily wailings fill the land."

15 If I had said, I'll thus speak out,
      I had thy children drugged with lies:
16 Yet when I thought to solve my doubt,
      It was too painful in my eyes,

17 Till to the House of God I went,
      And knew their end ; and how they stood
18 Upon a slippery descent ;
      That false and fleeting was their good.

19 Behold, the doom that long had slept
    An utter desolation makes ;
  They instantly away are swept,
20 Like to a dream when one awakes.

  Now that I know Thou dost despise
    Their image, th' unreal show
21 No longer dupes and grieves mine eyes:
    I brutish was and did not know.

22 A beast before Thee I have been,
    But Thou hast with my folly borne ;
  And hast forgiven me my sin ;
23 And I'm still with Thee night and morn.

  Thou hast of my right hand kept hold :
24 Thou by Thy counsels wilt me guide,
  A straying sheep of Thy dear fold,
    And wilt receive me to Thy side.

25 For whom in heaven have I but Thee?
    With Thee on earth I none require :
26 My everlasting fortress be,
    Rock of my heart ! my sole Desire !

27 Those far from Thee Thou wilt destroy,
    Who 'gainst their marriage vows rebel ;
28 But to draw near Thee is my joy,
    In thee to trust, Thy works to tell.

PSALM LXXIV.

O GOD, why dost Thou cast us off?
    Thy tenderness revoke?
Against Thy once loved flock, O why
    Doth Thy long anger smoke?

2 Remember Thine own Israel,
    Thy purchase long ago;
And this Mount Zion which has been
    Thy Dwelling here below.

3 Lift up Thy feet, draw near and see
    Perpetual ruins piled;
The ill Thy Sanctuary done,
    How ravaged and defiled.

4 Thine adversaries mid the place
    Of Thine assembly roared;
Their ensigns they set up for signs,
    Who other gods adored.

5 They like to men with lifted axe
    Among thick-growing trees,
6 With sledge and hatchet broke and hacked
    The carvings of the frieze.

7 They set Thy Sacred House on fire,
    Thy Dwelling-place profaned;
8 They burned up all God's synagogues
    That in the Land remained.

9 No signs we see, there proof is none
    Of gift of prophecy:—
  No one among us knows how long
    Before the end will be.

10 How long, Lord, shall the foe blaspheme?
    Shall he forever stand?
11 Why from thy bosom dost Thou not
    Pluck Thy destroying Hand?

12 Yet God's my King of old, who wrought
    Salvation in the earth:
13 Thou by Thy strength the sea didst part,
    And gav'st a nation birth:

  Didst heads of huge sea-monsters crush;
14   Leviathan didst quell,
  And gavest him for food to them,
    That in the desert dwell:

15 Didst cleave the fountain and the flood,
    Didst mighty rivers dry:
16 The day is Thine, the night is Thine,
    The sun that climbs the sky.

17 Thou all the bounds of earth hast set,
    Summer and winter made—
  The frame of mighty nature formed,
    And her foundations laid.

18 Remember this, Lord! how the foe
    Blaspheme Thee and contemn—
19 A greedy herd, the turtle-dove
    Surrender not to them.

20 Have to Thy covenant respect:
    For earth's dark places are
Full of the homes of cruelty,
    And everlasting jar.

22 Arise, O God! plead Thine own cause:
    Make their reproaches end:
23 The tumults of Thine enemies,
    Continually ascend.

PSALM LXXV.

WE give Thee thanks, O God!
    We give Thee thanks sincere:
Thy wondrous doings in our midst
    Declare Thy Name is near.

2 "I will a set time take;
    The judgment-seat ascend;
Myself will judge in equity;
    Myself the right defend.

3 "The earth and its inhabitants
    Are falling into wreck:
I poise the pillars; I alone
    The rushing ruin check.

4 "I said unto the arrogant :
   ' Do not lift up your horn ;
5 Speak not with a stiff neck proud words
   Of insolence and scorn.' "

6 For not from east or west
   Nor south promotion springs :
7 But God is judge, He puts down one,
   To power another brings.

8 A cup is in His hand,
   It foams high o'er the brink ;
The wine is mixed, the wicked shall
   Its dregs wring out and drink.

9 But as for me, I will
   Forever sing Thy praise ;
10 Horns of the wicked I will lop,
   Horns of the righteous raise.

PSALM LXXVI.

IN Judah God is known ; His Name
   To Israel He showed ;
2 In Salem His Pavilion spread,
   Made Zion His Abode.

3 Bolts of the bow He shattered there,
   Swift flashing from afar ;
Buckler He broke, and sword, and all
   Th' implements of war.

4 High up Thy dread magnificence
    Majestically towers
  Above the mountains, whence descend
    Fierce predatory powers.*

5 Spoiled are the stout of heart—they slept,
    Bound in death's iron bands—
  And all the men of might have found
    No use for their strong hands.

6 At Thy rebuke, O God, they lay,
    Both chariot and horse,
  In a deep sleep and motionless—
    On every side a corse.

7 Thou, even Thou, art to be feared:
    When once Thou angry art,
  Ah! who can stand before Thee then,
    With guilt within his heart?

8 Sentence from heaven was heard proclaimed:
    The earth feared and was still,
9 When God to judgment rose to save
    Meek doers of His will.

10 Man's wrath is made to praise Thee; Thou
    Shalt future wraths† restrain—
  Shalt hold in check the residue
    While any shall remain.

---

* Assyrian hosts under Sennacherib. See 2 Kings xix. 35.
† The Hebrew original is plural.

11 Vow to the Lord your God and pay:
    Bring tribute to your Dread—
12 Kings of the earth! lest He cut off
    And count you with the dead.

PSALM LXXVII.

I'LL lift my voice to God,
   And He my cry will hear;
I'll lift my voice to God, who will
   Incline a gracious ear,

2 As when I sought the Lord
   In time of heavy grief,
All day and night, with hand stretched out—
   My soul refused relief.

3 I think on God, and sigh;
   I moan, my spirit's weak;
4 Mine eyes Thou waking hold'st, I am
   So tost I cannot speak.

5 I days of old recall;
6   My carol in the night;
I with my heart communion hold,
   And grope and seek for light.

7 Will God for aye cast off?
   Be favorable no more?
8 Forever has His mercy ceased?
   Is there no hope in store?

Has the old promise failed?
9 The Mighty One forgot?
No longer do His bowels yearn,
His anger is so hot?

10 I said, these ghastly doubts
Of a sick mind deny
Facts of the years of the right hand,
And arm of the Most High.

11 I will commemorate
The doings of the Lord:
12 The wonders which of old He wrought
Will gratefully record.

13 Thy way, O God, is pure:
Who mighty is like Thee?
14 Among the nations Thou hast shown
Thy power and majesty.

15 Thy people were set free,
By Thy delivering aid:
16 The waters saw Thee, O our God,
They saw and were afraid.

They trembled in their depths;
17 The clouds their waters poured:
18 The firm earth shook, while lightnings blazed
And skies with thunder roared.

19 Thy way was in the sea ;
   Thy footsteps were not known ;
20 Thou led'st Thy people like a flock
   Through all the desert lone.

PSALMS LXXVIII.

HEAR, O my people, I will tell
   Deep meanings in a parable ;
Repeat dark sayings from of old
3 To us by our grey fathers told :

The things they did to us confide,
4 We will not from their children hide :
Jehovah's praises we 'll recite,
And all the wonders of His might.

5 For to this end and for this cause,
In Jacob He established laws ;
That handed down from sire to son,
They might be known, observed and done :

6 That children which should yet be born
To theirs might tell them night and morn ;
7 Their hope in God might firmly set,
And not His mighty works forget :

8 And not be as their fathers were,
Stubborn, perverse and prone to err ;
Their hearts unsteadfast and untrue
From God withholding service due.

9 The sons of Ephraim* turned back,
  In time of conflict and attack;
10 Kept not the covenant of God,
  But, faithless, left His ways untrod:

11 Forgot the doings of His Hand
  Of which the fame filled all the land—
12 His wondrous works, with judgment fraught,
  In Egypt for their fathers' wrought.

13 The Red Sea waves He cleft in two,
  And caused them, dry-shod, to pass through—
  Making the waters of the deep
  To stand suspended as a heap.

14 By day He with a cloud them led;
  By night with light of fire instead;
15 The rock He in the desert clave,
  And drink abundantly them gave;

16 Out of the cliff, beneath the sun
  He streams like rivers made to run:
17 But 'gainst the Highest none the less
  Rebelled they in the wilderness.

18 They tempted God with lustful greed,
  Asking for food they did not need:
19 Doubted His power; "Can God," they said,
  "A table in the desert spread?"

---

* The chief of the Ten Tribes that revolted, representing the whole.

20 "He smote the rock and streams did flow,
  But can he give us bread also?
  He water has, 't is true supplied,
  But can He flesh for us provide?"

21 Jehovah heard this, and His ire
  Burned against Jacob like a fire;
22 Because they, impious and unjust,
  Did not in His salvation trust.

32 For all this, they ceased not to sin,
  Grey unbelievers hard to win;
33 Therefore, in vanity and fears,
  Did He consume their days and years.

34 When He them slew, they sought Him then,
  Made eager quest for God again
35 Their sometime Rock, their Refuge nigh,
  Their strong Redeemer, God Most High.

36 But with the mouth they Him deceived;
  Lied with their tongues and disbelieved.
37 Their heart, not fixed the right to do,
  Was to His covenant untrue.

38 But pitiful He did not slay;
  His anger often turned away;
39 Forgave, when they transgressed afresh,
  Remembering they were but flesh.

40 How oft against Him they rebelled,
   The Holy One of Israel!
41 Each day they tempted God anew,
   And grieved Him all the desert through.

42 It was, as if they did not know
   Whose hand redeemed them from the foe—
43 As if the signs in Egypt wrought
   Were strangers to their mind and thought.

44 He turned their rivers into blood,
   So none could drink the crimson flood:
45 Devouring flies among them sent,
   And frogs for their destruction meant.

46 He gave their labor and produce
   Up to the caterpiller's use:
47 Destroyed their vines (by hailstones lost),
   Their sycamores with fatal frost;

48 Gave over, to hail-slaughtering knocks
   And thunderbolts, their herds and flocks:
49 Let loose the fierceness of His wrath,
50 And made for it a level path:

51 Sent on an embassy of death,
   Angels of evil with hot breath,
   The pestilence with fiery throat—
   All the first-born of Egypt smote,

52 But like a flock His people led
    Into the wilderness, and fed.
53 While they passed safe from terror free,
    Their foes were buried in the sea.

54 He brought them to the Holy Land,
    The Mountain won by His right hand—
55 Proceeded nations to expel,
    That so the tribes might therein dwell.

56 Yet they resisted God Most High,
    And would not with His laws comply—
57 Aside, as did their fathers, so
    They turned like a deceitful bow:

58 High places built which He forbade;
    Him with their idols jealous made:
59 So high their impious daring soared,
    God greatly Israel abhorred.

60 The Tent at Shiloh He forsook;
    Ark of His Strength they captive took—
61 His Glory* passed to heathen hands,
62 And blood and carnage filled the lands.

63 The fire devoured their young and strong;
    Their maidens were unpraised in song;
64 Priests by the sword in numbers slept,
    And by their widows were unwept.

---

* The Ark, where the "Glory of the Lord" or Shekinah had rested, was still called His Glory, when this visible token of His Presence was withdrawn.

65 Then waked the Lord as out of sleep,
66 Drove back His foes with dreadful sweep,
And fastened to their hated name
Perpetual reproach and shame.

67 The house of Joseph pleased not Him,
So He rejected Ephraim;
68 But Judah's loyal tribe approved;
And on Mount Zion which He loved,

69 He built His Sanctuary, cast
Foundations made for aye to last:
70 David his servant too did choose,
71 Took Him from following the ewes,

To feed His people Israel,
72 And he fulfilled his office well—
With honest heart, and skillful hand,
And shepherd-care, he ruled the Land.

PSALM LXXIX.

THE heathen in Thine heritage,
O God, have hostile inroads made;
Thy Holy Temple have defiled,
Jerusalem in ruins laid.

2 They have Thy servants' bodies given
As food to birds and beasts of prey;
3 Their blood, like water, shed—all round
Thy slaughtered saints unburied lay.

4 We have become our neighbors' scorn:
5   How long, O Lord? Will Thy just ire
  And jealousy forever last,
    And burn unquenchably like fire?

6 Wrath rather on the nations pour,
  That know Thee not, nor on Thee wait;
7 For they have Israel devoured,
  And made his dwellings desolate.

8 Remember not against us, Lord,
  Our fathers' sinnings long ago:
Let us Thy tender mercies meet,
  For we are brought exceeding low!

9 O God of our salvation, help!
  Help for the glory of Thy Name!
For Thy Name's sake deliver us,
  And purge away our guilt and shame.

10 O wherefore should the heathen say,
  Where is their God? Display Thy might;
And be Thy servants' blood avenged,
  Among the nations in our sight.

11 Incline a favorable ear,
  And hear the groaning captive's cry:
After the greatness of Thy power
  Preserve Thou those condemned to die

12 Return our neighbors' scorn sevenfold :
13   So we, Thy flock, will give to Thee
    Eternal thanks : Thy praise show forth
      To generations yet to be.

PSALM LXXX.*

SHEPHERD of Israel, give ear—
  Who like a flock dost Joseph lead !
Throned on the Cherubim, shine clear,
  Forth from Thy Cloud let light proceed !
2 Arouse Thy might ; Lord, save, restore !
3 Let Thy Face shine on us once more !

4 Lord God of Hosts, how long wilt Thou
    Be angry 'gainst Thy people's prayer ?
5 For food, for drink Thou giv'st them now
    Abundant tears, their only fare.
6 Our neighbors laugh : Lord, save, restore !
7 Let Thy Face shine on us once more !

8 Thou didst a Vine from Egypt fetch,
    And plant, and drive the nations out
9 To give it room—and let it stretch
    Its mighty roots and boughs about,
10 To fill and cover all the Land,
11 Extending to Euphrates' strand.

---

*The occasion of this Psalm is supposed to have been the overthrow and deportation of the Ten Tribes—known as the Kingdom of Israel, in distinction from the Kingdom of Judah.

12 Why hast Thou broken down its wall,
    So all may pluck it in their greed?
13 Boar from the wood it strips, and all
    Beasts roaming wild upon it feed.
14 Visit the Vine, which Thou didst plant,
15 O God of Hosts, and shelter grant!

16 'T is burned with fire; it is cut down:
    At Thy rebuke they cease to be.
17 Make strong our Champion of renown,
18   So we shall not backslide from Thee.
19 Lord God of Hosts, revive, restore!
    Let Thy Face shine on us once more!

PSALM LXXXI.

SHOUT to the Lord, our Strength!
    To God of Israel sing!
2 Take up the psalm! The timbrel strike!
    Wake every tuneful string

Of the sweet harp and lute!
    And let the trumpets sound!
3 As at new moon, so now at full,
    Spread the announcement round,

4 This is the happy day
    Of the Passover Feast,
5 Appointed to commemorate
    When Jacob was released,

And out of Egypt went—
  To him a foreign land,
Where he another language heard,
  He did not understand.

———

6 "From his tasked shoulders I
  Removed the crushing load;
His hands I from the basket freed,
  Great favor to him showed.

7 "In trouble thou didst call:
  And I did set thee free—
I from the cloud, the secret place
  Of thunder, answered thee.

"When thou at Meribah
  Didst murmur, I thee tried;
I gave thee water from the rock,
  Miraculously supplied.

8 "O, Israel, bend now
  To me a listening ear,
And I will to thee testify,
  If thou wilt only hear.

9 There shall no foreign god
  In thee permitted be;
And thou shalt worship no strange god,
  But worship only Me.

10 "I am the Lord thy God,
      Who did from Egypt bring:
   Ope wide thy mouth, and I'll it fill
      With every needful thing.

---

11 "When Israel refused
      To hear Me and obey,
12 I gave them up to stubbornness
      To walk in their own way.

13 "O that My people would
      But hearken to My voice!
14 I'd soon subdue their enemies,
      And make their hearts rejoice.

15 "The haters of the Lord
      Should unto Him submit;
   The nation then should long endure,
      No end should be to it.

16 "I would them also feed
      With finest of the wheat,
   And satisfy them from the rock
      With honey too to eat."

PSALM LXXXII.

THE mighty God of Heaven
   In His assembly stands,
Judging the gods who judge below—
   The princes of the lands.

2 "How long will ye judge wrong;
 Just laws corruptly wrest?
3 Right ye the weak and fatherless,
4 And rescue th' opprest!"

5 Perversely, they prefer
 In darkness still to walk;
 The earth's foundations shake, while they
 The ends of justice balk.

6 "Though I said, 'Ye are gods,
 All sons of the Most High,'
7 Yet ye shall from your places fall,
 Like common men shall die!"

8 Arise, O God! and judge
 The earth in righteousness:
 Assert thy claim, whose right it is
 All nations to possess!

PSALM LXXXIII.

KEEP silence not, O God!
 Hold not Thy peace, nor rest;
2 For, lo, Thy foes a tumult make,
 Proud hatred swells their breast.

3 They craftily combine;
 "Come," say they, "we will plot,
4 And from the roll of nations will
 The name of Israel blot."

6 Edom and Ishmael,
    Philistia and Tyre,
7 Asshur and Amalek, to help
8   The sons of Lot, conspire.

9 Do as to Midian,
    And as to Sisera,
  When Thou at the brook Kishon didst
    The hosts of Jabin slay :

10 Destroyed at Endor, these
    Were dung unto the ground ;
  The bodies of ten thousand slain
    Lay festering around.

11 Their nobles do Thou like
    Oreb and Zeeb make ;
  Like Zeba and Zalmunna, let
    Destruction them o'ertake,

12 Who impudently said :
    "Let us the dwellings seize
  And fertile pasture grounds of God,
    And henceforth live at ease."

13 Make, O my God, them like
    The whirl of flying wheels ;
  Like chaff before the wind them drive,
    Grim slaughter at their heels.

14 As fire the forest burns,
    Flame kindles mountains, so
15 Do Thou pursue them with Thy storm—
    Make them Thy terrors know:

16 Their face fill with contempt,
    Till they shall seek Thy Name—
17 Let them forever be abashed,
    And perish in their shame.

18 Then shall men know that Thou,
    Jehovah! Thou alone,
  Art the Most High o'er all the earth,
    And worship at Thy throne.

PSALM LXXXIV.

HOW lovely are Thy Dwellings, Lord!
  My spirit longs, yea faints to see
Thy far-off Courts, where praise is poured
  By lips thrice-privileged to Thee.
    My heart and flesh
    Cry out afresh
For those dear precincts, long untrod,
And most for Thee, the Living God.

3 The favored sparrow there appears;
    And there the swallow has her nest,
  In which her callow brood she rears,
    A fearless unforbidden guest,

  Thine altars nigh,
  O Lord Most High—
While I am banished from the place,
Thy Mercy Seat and Throne of Grace.

4 Happy the dwellers in Thy Courts,
  Who permanently spend their days
Within Thy Temple's sacred ports,
  In offerings of prayer and praise:
5   Happy is he,
   Whose strength's in Thee,
With highways in his heart that lead
To Zion's Hill, cast up for speed.

6 They, passing through the Vale of Tears,
  Make it a place of welling springs:
The early rain the pilgrim cheers,
  And seasonable blessings brings.
   From strength to strength
   They go—at length
They all appear, their journey done,
'Fore God in Zion, every one.

8 Jehovah, God of Hosts, incline
  A gracious ear, and hear my cry!
9 O God, my Shield! look Thou on Thine
  Anointed with a loving eye!
10   Better one day
   Is it to stay
Within Thy House, and keep the door,
Than tents of sin a thousand more.

11 Jehovah is a Sun and Shield;
    He grace and glory will bestow;
    No good but He will to them yield
    Who walk uprightly here below.
12   O Lord of Hosts,
        Guard Thou our coasts;
    Our light and our protection be—
    Happy the man who trusts in Thee!

PSALM LXXXV.

THOU hast, O Lord, in former years
    Been gracious to Thy Land;
Hast captive Israel brought back,
    By Thy restoring hand.

2 Thy people's guilt Thou hast removed,
    Their sins hast covered o'er;
3 Withdrawn the fierceness of Thine ire,
    So that it smoked no more.

4 O God of our Salvation, now
    Return to us; and make
Thine indignation towards us cease,
    For Thine own mercy's sake.

5 Wilt Thou be angry, and draw out
    Thine anger evermore?
6 Wilt Thou not quicken us again,
    And former joys restore?

7 Show us Thy mercy, gracious Lord !
    And Thy salvation grant :
8 I wait to hear Thee speak the peace
    For which Thy people pant.

   Let them no more to folly turn ;
    But fear, and steadfast stand ;
9 That Thy indwelling presence may
    Make glorious the Land.

10 Mercy and Truth together meet,
    And Righteousness and Peace
   Embrace and kiss—Thy covenant
    Is sure and does not cease.

11 Attesting Truth springs up like grain
    Out of the teeming sod ;
   And Righteousness looks down from heaven,
    Like rainbow-pledge from God.

12 The Lord the promised good shall give ;
    Our Land her increase pour :
13 And Righteousness, His harbinger,
    Shall go His steps before.

PSALM LXXXVI.

BOW down Thine ear, O Lord, to me,
   Needy and poor I succor crave :
2 Preserve my soul, beloved of Thee,
    Thy servant trusting in Thee, save !

3 Be merciful to me, for I
 The whole day long unto Thee cry.

4 Rejoice Thy servant's soul ! I lift
   To Thee a meek, confiding heart :
  Descends from Thee each perfect gift—
5 Good and forgiving, Lord, Thou art ;
  Plenteous in mercy unto all
  Who unto Thee contritely call.

6 Give ear, O Lord, unto my prayer ;
7 In trouble Thou wilt hear my cry ;
8 No gods with Thee can e'er compare,
   No works of theirs with Thine can vie ;
9 All nations shall their Maker own,
10 And worship Thee and Thee alone.

11 Teach me to walk in wisdom's ways ;
    Unite my heart to fear Thy Name ;
12 With my whole heart I will Thee praise,
    And evermore resound Thy fame.
13 Great is Thy mercy, for 't was it
   That snatched me from the lowest pit.

14 Proud ones against me have rebelled—
    The violent, the sons of strife—
   Thy fear they 've not before them held,
    Ungodly men that sought my life ;
15 But Thou a God art, full of ruth—
   Plenteous in mercy and in truth.

16 O to me turn and gracious be!
  Strength and salvation to me give!
17 A sign of favor show to me,
  That, seeing by whose help I live,
  All those towards me with hate inflamed,
  May be confounded and ashamed.

PSALM LXXXVII.

O N consecrated ground,
  The holy mountains round,
Rest Zion's bulwarks and her lofty domes:
2   Jehovah loves her gates,
  And them more precious rates
Than all the lordliest of Jacob's homes.

  Dear City of our God,
  The Place of His Abode!
3 Most glorious things are prophesied of thee;
  To the true worship won,
4   Egypt and Babylon,
Philistia and Tyre and Cush shall be.

  By God establishéd—
  In Thee, it shall be said,
5 This man was born and that; and so when He
6   The nations shall convert,
  Of each He will assert,
7 There this was born—the mother of the free.

PSALM LXXXVIII.

LORD God of my salvation, I
  By day, by night before Thee cry,
2 O let my prayer to Thee ascend,
  Thine ear to my petition bend!

3 For, oh, my soul is full of fear,
  And my life draws to Sheol near:
4 I'm counted with th' already dead,
  And all my manly strength is fled.

5 Cast off, I with the dead remain,
  Forsaken, like the buried slain,
  Whom Thou Thyself rememberest not,
  From Thee cut off and doomed to rot.

6 Thou hast in lowest pit me hurled,
  Th' abysses of the underworld;
7 Thy wrath lies heavy on my soul,
  Great waves of sorrow o'er me roll.

8 Thou my acquaintance hast estranged,
  And hast their love to loathing changed;
  Shut up, I can go forth no more,
9 Mine eye decays through weeping sore.

  I Thee invoke, Lord, every day;
  I stretch forth wearied hands and pray:
10 Wilt Thou show wonders to the dead,
  Shall shades * arise Thy praise to spread?

---

* Disembodied spirits, implying the separate existence of the soul after death.

11 Shall any in the grave rehearse
   Thy loving kindnesses in verse?
   Or any in Abaddon* bless
   And celebrate Thy faithfulness?

12 Any in that lone darksome land
   Recite the wonders of Thy hand?—
   Land of forgetfulness and night
   Where reaches not one ray of light.

13 To Thee I come with tears and cries;
   At early morn my prayer shall rise—
14 Why cast me off, O God of grace?
   Why dost Thou hide Thy lovely Face?

15 I long have drawn uncertain breath,
   A ready candidate for death :
   Have borne Thy terrors and still bear,
   A wretched victim of despair.

16 Thine indignations like a sea,
   Loud roaring, have passed over me :
17 Thy terrors have made me a prey,
   Like waters compassed me all day.

18 Of lover and of friend bereft,
   Darkness to me alone is left—
   My path is lost.   Great Shepherd, say,
   Shall I still wander from Thy way?

---

* A poetical equivalent of Grave and Death.   See Prov. xvii. 11 ; Job xxvi. 6 ; xxviii. 22.

PSALM LXXXIX.

THE mercies of the Lord
    I will forever sing;
2 Make known th' enduring faithfulness
    Of our Eternal King.

3 For, Mercy, I have said,
    Shall be built up for aye:
Thy faithfulness, fixed in the heavens,
    Be permanent as they.

  "I have with David made
    A covenant, and sworn:
4 'I stablish will thy seed; build up
    Thy throne for sons unborn.'"

5 The heavens shall celebrate,
    The skilled angelic choirs,
The wonders of Thy faithfulness
    Upon their golden lyres.

6 For who in all the Sky—
    Sons of the mighty there,
The angels that excel in strength—
    Can with the Lord compare?

7 A God most terrible,
    With awful glory crowned—
High seated at His council board,
    The holy ones around.

8

8 Jehovah, God of Hosts,
    Who mighty is like Thee?
  Thy faithfulness the girdle is
    Of Thy eternity.

9 The proud imperious deep
    Acknowledges Thy sway:
  Th' obsequious waves Thy mandate hear
    And instantly obey.

10 Thou hast proud Egypt crushed,
     Inflicting mortal harm;
   Thy foes hast scattered by the strength
     Of Thine almighty arm.

11 The heavens and earth are Thine,
     Thou didst all nature frame:
12 All quarters of the world rejoice
     In their Creator's Name.

14 Justice and judgment are
     Thy throne's eternal base;
   Mercy and Truth, celestial forms,
     Shall go before Thy face.

15 Happy the people, who,
     Knowing the joyful sound,
16 Walk in the sunshine of Thy Face,
     Glad daylight all around.

17 For Thou, Lord, art our Strength ;
   Our Ornament, as well ;
18 Our Shield, our King, the Holy One
   Of favored Israel.

---

19 In vision Thou didst speak
   And saidst : " I help have laid
   Upon a Mighty One and fit,
   Of whom I choice have made—

20 " David, my servant, him
   I have anointed King ;
21 My hand and arm shall present be
   For his establishing.

22 " No foe shall him compel,
   Or vanquish him in fight ;
23 His adversaries I 'll beat down,
   And those who hate him smite.

24 " My faithfulness and love
   Shall him exalt and bless ;
25 I 'll set his hand too on the seas
   And rivers to possess.

26 " From his warm lips to Me
   Shall burst the filial cry :
   'Thou art my Father, Thou my God,
   The Rock to which I fly.'

27 "I'll make him my First-born,
    Highest of earthly kings;
28 His throne shall, like the days of heaven,
29   Exceed all reckonings.

30 "If Me his sons forsake,
31   And from my laws diverge,
32 Their sin I'll visit with a rod,
    Their trespass with a scourge;

33 "But I'll not utterly
    My mercy from him take;
I'll not My faithfulness let fail,
34   My covenant not break.

35 "Once by My holiness
    I have to David sworn,
36 His seed shall last, his throne abide
37   While night succeeds to morn.

---

38 And yet Thou hast cast off,
    On Thine anointed frowned,
39 Abhorred his covenant, profaned
    His crown hurled to the ground;

40 Hast broken down his walls,
    His strongholds hast uptorn:
41 All spoil him that pass by—he has
    Become his neighbors' scorn.

42 Thou hast made strong his foes,
    And triumph to them given;
43 Turned back the keenness of his sword,
    And from the field him driven.

44 And Thou hast made to cease
    The brightness of his fame;
45 His throne cast down, his days cut short,
    And covered him with shame.

46 How long, O Lord? wilt Thou
    Thyself forever hide?
   How long shall burn like fire Thy wrath?
    How long shall foes deride?

47 Remember, Lord, how short
48   My time is: To what use
   Hast Thou made man? No one the grasp
    Of Sheol's hand* can loose.

49 Where are Thy mercies which
    Thou didst to David swear?
50 Remember, Lord, I the reproach
    Of many peoples bear.

      Blessed be Jehovah forevermore,

          Amen, and Amen.

* So the Hebrew.

BOOK IV.

PSALM XC.

LORD, Thou hast been our dwelling-place,
   Our refuge in the past:
2 Before the mountains were brought forth
   Or earth's foundations cast,

Thou wast, and art, and wilt be God:
   From everlasting Thou
To everlasting still the same,
   An unbeginning NOW.

The generations come and go,
   Appear, and perish then;
3 Thou turnest man to dust, and say'st:
   "Return ye sons of men!"

4 For in Thy sight a thousand years
   Are but as yesterday,
And as a brief watch in the night
   When it hath passed away.

5 Thou bearest them as with a flood
    On to the silent deep;
  So unsubstantial and so vain
    Their life is as a sleep.

  They are like grass, which groweth up
6   In the sweet morning light,
  And in the evening is cut down,
    And withered to the sight.

7 We by Thine anger are consumed;
8   Our secret sins are known;
9 The troubled years in sorrow pass,
    Their end a sigh,* a groan.

10 Three score and ten complete our term,
     And should it reach four score,
   'T is soon cut off, we fly away,
     And here are seen no more.

11 Who knows the power of love incensed?
     Of Thy just anger, who?
   Of wrath proportioned to Thy fear,
     And awe that is Thy due?

12 Teach us to so compute our days,
     That we each hour may prize;
   Apply our hearts to learn the lore
     And wisdom of the skies.

* Marginal reading.

13 Return, O Lord, how long? Do Thou
    Compassionate our case;
  Let it repent Thee so to hide
    The comfort of Thy Face.

14 With early mercy satisfy,
    And all our days make glad,
15 According to the days and years
    Wherein Thou mad'st us sad.

16 Let Thy redeeming work be seen;
17   Thy beauty on us rest;
  Establish Thou what we attempt,
    And be our labors blest.

PSALM XCI.

WHO has his refuge in the sky,
    And secret place of the Most High,
On whom the Almighty's shadow falls,
Can have no need of towers and walls:
2 Who puts in God his trust sublime,
Is safe from all the ills of time.

3 The Lord is his deliverance
  From fowler's snare, and pestilence:
4 His wings shall a safe covert yield;
  His truth a buckler be and shield.
5 Thee shall no terror of the night,
  Nor dart that flies by day affright;

6 No pest that in the darkness hastes,
　Nor sickness that at noon-day wastes;
7 Thousands shall fall at thy right hand,
　But unmolested thou shalt stand:
8 Thou only with thine eyes shalt see,
　Shalt only a spectator be,

　Of the reward and recompense
　God doth to wicked men dispense.
9 And inasmuch as thou hast said,
　"The Lord my refuge is;" and made
　Thy habitation the Most High;
10 No plague shall come thy dwelling nigh:

11 For He shall give His angels charge.
　With heavenly orders strict and large,
　To keep thee safe in all thy ways,
12 And in their hands to thee upraise—
　Lest, left unto thyself alone,
　Thou dash thy foot against a stone.

13 Thou shalt upon the lion tread,
　And trample on the serpent's head.
14 Jehovah saith: "Because that he
　Hath set his love supreme on Me—
　Because that he My Name hath known,
　I will deliver him and own.

15 "He shall upon Me call, and I
　Will answer, and to him draw nigh:

Will with him in his trouble be,
Will honor him and set him free:
16 Long life I will on him bestow,
And to him My salvation show."

PSALM XCII.

TO give Jehovah thanks,
    And Thy high praises sing,
O Thou Most High, is a most good
    And necessary thing.

2 Thy kindness to show forth
    Is meet at morning light;
And laud Thy love and faithfulness,
    At each return of night,

3 Upon the decachord,
    With psaltery and lute,
And harp of soft and solemn sound
    The holy strains to suit.

4 For Thou hast made me glad,
    Through knowledge of Thy works—
In all a glorious goodness shines
    An awful beauty lurks.

3 How infinite Thy works!
    Thy thoughts are an abyss;
6 The brutish man and fool alike
    Are ignorant of this.

7 When spring they as the grass,
   The wicked, overjoyed,
  Know not it is that they may soon
   Forever be destroyed.

8 But Thou, Jehovah, art
   For evermore on high :
9 Thy foes shall perish, all their hosts
   Be scattered from the sky.

10 Thou hast my honored head,
   Anointed with fresh oil—
11 Mine eye hath seen Thy Hand stretched out
   Mine enemies to foil.

12 The righteous as a palm
   Shall grow and flourish, like
  Cedars of Lebanon whose roots
   In soil congenial strike.

13 They, planted in Thy House,
   Shall in Thy Courts be seen
14 Producing fruit—ev'n in old age
   Still full of sap and green.

15 Just is the Lord, who sits
   Between the Cherubim—
  He is my Rock, and there is no
   Unrighteousness in Him.

PSALM XCIII.

JEHOVAH reigns, and reigns alone :
    Earth is His footstool, heaven his throne ;
He, with omnipotence arrayed,
Of old the world 's foundations laid.

2 O universal is Thy sway ;
The loyal atoms Thee obey ;
All being, Lord, proceeds from Thee,
Who dwellest in eternity.

3 Let angry waves lift up their roar,
And dash themselves against the shore ;
4 Above the voices of the deep,
Thine shall be heard commanding sleep.

5 Thy testimonies, Lord, endure ;
Thy promises are very sure ;
While holiness Thy house and door
Makes beautiful forevermore.

PSALM XCIV.

LORD God of recompense,
    Shine forth with bickering flame ;*
2 Lift up Thyself, Judge of the earth,
Reward the proud with shame.

> * And from about Him fierce effusion rolled
> Of smoke, and *bickering* flame, and sparkles dire.
>   —*Milton*, *P. L.*, *B. VI*, *l.* 766.

3 How long, O Lord, how long
    Shall wicked men exult?
4 In saucy triumph speak hard words,
    And cruelly insult?

5 They grind the people, they
    Thy heritage oppress;
6 The widow and the stranger kill,
    Murder the fatherless.

7 They say: "Jah will not see,
    The God of Jacob know"—
8 Reflect, ye brutish ones; ye fools,
    When will ye wiser grow?

9 Who made the ear and eye,
    Shall He not hear and see?
10 From Him who gives the power to know,
    Shall knowledge hidden be?

11 He knows men's thoughts are vain,
    And like the breath they draw:
12 Happy is he whom Thou dost warn,
    And teach, Lord, from Thy law.

13 Thy chastisements are meant
    To profit not to grieve,
  Against the time the pit is dug
    The wicked shall receive.

14 The Lord will not cast off
    His people, nor forsake :
15 For banished Justice shall return,
    And righteous judgment make.

16 Who will for me against
    The evil-doers rise?
  For me stand up against those who
    Iniquity devise?

17 Unless Jehovah were
    A present help for me,
  My soul would soon in Silence dwell—
    My struggles ended be.

18 When I said, My foot slips,
    Thy mercy, Lord, was near;
19 Mid whirling thoughts Thy comforts did
    My troubled spirit cheer.

20 Shall Crime beside Thee sit,
    High seated on a throne,
  To frame iniquity by law
    And right be overthrown?

21 They haste to congregate,
    They rush in crowds, they hem
  Souls of the righteous in, the blood
    Of innocence condemn.

22 But God has been my Tower,
   My Rock, my sure Defence;
23 He in their sins will cut them off,
   Their evil recompense.

PSALM XCV.

LET us to Jehovah raise,
   Rock of our Salvation, praise!
2 Let us come with lifted palms!
   Let us shout to him in psalms!
   Let our joyful thanks arise
   To the Monarch of the Skies!
3 Inexpressible the odds
   'Twixt Him and all other gods.

4 Depths of earth to Him belong,
   And the heights of mountains strong:
5 His the sea, made by His hand
   That created the dry land.
6 Let us worship! let us bow
   'Fore the Lord, our Maker now!
7 He's our God, our Shepherd He,
   People of His pasture we,

   Objects of His shepherd-care—
   Thus He doth His mind declare:
   "O that ye to-day would hear!
8 Steel your hearts not 'gainst my fear,

As at Meribah, no less
  Massah in the wilderness,
9 When your fathers tempted Me,
  Proved Me, and My work did see!

10 " Forty years I, grieving sore,
   With that generation bore:
   ' They a people are,' I said,
   ' That have always erred and strayed ;
   Irreclaimably preverse,
   Aye addicted to the worse ;'
   So in wrath I did protest
   They should enter not my rest."

PSALM XCVI.

SING to Jehovah a new song,
　　His great salvation sing :
2 Sing to Jehovah, bless His name,
　　The good news publishing ;
  Let earth her guilty silence break,
  And sweet melodious thunder make.

3 Among the nations day by day
　　Declare His power and love.
4 How greatly He is to be feared
　　All heathen gods above—
5 Vain senseless things of wood and stone—
  Jehovah made the heavens alone.

6 Honor and majesty attend,
   And go before His Face;
 Beauty and excellence and strength
   Are in His Holy Place:
7 Ye peoples, long estranged, proclaim
 The glory of Jehovah's Name.

8 An offering bring and come into
   His Courts, His throne address!
9 O worship Him in beauty clad,
   Adorned with holiness!
 Tremble before Him all the earth,
 From whom all creatures have their birth.

10 Among all nations publish ye,
   Jehovah reigns on high:
 The world stands fast: His equity
   From the impartial sky
 He'll make on all alike descend,
 And Right be honored in the end.

11 Let heaven and earth be glad, the sea
   With all its fullness roar:
12 Let fields exult, let happy trees,
   Their whispered gladness pour:
13 For, lo, He comes in glorious dress
 To judge the world in righteousness.

PSALM XCVII.

JEHOVAH reigns : let earth rejoice ;
   Let all the isles be glad !
He rules the world in equity,
   And is with mercy clad.

2 Thick clouds and darkness Him surround ;
   But this great truth is known,
That righteousness and judgment are
   The basis of His throne.

3 Before Him went a fire that burned ;
   The kindlings of His look
4 His foes consumed : His lightnings flamed,
   The earth beheld and shook.

5 Melted the hills like wax before
   The presence of the Lord ;
6 Loud thundering the skies declared
   His right to be adored.

7 Put shame on those who idols serve—
   Things deaf and dumb and blind ;
Bow down yourselves to Him, ye gods,
   Vain phrenzies of the mind.

8 Lo, Zion heard it and was glad ;
   And Judah's daughters sang,
How just Thy judgments are, O Lord !
   Till all the mountains rang.

9 For Thou, O Lord, art high above
    All that on earth bear sway :
  Thy throne is in the heaven of heavens
    And doth not pass away.

10 O ye that love the Lord, be sure
    Ye evil hate, and fight :
11 For light is for the righteous sown,
    And joy for the upright.

PSALM XCVIII.

SING a new song of matchless charm !
    The Lord most wondrous things hath done :
With His right hand and holy arm
  He hath a victory for Him won ;
2 Before the nations hath displayed
His righteousness and saving aid.

3 He hath been faithful to His word,
    Each holy pledge remembered still ;
And in His mercy hath conferred
    This crowning grace on Israel—
Famous where'er man's foot hath trod
As " THE SALVATION OF OUR GOD."

4 Make to the Lord a joyful noise ;
    Break forth ; His praise with rapture sing ;
5 Make melody with harp and voice,
6   And sound of trumpet to our King ;
Join, all ye dwellers on the earth,
To give the mighty transport birth.

7 Let the sea roar, each wave a tongue;
8   And let the rivers clap their hands;
  And joy resound the hills among;
    And shouts of welcome fill all lands:
9 For, lo, He comes in holy dress
  To judge the world in righteousness.

PSALM XCIX.

JEHOVAH reigns, the Mighty God,
  Let all the nations shake!
He's throned above the Cherubim,
  Let conscious Nature quake!

2 Jehovah is in Zion, great;
  Above all people, high;
3 Let them extol Thy dreadful Name,
  And give the reason why,
    For it is holy.

4 Thy kingly strength doth judgment love;
  Thou dost establish right;
Thou innocence dost vindicate,
  And wickedness requite.

5 Exalt the Lord our God; approach
  His awful Mercy Seat;
Prostrate yourselves before His throne,
  And worship at His feet,
    For He is holy.

6 Moses and Aaron were to God
    As priests to intercede ;
  And Samuel called upon His name,
    And did for Israel plead.

7 They called, He answered them ; He in
    The cloudy pillar spake ;
  They kept His statues which He gave
    And warned them not to break.

8 Thou didst, Jehovah, answer them—
    Wast a forgiving God ;
  But mad'st them feel for their misdeeds
    The vengeance of Thy rod.

9 Exalt the Lord our God, bow down ;
    Ye people all draw near !
  Assemble at His Holy Mount
    And worship in His fear,
            For He is holy !

PSALM C.

O ALL ye lands, unite your joys ;
    Make to the Lord a joyful noise ;
2 Serve Him with gladness ; come before
    His presence, and with songs adore !

3 The Lord is God, for He it is
    Who us has made, and we are His ;
  We are His people, we His sheep
    Whom He delights to tend and keep.

4 Enter His Temple gates with praise ;
   Songs of thanksgiving to Him raise,
5 For He is good, His mercy vast
   And faithfulness forever last.

PSALM CI.

MERCY and judgment will I sing ;
   To Thee, O Lord, will I sing praise ;
2 When Thou shalt come, I, in Thy strength,
   Will walk in wisdom's perfect ways ;
   I will at home perform my part,
   And serve Thee with an honest heart.

3 I'll no base thing before me set ;
   I hate their work who turn aside ;
4 Their vileness shall not cleave to me,
   Naught evil shall with me abide.
5 The slanderer I will not spare,
   The proud of heart I will not bear.

6 I'll seek them out, mine eyes shall be
   Upon the faithful of the Land,
   That they may dwell with me, and be
   The trusted men of my right hand.
7 Men of deceit I'll not employ,
8 All evil-doers I'll destroy.

PSALM CII.

HEAR, O Jehovah, let my cry
  Reach Thy high dwelling-place:
2 In this dark day of my distress
  Hide not Thy loving Face.

3 Make haste to answer, for my days
    Have vanished into smoke;
  My fevered bones cease not to burn,
    And fiery pangs provoke.

4 My heart is smitten, like the grass
    All withered, scorched, and dried;
  For I forget to eat my bread,
    By groans preoccupied.

5 So lean, my skin cleaves to my bones,
    I solitary moan,
6 Like pelican in the wilderness,
    Like owl 'mid ruins lone;

7 Like sparrow on the house-top, I
    Unsleeping sit forlorn;
8 While all day long my maddened foes
    Belch curses mixed with scorn.

9 Sitting in sackcloth, ashes vile
    I eaten have like bread;
  My tears have mingled with my drink,
10   For Thy displeasure shed.

As by the whirlwind taken up,
  Thou hast me borne away:
11 My life is as the lengthened shade
  That marks the close of day.

12 I withered am like grass, but Thou
  Forever shalt endure ;
And to all generations, Lord !
  Is Thy remembrance sure.

---

13 Thou wilt arise and Zion build ;
  For the set time and right
14 Is when Thy servants love her stones,
  And in her dust delight.

15 So shall the nations fear Thy Name ;
  All kings Thy greatness own ;
16 Because the Lord has Zion built,
  And made His glory known ;

17 And stooped to hear the destitute,
  Despising not their prayer—
18 The grace of which the written page
  To after times shall bear.

19 Jehovah looked down from the height
  Of heaven itself to hear
20 The groaning of the prisoner
  And loose him from his fear ;

21 That men in Zion might declare
   His pity to the race,
22 When gathered at Jerusalem
   The kingdoms seek His face.

---

23 My strength He weakened in the way;
   My days He has made few:
24 I said, "Remove me not, my God,
   Before my life's half through!

   "Thy years are endless; grudge me not
   The remnant of my term—
   Thou art the Everlasting God
   And I am but a worm!"

25 Of old hast Thou, Almighty One!
   The earth's foundation laid;
   The heavens the work are of Thy hands,
   And are by Thee upstayed.

26 While they shall perish, Thou shalt last—
   These, like a garment worn,
   Thou wilt put off, new dress to wear
   On that eternal morn.

27 But Thou art evermore the same,
   Thy years shall have no end;
28 Thy servants shall endure, their seed
   Prosperity attend.

PSALM CIII.

O BLESS the Lord, my soul!
   Let all within me bless;
Join, all my powers, in psalms of praise
   And hymns of thankfulness!

2 O bless the Lord, my soul!
   Let memory awake,
And think of all His benefits,
   And grateful mention make:

3 Who all thy sins forgives;
   All thy diseases heals;
4 Who saved thy life from threatened death,
   And for thee pity feels.

5 Who gives thee pleasant food,
   And makes an end of pain;
So, like an eagle, is renewed
   Thy faded youth again.

6 He judgment executes
   For all that are oppressed;
7 He made to Israel of old
   His goodness manifest.

8 The Lord is merciful,
   And is to anger slow;
The plenteous fountains of His grace
   Continually o'erflow.

9 He will not always chide,
    His anger always keep;
10 He has not dealt with us to match
    Our soul's demerit deep.

11 For as the heaven is high
    Above this lower sphere,
  So great His mercy is toward them,
    Who reverence Him and fear.

12 Far as from east to west,
    He doth our sins remove;
13 He pities us, as parents do
    The children of their love.

14 For He knows well our frame;
    How frail we are, He knows;
  How man's original is dust,
    And back to it he goes.

15 His days are as the grass;
    He blossoms like the flower,
16 The wind sweeps o'er it, and 't is gone—
    The vision of an hour.

17 But then His mercies are
    Forever and for aye,
18 To such as keep His covenant,
    And His commands obey.

19 His throne is in the heavens,
   His kingdom over all :
20 Ye angels—that excel in strength,
   Who hearken to His call,

   Then fly to execute
   His powerful decrees—
21 Bless ye the Lord ; and thou, my soul !
22   Bless Him on bended knees.

PSALM CIV.*

O LORD, my God ! Thou art
   Above conception great ;
Nature Thy wardrobe is in part—
   The purple of Thy state.

2 Thy garment is the light—
   Around Thee, lo, are drawn
The starry mantle of the night,
   The vesture of the dawn.

---

* Alexander Von Humboldt, in his "Cosmos," remarks : "It might be said one single Psalm (the 104th) represents the image of the whole Cosmos. . . We are astonished to find in a lyrical poem of such limited compass, the whole universe—the heavens and the earth—sketched with a few bold touches." Bishop Lowth in his Lectures refers again and again to this Psalm (or Idyllium, as he somewhere calls it) in terms of unbounded admiration. He says : "There is nothing of the kind extant (indeed nothing can be conceived) more perfect than this Hymn, whether it be considered with respect to its intrinsic beauties, or as a model to this species of composition." Lord Bacon dedicates to his " very good friend, Mr. George Herbert," a version executed in the heroic couplet:

" Father and King of Powers, both high and low,
   Whose sounding fame all creatures serve to blow," etc.

The heavens Thou dost extend
As a pavilion fair ;
3 Thy chambers' beams Thou dost suspend
In watery depths of air.

The clouds Thy chariots are ;
4   The winged winds Thy steeds ;
To bear Thy messages afar
The flaming lightning speeds.

5 Thou founded hast the earth
On law's eternal base,
That nothing should, while time shall last,
Remove it from its place.

6 The garment of the deep
Around it all was poured ;
Above the mountains' highest steep
The haughty waters roared.

7 Thy dread rebuke they heard ;
They fled, they hasted down,
Before the thunder of Thy word,
The terror of Thy frown.

8 They climb the mountains' height,
They down the valleys roll,
Wave chasing wave in headlong flight,
To the appointed goal.

9 There Thou a bound hast set,
    That nevermore the main,
  Howe'er the loud waves rage and threat,
    May drown the earth again.

10 Among the vales and hills
    A thousand fountains burst ;
11 There run cool brooks and murmuring rills
    For beasts to slake their thirst.

12 The fowls of heaven have near
    Their favorite retreat,
  Among the branches singing clear
    Their happy songs and sweet.

13 From out the blessèd sky
    Thou send'st the genial rain ;
  And thirsty vales and hill-tops dry
    Revive and laugh again.

14 Thy breath is in the fields ;
    Thy power beneath the sod ;
  Each mead and cornfield tribute yields,
    And owns the present God.

15 For sake of man and beast,
    To satisfy their needs,
  Exhaustless Nature spreads this feast,
    This miracle proceeds.

16 Majestic cedars prop
   The nests on Lebanon ;
17 The stork prefers the fir-tree's top
   To build her house upon.

18 On craggy summit, where
   Can tread no other feet,
   The wild goats and the conies there
   Find both a safe retreat.

   Thou dost for all provide
   Whate'er their natures ask,
   A sphere and faculty to guide,
   A purpose and a task.

19 Alike the sun and moon
   Their proper seasons wait—
   For punctual Nature's ne'er too soon,
   Nor ever yet too late.

20 As down heaven's headlong steep
   The dewy night is hurled,
   Forth from their dens all wild beasts creep,
   While darkness wraps the world.

21 Young lions roar for prey,
   And seek their meat from God ;
22 But when the sun arises, they
   No longer roam abroad.

23 Man, now, refreshed by sleep,
    Goes forth at morning light
 To plough the fields, to sow, or reap,
    Till the return of night.

24 O Lord, how manifold
    The products of Thy hand—
 How wise! how wondrous to behold!
    How admirably planned!

25 And not the earth alone,
    But the unfathomed sea
 Is filled with myriads unknown,
    Whose being is in Thee.

26 There go the ships; and there
    Leviathan disports,
 And other beasts the waters bear—
    Innumerable sorts.

27 These all on Thee depend;
    All wait on Thee for food;
28 Thine open hand Thou dost extend,
    And they are filled with good.

29 That moment Thou dost hide,
    Benignant Lord, Thy Face,
 They down to swift destruction glide,
    They die and leave no trace.

30 Thou spread'st Thy brooding wing :
    Thou sendest forth Thy breath,
  And countless forms of life upspring
    From out the dust of death.

  The earth, that late was seen
    Shrunk by the fatal cold,
  Warmed by Thy smile appears as green
    And beauteous as of old.

31 Thy glory doth endure,
    Thy goodness doth not pass,
  Thy works reflect Thine image pure
    Distinct as in a glass.

32 Awe-struck beneath Thy gaze,
    Earth shakes from south to north—
  At Thy bare touch the mountains blaze,
    Volcanic fires burst forth.

33 While I have power to praise,
    And being have and breath,
  My joyful songs to Thee I'll raise,
    Nor shall they cease at death.

34 What tongue cannot repeat,
    That silence shall express ;
  My thoughts of Thee shall still be sweet,
    Whose love is fathomless.

35 Though Thou canst be severe,
    As impious men shall know,
Yet to the humble and sincere
    Thy grace doth overflow.

My soul, bless thou the Lord!
    Glad hallelujahs sing!
Let rapturous praise be ever poured
    From an exhaustless spring.

SECOND VERSION.

O LORD my God! Thou art
    Of all that is the soul—
The mystery of every part,
    The glory of the whole.

2 Thou art the Light of light,
    Light is Thy dazzling veil—
Compared with this, Thy raiment white,
    The light of suns is pale.

With high aerial grace,
    The azure firmament
Thou hangest o'er the empty place,
    In likeness of a tent.

3 Thy chambers' buoyant beams
    Rest on that upper sea,
Where unseen rivers flow, and streams
    Pour tribute silently.

Thou makest clouds Thy car,
　　By winds tempestuous driven ;
4 Th' obedient lightnings bear afar
　　The messages of Heaven.

5 Immovably Thy hand
　　The earth established—still
Beneath its strong foundations stand
　　The pillars of Thy will.

6 Thou poured'st the deep around,
　　Whose waters roared and swirled
Above the mountains of a drowned
　　And ocean-buried world.

7 At Thy rebuking word,
　　They trembling fled away—
The thunder of Thy voice they heard
　　And hastened to obey.

8 In endless ebb they shrink
　　To lower levels fast ;
The mountains rise, the valleys sink,
　　Till, gathered at the last,

9 They keep the place assigned—
　　Th' unsounded depths of seas,
By bars of adamant confined,
　　And Thy unchanged decrees.

10 In valleys cool and sweet,
　　Spring brooks and murmuring rills,
　That walk the meads with shining feet,
　　And run among the hills.

11 Beasts of the field there drink :
　　Wild asses thirst allay ;
12 Among the trees that shade the brink
　　Sing happy birds all day.

13 Thou water'st all the land,
　　And makest glad the sod ;
　The earth contented owns the hand
　　And husbandry of God.

14 Thou makest grass to spring
　　For cattle ; and dost plan
　Supplies of every needful thing
　　For the support of man.

15 The tilled and teeming soil
　　Brings forth the foodful wine,
　That cheers the heart of man, and oil
　　That makes his face to shine.

16 The cedars of the Lord,
　　The pride of Lebanon,
　With plenteous sap and vigor stored,
　　Thou planted'st every one.

17 The birds there build, and hide
    Their nests from human ken ;
  Fir trees for storks a house provide,
    Far from the haunts of men.

18 The wild goats climb the steep
    Of friendly hills that mocks
  Pursuing feet ; and conies creep
    For safety in the rocks.

  All these Thy thoughts employ ;
    Thy tender mercies share ;
  The great and mean alike enjoy
    Thy universal care.

19 The changeful moon observes
    Thine ordinances yet ;
  The sun his orbit keeps, nor swerves,
    And knows his time to set.

20 Thou makest dark : 't is night,
    Mid settling shadows brown,
  Wild beasts with eyeballs flashing light
    The forests trample down.

21 Young lions roar for prey,
    And food from Thee require ;
22 But, when the sun arises, they
    Back to their dens retire.

23 After the night's repose,
   Refreshed in every power,
Man to his work and labor goes,
   Until the evening hour.

24 O Lord, how manifold
   Thy works, in wisdom framed;
The earth is full of wealth untold,
   Beneficence unnamed.

25 So this great sea and wide,
   Where things unnumbered creep;
Beasts small and great there swiftly glide
   And populate the deep.

26 There go the ships; there plough
   Monsters of mighty fin—
That huge leviathan, whom Thou
   Hast made to play therein.

27 These wait without alarm
   On Thee, their bounteous Lord,
Who hang'st Creation on Thine arm,
   And feed'st it at Thy board.

28 Thy love and pity grand
   Assure them timely food;
Thou op'nest Thy paternal hand,
   And they are filled with good.

29 Thou hid'st Thy Face and they
    Are struck with mortal fear;
  Thou takest soon their breath away,
    They die and disappear.

30 Thy Spirit broods above,
    They live, in numbers more;
  The earth beneath Thy smile of love
    Seems fairer than before.

31 The glory of Thy power
    Shall stand as it has stood,
  Since that divine rejoicing hour
    When Thou mad'st all things good.

32 Earth trembles at the stroke
    Of Thy swift-glancing eyes;
  The hills Thou touchest and they smoke—
    Volcanic flames arise.

33 O Lord my God! I fling
    Me down at Thy dear feet;
  There will I lie and gladly sing
    Adoring anthems sweet.

34 Bless thou the Lord, my soul!
    Permitted as thou art,
  Of this majestic cosmic whole
    To form a noble part.

PSALM CV.

GIVE to Jehovah thanks and praise!
    And call upon His Name—
Th' Eternal, Self-existent One,
    From age to age the same.

    Among the nations it declare,
      And make His doings known;
2 Talk ye of all His wondrous works,
    His grace to Israel shown.

3 O glory in His Holy Name!
    Who seek Him shall rejoice:
4 Ye people, seek; Jehovah choose,
    And triumph in your choice;

5 And keep perpetually in mind
    The miracles He wrought;
The judgments of His mouth, likewise,
    With dreadful warning fraught.

6 Ye faithful Abrah'm's chosen seed,
    Jehovah is our God!
7 His judgments are in all the earth—
    He wields a chastening rod.

8 He made a lasting covenant
9   With Abrah'm, and it sealed
10 By oath, and it a statute made
    Never to be repealed;

11 Saying, "To thee I'll give the land
    Of Canaan; it shall be
　　The lot of your inheritance
    By title got from Me"—

12 A promise made, what time they were
    In number very few,
　　And strangers there, mere travelers,
    The country passing through.

13 From nation they to nation went;
    Their trust in God they put;
　　From realm to realm they journeyed safe,
    With free unfettered foot.

14 He suffered none to do them wrong;
    Rebuked kings for their sake;
15 Said, "Touch not my anointed ones;
    Let them no injury take!"

16 He brought a famine on the land;
    He brake the staff of bread;
17 He sent a man before them, that
    The starving might be fed.

18 Joseph was sold in Egypt, where,
    Upon false charges made,
　　His feet they with strong fetters hurt
    And him in irons laid:

19 Till when his word had come to pass,
   And him the Lord had proved,
The ruler of the people sent
   And had his chains removed;

21 And made him lord of all his house,
   And gave him full control
Of all his wealth, to follow out
   The pleasure of his soul;

22 To bind his chiefs; his elders teach
   The arts of wise command.
23 Then Israel into Egypt came
   And sojourned in the land.

24 When much increased, and stronger grown
   Than those they served, these say:
25 "We'll shrewdly deal, we'll them oppress,
   Each son at birth will slay."

26 He Moses did depute and send,
   And Aaron whom He chose;
27 They signs and prodigies displayed
   Among their cruel foes.

28 He darkness sent, and made it dark,
   Their hearts with terror filled;
29 He turned their waters into blood,
   And all their fish He killed.

30 Their land was filled with countless frogs,
   Ev'n chambers of their kings :
31 He spake, there came great swarms of flies,
   And gnats inflicting stings.

32 He gave them hail instead of rain,
   And flame swept through the land ;
33 Their vines and fig trees smote, and brake
   The trees on every hand.

34 He spake, and straight the locusts came
   In numbers without bound ;
35 Grasshoppers, too, that ate up all
   The products of the ground.

36 He smote likewise all their first-born,
   The chief of all their strength :
37 Laden with silver and with gold
   He brought them forth at length.

   Among the tribes there was not one
   That feebleness betrayed :
38 Egypt was glad when they were gone,
   Because she was afraid.

39 A cloud He for a covering spread ;
   For light at night a fire ;
40 Fed them with bread from heaven, and quails
   To answer their desire.

41 He smote the rock, and waters gushed,
    That like a river ran
Through dry and thirsty places where
    There was no drink for man.

42 He kept His holy word in mind
    To Abrah'm pledged, and brought
43 His chosen people forth with joy
    Unto the Land they sought.

44 The Land of many peoples gave
    Them richly to possess;
45 That they might all His statutes keep—
    Praise ye the Lord and bless.

PSALM CVI.

PRAISE ye the Lord, for He is good,
    His mercy lasts the ages through:
2 What tongue can tell His mighty acts
    Or utter all His praises due?

3 Happy are they who judgment keep;
    Who never from Thy law depart;
Who love the ways of righteousness
    And serve the Lord with perfect heart.

4 Regard me with the favor, Lord,
    Thou bear'st Thy people; visit me
5 With Thy salvation, that I may
    The welfare of Thy chosen see!

6 But we have with our fathers sinned ;
    Have from Thy testimonies swerved ;
  Our covenant with Thee have broke ;
    And all we suffer have deserved.

7 Mindless of signs in Egypt wrought,
    Rebellious words our fathers spake
8 At the Red Sea ; He yet them saved,
    By His great power for His Name's sake.

9 The Sea dried up at His rebuke :
    He through its hidden depths them led—
  That seemed a low and level plain,
    Solid and firm beneath their tread.

10 When safe upon the further shore,
     The waters, which for them were cleft,
11 Closed over the pursuing foe,
     Not one of their whole member left.

12 Then they believed His words ; they sang
13   His praise, but soon His works forgot—
   Self-willed, impatient, they made haste,
     And waited for His counsel not.

14 They lusted in the wilderness,
     And tempted God—on having bent—
15 Displeased, He gave them their request,
     But in their souls He leanness sent.

16 They Moses envied in the camp,
    And Aaron, made high priest to be;
17 Earth oped—with Dathan swallowed were
    Abiram and his company.

18 A fire was kindled, and consumed
    Korah and all his wicked crew.
   In spite of judgments Israel still
    Remained rebellious and untrue.

19 They made a calf at Horeb; thus
20   They changed their Glory for, alas!
   The molten likeness of an ox
    That chews his cud and feeds on grass.

21 They God forgat, their Saviour, who
    Had graciously, to set them free,
22 In Egypt done great things for them
    And terrible by the Red Sea.

23 Therefore He said: "I'll them destroy!"
    But nevertheless allowed to plead,
   Moses His chosen—who in the breach
    Before Him stood to intercede.

24 Yea, they despised the pleasant Land;
    And they discredited His word;
25 They daily murmured in their tents,
    And harkened not unto the Lord.

26 So with uplifted hand He sware
   They should the Promised Land not see—
27 Their seed should 'mong the nations fall,
   And in all lands should scattered be.

28 To Baal-Peor they them joined;
   Things offered to dead idols ate;
29 By their nefarious deeds provoked,
   A plague them slew in numbers great.

30 Then stood up Phinehas alone,
   And executed judgment fell!
   The plague was stayed—in this bold act
31 'T was ever held that he did well.

32 At Meribah they angered Him;
   And Moses suffered for their sake,
33 Because, beyond endurance vexed,
   He foolishly and rashly spake.

34 The peoples they did not destroy—
   Unmindful of the Lord's commands—
35 But mixed with them, and learned their works,
36   And served their idols made with hands;

   And these became a snare to them;
   By horrible example led,
37 They sons and daughters sacrificed—
38   Their guiltless blood to demons shed.

39 Thus they the Land with blood defiled,
    And played the harlot 'fore the Lord ;
40 Therefore His wrath was kindled so
    He His inheritance abhorred.

41 He to the nations gave them up,
    Up to the tyranny of those
42 Who hated them—caused them to bow
    Their stiff proud necks to cruel foes.

43 He many times delivered them,
    But they, rebellious and perverse,
    Were by their crimes, full oft, brought low—
    Such their propension to the worse.

44 Yet when He heard their moaning cry,
45   His covenant He called to mind,
46 And pitied them, and made the hearts
    Of captors pitiful and kind.

47 Save us, O Lord ! and gather us
    From out the nations, and restore,
    That we may give Thee sounding thanks
    And triumph in Thy praise once more.

Blessed be the Lord God of Israel from everlasting to everlasting ; and let all the people say, Amen. Praise ye the Lord.

BOOK V.

PSALM CVII.

GIVE Jehovah thanks, for He
   Is most good; His mercy vast
Compasses eternity,
   Future ages and the past.

2 So let His redeemed attest,
3   Whom He gathered and led forth
From the east and from the west,
   From the south and from the north.

4 They the desert wandering o'er,
   Found no permanent abode;
5 Hungry and athirst, foot-sore,
   Faint they sunk beneath the load.

6 Then unto the Lord they cried,
   In their hour of bitter need;
He with their requests complied,
   And from their distresses freed.

7 By a straight way He them led
   From the wilderness, to go
  To a land inhabited,
   Where abundant harvests grow.

8 O that men would praise the Lord,
   And Him never grieve again,
  For His goodness that restored,
   And His wondrous works to men!

9 For He satisfies the needs
   Of the longing soul with food,
  And the hungry soul He feeds
   With a plentitude of good.

———

10 Those that in dark prisons lay,
    Being bound with iron bands—
11 Having dared to disobey,
    And contemn the Lord's commands—

12 Were brought down with heavy toil,
    Victims of oppression made,
   Slaves compelled to drudge and moil,
    With no hand to render aid:

13 Then unto the Lord they cried,
    In their hour of bitter need;
   He with their requests complied,
    And from their distresses freed.

14 Out of death-shade made them pass,
    Iron bands asunder broke,
  Burst the mighty gates of brass,
    Loosed the captive from his yoke.

15 O that men would praise the Lord,
    And Him never grieve again,
  For the goodness that restored,
    And His wondrous works to men!

---

17 Fools, because of their misdeeds,
    Painful fetch uncertain breath;
18 Mid the loathings sickness breeds,
    They draw near the gates of death.

  They but reap what they have sown—
    Tossed with fever, racked with pain,
  Conscious they deserve each groan,
    Guilt forbids them to complain.

19 Then unto the Lord they cry,
    Bending unaccustomed knees:
  He beholds with pitying eye,
    And from their distresses frees.

20 He sends forth His healing word,
    Pain and weakness to dispel:
  With new life the frame is stirred,
    And the sick again are well.

21 O that men would praise the Lord,
    And Him never grieve again,
For the goodness that restored,
    And His wondrous works to men!

---

23 They that with stout hearts and bold
    O'er the sea in vessels sweep,
24 These Jehovah's works behold,
    And His wonders in the deep.

25 He commands: a stormy wind
    Lifts the ocean from its bed;
In fierce battle now combined
    Each mad billow lifts its head.

26 Up to heaven the bark is tost;
    Poised upon the steep wave's brink,
They give up themselves for lost,
    As again they downward sink.

27 Like a drunken man they reel,
    Pitching, staggering to and fro;
All their skill is vain they feel—
    What to do they do not know.

28 Then unto the Lord they cry,
    Bending unaccustomed knees;
He beholds with pitying eye,
    And from their distresses frees.

29 Howls the tempest now no more;
　　Calm and peaceful is the sea;
30 So He brings them safe to shore,
　　To the port where they would be.

31 O that men would praise the Lord,
　　And Him never grieve again;
　For the goodness that restored,
　　And His wondrous works to men!

---

32 Let the people Him extol,
　　When they in th' assembly meet!
　Let the elders one and all
　　Praise Him in the council-seat!

33 He a barren desert makes
34 　Of fair fields and watered plains;
　For the sinful dwellers' sake,
　　Fire and brimstone on them rains.

35 He the burning desert cools;
　　Springing waters upward burst;
　Sky-reflecting crystal pools,
　　Running streamlets slaking thirst,

　Turn the sand to fruitful loam;—
36 　And He makes the hungry there
　Dwell in peace, that they a home
　　And a city may prepare,

37 Sow the fields, and plant the vine :
  He doth them increase and bless,
38 Fostered by His power divine,
  Lets their cattle grow no less.

39 They are minished and bowed down,
  By oppression's hand abased ;
40 Princes blasted by His frown,
  Wander in a pathless waste.

41 He the poor in families
  Sets, where no afflictions come ;
42 It the upright gladly sees
  And iniquity is dumb.

43 Who is wise will ponder well,
  Nor despise the warning voice ;
  Will upon His mercies dwell,
  And with trembling heart rejoice.

PSALM CVIII.*

MY heart is fixed, my heart is fixed,
  I will, O God. Thy praises sing :
2 Awake, my soul! with voice be mixed,
  Both lute and harp ! your every string.

3 I'll wake the dawn ; I'll celebrate
  Thy praise among the nations, for
4 Thy Mercy and Thy Truth are great,
  High o'er the heavens for evermore.

*This Psalm is compiled from two others—verses 1-5 are substantially the same as Ps. 57 : 7-11 ; vs. 6-12 as Ps. 60 : 5-12.

5 Be Thou exalted, God Most High!
    Above all praise, all thought above,
  Above the earth, above the sky,
    High seated on Thy throne of love!

---

6 That Thy belovéd ones
    May be delivered, save
  With Thy right hand, and o'er us let
    Victorious ensigns wave!

7 God in His holiness
    Hath spoken—I, therefore,
  Will triumph in the confidence
    He will the lost restore:

  Then the reconquered Land
    I will again divide—
  Succoth and Schechem—and his part
    Mete out to every tribe.

8 Mine's Gilead; and mine's
    Manasseh's either half;
  My head's defence is Ephraim;
    Judah's my royal staff;

9 Moab my wash-pot is,
    Wherein I'll wash my feet;
  O'er Edom I'll extend my sway,
    Philistia I'll unseat.

---

10 Who will me bring into
    Edom's fenced capital?
  Surmount its muniment of rocks,
    Impregnable high wall?

11 Thou who hast cast us off,
    Wilt Thou not lead our van?
12 O give us help from trouble, for
    Vain is the help of man:

13 Go forth Thou with our hosts,
    And marshal and dispose!
  We shall through God do valiantly,
    For He 'll tread down our foes.

PSALM CIX.

HOLD not Thy peace, God of my praise!
  For they against me slanders raise;
With tongue of falsehood and deceit
3 They words of causeless hate repeat.

4 They for my love return ill-will,
  But I to prayer devote me still;
5 Evil for good they 've on me laid,
  My love with hatred have repaid.

6 Measure for measure him be given,
  By the dispensing hand of heaven;
  The woes he loves to others deal,
  Let him in his own person feel.

O'er him the wicked give command ;
Th' accuser set on his right hand ;
7 When tried, let him no favor win,
His prayer for mercy be for sin.

8 His days make few and evil make ;
His office let another take ;
9 His children be of sire bereft,
And be his wife a widow left.

10 And let his orphaned children roam,
Poor vagabonds without a home—
From some decayed and ruined shed
Let them creep forth to beg for bread.

11 Let the extortioner lay toils ;
And strangers from him gather spoils ;
12 Pity to show let there be none
Either to father or to son.

13 Let him posterity have not ;
His name be blotted and forgot ;
14 His father's guilt, his mother's sin,
15 Make him as though he 'd never been ;

16 Because that he no pity knew,
And did th' afflicted one pursue ;
With deadly malice and hot breath
The broken hearted hunt to death.

17 Cursing he loved, and so the same
   Down on himself revolving came :
   He had in blessing no delight
   And so 't was far from him of right.

18 He on him as a garment put
   Cursing, that reached from head to foot—
   Close fitting, clinging to the skin
   That sucked the raging madness in.

19 Be it to him a poisoned vest ;
   And let his bones imbibe the pest ;
20 And let this be his just reward,
   A righteous judgment from the Lord.

---

21 But, Thou. Lord, gracious be to me,
   (For Thou art good) and set me free ;
   Because I needy am and poor,
22 And wounded is my heart and sore.

23 Like shadows, which at close of day
   Lengthen, I passing am away ;
   Like locust, tost and helpless driven
   Before the stormy winds of heaven.

24 My tottering knees beneath me fail ;
   Through fasting I 've grown lean and pale ;
25 Reproach, of scorn and hatred bred,
   They cast on me, and wag their head.

26 Thy help, O Lord my God, I crave;
   According to Thy mercy, save!
27 That they the act may understand
   Is done by Thy delivering hand.

28 They will me curse, but Thou wilt bless;
29 Shame shall them cover as a dress;
   Like to a mantle shall their own
   Confusion be around them thrown.

30 I to the Lord great thanks will give,
   And sound His praises while I live;
31 For He is present to console
   And save from them that judge my soul.

PSALM CX.

JEHOVAH said unto my Lord:
   "Sit Thou on My right hand,
Till I Thy foes Thy footstool make,
   Thy foes of every land."

2 Jehovah out of Zion shall
    Rod of Thy strength extend;
  Thine enemies shall own Thy rule,
    All nations to Thee bend.

3 Thy people free-will offerings* are,
    Men to Thy service sworn;
  Decked with the pearls of holiness,
    Like dew-drops of the morn.

* So the Hebrew.

4 Sworn hath Jehovah, He 'll not change :
   "Thou shalt forever be,
  After the order of Melchizedek,
   A Royal Priest to Me!"

5 The Lord, the strength of Thy right hand,
   Opposing kings shall smite :
  He will among the nations judge,
   And vindicate the right.

6 In many countries o'er broad lands
   The warrior heaps the dead ;
7 Quenches his thirst by way-side brook
   And victor lifts his head.

PSALM CXI.

PRAISE Jehovah! I will bring
   All my powers His praise to sing ;
  Mid the consecrated ranks
  Of the upright will give thanks.

2 Great the works Jehovah wrought,
   To be diligently sought,
3 Memorable, matchless, grand—
   Aye His righteousness shall stand :

4 Kind, compassionate, and dear,
5 Food He gives to them who fear :
   Of His covenant He will be
   Mindful to eternity.

6 To His people He made known
His great power, in Canaan shown ;
'Gainst the nations war did wage ;
Made the Land their heritage.

7 All His works are just and pure ;
And His precepts all are sure ;
8 Stablished are for aye each one,
Truly spoke and rightly done.

9 Their redemption He obtained ;
He His covenant ordained ;
True to His eternal pact—
Gracious promise turned to fact.

All His mighty works proclaim
Fearful is His Holy Name :
10 Whosoever wisdom wins
With Jehovah's fear begins.

He is wise who understands,
Keeps His precepts and commands ;
Whose great goodness ceases never,
And His praise endures forever.

PSALM CXII.

HALLELUJAH! This attest
He who fears the Lord is blest ;
Knowing His commands are right
He in them finds great delight.

2 Mighty shall his offspring be;
  Blest with great prosperity;
3 Wealth be in his house and hand;
  Aye his righteousness shall stand.

4 There arises to the upright,
  In the midst of darkness, light :
  Righteous he, compassionate,
  Kind to the unfortunate.

5 Happy he who favor shows,
  Lends, or generously bestows;
  He 'll his course by justice guide,
6 And unmoved shall e'er abide :

  And his righteousness shall be
  Always kept in memory—
  Fixed his heart and void of fear,
  Trusting, loving, and sincere.

7 Of bad news he 's not afraid;
  On the Lord his heart is stayed;
8 He shall no misgivings own,
  Till his foes are overthrown.

9 He has to the needy given;
  He accepted is of Heaven!
  High his horn shall lifted be;
10 Grieved the wicked shall it see.

PSALM CXIII.

HALLELUJAH ! praise accord,
  O ye servants of the Lord !
2 Let His Name exalted be
Now, and through eternity ;
3 From the rising of the sun
To its setting be it done !

4 High above all nations His
Everlasting Kingdom is ;
Higher than His dwelling-place,
Is the glory of His grace.
5 Who's like Him who stoops to see
What in heaven and earth there be?

7 He the needy and the poor
Raises up to sit secure
8 With the nobles of the land,
Princes holding high command.
He the barren woman takes
And a joyful mother makes.
      Hallelujah !

PSALM CXIV.

WHEN Israel, held in bondage long,
  Out from the land of Egypt went,
2 She was His sanctuary strong,
  And from her midst His law was sent.

3 The Sea affrighted saw, and fled;
   Jordan amazed was driven back;
 While down across the waters' bed
   Dry-shod, she kept her onward track.

4 The conscious Mountains skipped like rams—
   Sinai and Horeb in their place—
 The quickened Hills leaped up like lambs,
   Thrilled with deep awe from top to base.

5 Why fleddest thou, O Sea? and why
   O Jordan, did thy waters shrink?
 Why then were left your channels dry,
   That moment Israel touched your brink?

6 Ye Mountains, why skipped ye like rams,
   Sinai and Horeb in your place?
 And why, ye Hills, leaped ye like lambs,
   Thrilled with deep awe from top to base?

7 Tremble, thou Earth, and be afraid!
   The Lord, the God of Israel hear;
8 Whose presence turned the rock, and made
   The flint a fount of waters clear.

PSALM CXV.

NOT unto us, but glory give,
   O Lord, to Thy dishonored Name!
 Thy truth and mercy vindicate,
   And impious rulers put to shame.
2 Why should the taunting nations say:
   "Where's now their God, where is He, pray?"

3 Our God's in heaven, He reigns supreme,
   And whatsoe'er He pleased has done:
4 Their gold and silver idols, made
   By human hands, have functions none—
5 Mouth, eyes, ears, noses, hands and feet,
6 That cannot move, perceive, nor eat.

7 They make no sound, poor senseless things:
8   Like them shall be those who them made;
   And every one who trusts in them—
   Blockish, incapable of aid:
9 Trust, Israel! and keep the field—
   Jehovah is thy Help and Shield.

10 O house of Aaron, in Him trust:
11   All who Him fear in Him confide;
   It matters not what threatens, while
   Omnipotence is on your side.
   Be not dismayed, refuse to yield,
   Jehovah is your Help and Shield.

12 Jehovah has remembered us;
   He will the house of Israel bless:
   Will bless the house of Aaron; crown
13   Those fearing Him with happiness,
   Both small and great; and He will add
   To you, diminished now and sad.

15 Ye of Jehovah blesséd are—
   Creator of the earth and heaven—

16 The heavens are for Himself; the earth
   He to the sons of men has given.
17 The dead praise not, their lips are dumb,
18 But we'll Him bless all time to come.
                    Hallelujah!

PSALM CXVI.

I LOVE the Lord, because to me,
   He audience deigned to give;
2 Inclined His ear, I'll on Him call,
   And bless Him while I live.

3 The cords of death encompassed me,
    The pains of death gat hold;
  I trouble and deep sorrow found,
    And terrors manifold.

4 Then called I on Jehovah's Name:
    "Deliver, Lord, and save!"
5 And He, who is most pitiful,
    Me kind deliverance gave.

6 Preserver of the simple, when
    I was brought very low,
  He helped me, and He raised me up,
    And did new life bestow.

7 Return, my soul, unto Thy rest;
    Be thankful for thy breath!
8 The Lord has with me kindly dealt,
    And rescued me from death;

Delivered has mine eyes from tears,
   My feet from falling ; so
9 I in the land of living men
   Before the Lord will go.

10 My faith enabled me to speak,
   I turned to God for aid ;
   I was afflicted greatly, but
   To trust man was afraid.

11 I in my haste and terror said :
   " All men are liars ; I
   Will put my trust in none of them,
   But on the Lord rely."

12 What shall I render to the Lord,
   From whom salvation came ?
13 I will the cup of blessing take
   And call upon His Name ;

14 Will to Jehovah pay my vows
   For His new gift of breath—
15 Most dear His saints are in His eyes,
   And precious is their death.

16 I am Thy servant, am the son
   Of Thy handmaiden, Lord !
   My fetters Thou hast loosed, and dost
   True freedom me afford.

17 I 'll in Thy Courts thank-offerings bring,
   And on Thy Name will call;
18 Among Thy people pay my vows,
   In presence of them all.
                    Hallelujah!

PSALM CXVII.

O PRAISE the Lord, His name extol,
   O all ye nations! all ye lands!
2 For great His mercy is toward all;
   His truth unchanged forever stands.
                    Hallelujah!

No. 2.

O praise the Lord, who reigns above!
   Ye nations, your allegiance own!
2 Great is His mercy and His love;
   His truth 's eternal as His throne.
                    Hallelujah!

No. 3.

Ye nations, praise the Lord!
   Before His footstool bend!
Great is His mercy, sure His word,
   His Kingdom without end.
                    Hallelujah!

PSALM CXVIII.

O THANK the Lord, for He is good—
   Let Israel, let Aaron say;
4 And all who fear Him, too, declare,
   His loving-kindness is for aye.

5 I called on Him in my distress,
    And He enlarged and set me free.
6 Since He is on my side, I will
7   Not fear what man can do to me.

8 It's better far to trust in Him,
9   Than help of princes to enjoy;
10 All nations compass me about,
    I in His Name will them destroy.

11 They compass me about like bees,
12   And use their stings to me annoy;
    Quenched are they like the fire of thorns—
    I in His Name will them destroy.

13 They thrust at me that I might fall;
    Jehovah hastened to my aid—
14 Jehovah is my strength and song,
    And He is my salvation made.

15 The voice of joy and triumph sounds
    In all the dwellings of the just;
16 Jehovah mightily has wrought,
    And lifted Israel from the dust.

17 I shall not die, but live; and will
    Recount His works while I have breath:
18 Though he has sorely chastened me,
    He has not given o'er to death.

19 Open the gates of righteousness,
20   And I will enter and give thanks;
21 The righteous shall march through, and praise
      Ascend from their exulting ranks.

22 The stone the builders did reject,
      And in their ignorance despise,
   Head of the corner He has made—
23   A thing most wondrous in our eyes.

24 This is the day the Lord has made;
      We'll triumph and rejoice therein!
25 Save now, Jehovah, I beseech;
      Let new prosperity begin.

26 Blessed be he, the coming one,
      That enters in Jehovah's Name!
   We from Jehovah's House you bless,
      From whom the great deliverance came

27 The Lord is God, He gives us light—
      The victim to the altar bind!
28 Thou art my God, I will Thee thank,
      Will Thee extol with heart and mind.

29 Give thanks to God, for He is good,
      His mercy is for evermore;
   Exhaustless is it as the sea,
      A sea unbounded by a shore.

PSALM CXIX.*

ALEPH.

BLEST are the perfect in the way,
Who never from God's *law* depart :
2 Blest who His *testimonies* keep,
And seek the Lord with all their heart.

3 Yea, no unrighteousness they do ;
Walk in His *ways* with careful feet ;
4 They keep the *precepts* He enjoins,
And find their strict observance sweet.

5 O that my ways directed were
To keep Thy *statutes*, void of blame ;
6 Then when to all of Thy *commands*
I have respect, I'll feel no shame.

---

* The 119th Psalm is wholly occupied with the praises of God's Word, under the various names of Law, Commandments, Precepts, Testimonies, Judgments, Statutes, Ways, and the like, of which at least one is expressly mentioned in every verse with the single exception of verse 122. In the metrical version here given, the particular name employed has been put into Italics to mark it rather than emphasize it. The Psalm is divided into Twenty-two Parts or Stanzas, corresponding to the twenty-two letters of the Hebrew Alphabet—Aleph, Beth, Gimel, etc.—each Stanza being composed of eight verses, couplets, or two-lined parallelisms, the first line of each parallelism beginning with the initial letter of the Stanza. Its *aphoristic* character fits it for pious meditation rather than for continuous perusal.

Since to love God is to love every thing that proceeds from Him—every intimation of His will, every spoken word—this explains the Psalmist's attitude towards the Divine Law whose praises are here celebrated. An object of passionate regard, we no longer wonder that he sets the Decalogue to music, and here as elsewhere indulges in frequent ecstatic outbursts, such as "O how I love Thy Law!" "It is more precious to me than gold and silver," "It is sweeter to me than honey and the honey comb." Truly,

> "Never praise of love or wine,
> Panted forth a flood
> Of rapture so divine."

7 With upright heart I will Thee praise,
    When I Thy righteous *judgments* learn ;
8 I all Thy *statutes* will observe—
    Forsake me not, nor from me turn.

BETH.

9 How shall a young man cleanse his way?
    By due attention to Thy *word*.
10 With my whole heart I have Thee sought,
    From Thy *commandments* have not erred.

11 I have Thy *word* hid in my heart,
    That I against Thee might not sin.
12 Thy *statutes*, blessed Lord, me teach,
    And firmly stablish me therein.

13 I have recounted with my lips
    The *judgments* of Thy mouth entire ;
14 Thy *testimonies* making glad,
    More than all riches I desire.

15 I'll in Thy *precepts* meditate,
    Thy ways by me shall be preferred ;
16 I in Thy *statutes* will delight,
    And I will not forget Thy *word*.

GIMEL.

17 Be to Thy servant kind that I
    May live, and I Thy *word* will keep ;
18 Open mine eyes, that in Thy *law*
    I may see wondrous things and deep.

19 I am a stranger in the earth,
   Hide Thy *commandments* not from me ;
20 My soul breaks from the longing it
   Has toward Thy *judgments* ceaselessly.

21 Thou hast rebuked the proud, accursed,
   Who have from Thy *commandments* swerved.
22 Roll off reproach from me, for I
   Thy *testimonies* have observed.

23 Princes against me sit and talk—
   Thy servant on Thy *statutes* pores ;
24 Thy *testimonies* also are
   My chief delight and counsellors.

DALETH.

25 My soul cleaves to the dust : Thou me
   Quicken according to Thy *word*.
26 I told my *ways*, Thou heardest me,
   Teach me Thy *statutes*, gracious Lord !

27 Make me Thy *precepts* understand,
   I'll on Thy wonders meditate.
28 My soul sinks down from heaviness,
   Make Thy *word* strong to lift the weight.

29 Cause me from falsehood to depart,
   And grant me graciously Thy *law*.
30 The way of truth I've made my choice,
   Thy *judgments*, I have held in awe.

31 I to Thy *testimonies* cleave,
   Preserve me clear from shameful charge.
32 I 'll run the way of Thy *commands*,
   Then when Thou shalt my heart enlarge.

HE.

33 Teach me Thy *statutes*, and I 'll keep
   Them to the end in every part.
34 Give understanding, and I will
   Observe Thy *law* with my whole heart.

35 Make me in Thy *commandments* tread,
   For I therein great joy obtain.
36 Me to Thy *testimonies* bend,
   And not to covetousness and gain.

37 Turn off mine eyes from vanity,
   Me quicken in Thy *ways*, and cheer;
38 Make to Thy servant good Thy *word*,
   Who is devoted to Thy fear.

39 Turn the reproach away I dread,
   For good Thy *judgments* are and true;
40 Behold, I for Thy *precepts* long,
   Me in Thy righteousness renew.

VAU.

41 And let Thy mercies come to me
   According to Thy *promise*, Lord!
42 Then I 'll him answer that reviles,
   For I have trusted in Thy *word*.

43 Take not the *word* of truth from me,
    Seeing I for Thy *judgments* wait.
44 So I Thy *law* for aye will keep,
    By it my conduct regulate.

45 And I will walk at liberty,
    For I to know Thy *precepts* seek :
46 And of Thy *testimonies* pure
    I unashamed 'fore kings will speak.

47 In Thy *commandments* which I love
    I'll take delight ; and will as well
48 To them lift up my hands and heart,
    And on Thy *statutes* fondly dwell.

ZAIN.

49 Thy *word* of promise call to mind,
    In which Thou hast caused me to hope.
50 This is my comfort in my grief,
    Thy quickening *word* new doors can ope.

51 The proud ones have laughed me to scorn,
    Yet from Thy *law* I've not declined.
52 Thy *judgments* I of old recalled,
    And they consoled my troubled mind.

53 Horror me seized, beholding men
    Forsake Thy *law*, its sanctions spurn.
54 Thy *statutes* still have been my songs,
    Here in the house of my sojourn.

55 Thy Name I've thought on in the night,
   And sought for strength to keep Thy *law*,
56 I have Thy *precepts* kept, and so
   Knowledge from sweet experience draw.

CHETH.

57 Thou art my portion, Lord, to keep
   Thy *words* will I devote my mind;
58 I sought Thy help with my whole heart,
   According to Thy *word* be kind!

59 I thought upon my ways, my feet
   I to Thy *testimonies* turned.
60 I hastened Thy *commands* to keep,
   With holy zeal my bosom burned.

61 Cords of the wicked wrapped me round,
   But on Thy *law* meanwhile I thought;
62 I'll rise at midnight to give thanks
   Because of righteous *judgments* wrought.

63 All those who fear Thee and who keep
   Thy *precepts*, my companions be.
64 The earth is of Thy mercies full,
   Make plain Thy *statutes*, Lord, to me.

TETH.

65 Thou with Thy servant has dealt well,
   According to Thy *word* relieved.
66 Me knowledge and good judgment teach,
   For Thy *commandments* I've believed.

67 Before I smitten was, I strayed,
   But now Thy *word* I keep fast hold.
68 Thou art most good and doest good,
   Thy *statutes* teach me and unfold.

69 The proud 'gainst me have forged a lie,
   But to Thy *precepts* I'll be true.
70 Their heart is fat and gross, but I
   Will with delight Thy *law* pursue.

71 'T is for my good I've been chastised,
   That I might learn Thy *statutes* old:
72 Law of Thy mouth is better than
   Thousands of silver and of gold.

JOD.

73 Thy hands they made and fashioned me,
   Make me Thy pure *commandments* learn:
74 All they that fear Thee will rejoice
   That to Thy *word* for hope I turn.

75 I know Thy *judgments*, Lord, are right,
   In faithfulness Thou smotest me.
76 According to Thy *word*, O let
   Thy mercy for my comfort be.

77 Be merciful that I may live,
   For my delight is in Thy *law*.
78 Shame those who wronged me without cause,
   I'll on Thy *precepts* muse with awe.

79 Let them that fear Thee, turn to me,
   Those that Thy *testimonies* know :
80 Make my heart in Thy *statutes* sound,
   Lest I meet shameful overthrow.

CAPH.

81 My soul for Thy salvation faints,
   I for Thy *word* with longing wait :
82 Mine eyes fail for Thy *promise*, made
   To comfort the disconsolate.

83 I 'm like a bottle in the smoke,
   Yet I Thy *statutes* keep in view :
84 When wilt Thou *judgment* execute
   On them who hotly me pursue ?

85 The proud ones have digged pits for me,
   Whose lives are by Thy *law* not swayed :
86 All Thy *commandments* faithful are,
   Against my persecutors, aid.

87 They nigh consumed me on the earth,
   I from Thy *precepts* did not swerve :
88 After Thy mercy quicken me,
   Thy *testimonies* I 'll observe.

LAMED.

89 Thy *word* in heaven forever stands,
   From age to age Thy faithfulness :
90 As earth abides which Thou didst found,
   Thy *truth* is permanent no less ;

91 By Thy *decrees* they stand this day,
　　For all Thy servants are, I know;
92 Had not Thy *law* been my delight,
　　I should have perished long ago.

93 Thy *precepts* I will ne'er forget;
　　For with them Thou hast quickened me.
94 Lord, I am Thine, me save, for I
　　Have sought Thy *precepts* diligently.

95 The wicked wait to me destroy;
　　But I Thy *testimonies* laud:
96 An end I've to perfection seen,
　　For Thy *commandment's* very broad.

MEM.

97 O how I love Thy *law*; it is
　　My meditation all the day.
98 Above my foes I am made wise
　　For Thy *commandments* with me stay.

99 I'm wiser than my teachers, for
　　Thy *testimonies* are my school;
100 Am wiser than the ancients, for
　　Thy *precepts* all my conduct rule.

101 My feet have shunned each evil way,
　　That in Thy *word* I might abide:
102 I have not from Thy *judgments* strayed,
　　For Thou Thyself hast been my guide.

103 How sweet Thy *words* are to my taste,
    Than honey to my mouth more sweet.
104 Instructed by Thy *precepts*, far
    From each false way I turn my feet.

NUN.

105 Thy *word's* a lantern to my feet,
    A light to make my pathway clear.
106 I've sworn, and will perform my oath,
    I'll hold Thy righteous *judgments* dear.

107 I am afflicted very much,
    According to Thy *word*, restore:
108 Accept my free-will offerings, Lord,
    Teach me Thy *judgments* to adore.

109 My soul is ever in my hand,
    Yet have I not thy *law* forgot:
110 The wicked laid a snare for me,
    Yet from Thy *precepts* strayed I not.

111 Because Thy *testimonies* are
    My heart's rejoicing, I them take
112 As my eternal heritage,
    And I'll Thy *statutes* ne'er forsake.

SAMECH.

113 Those of a double mind I hate,
    But love Thy *law* and do not feign.
114 Thou art my Hiding-Place and Shield,
    I from Thy *word* assurance gain.

115 Ye evil-doers, hence depart!
　　My God's *commands* I'll keep unblamed.
116 According to Thy *word* uphold,
　　That I may live, and not be shamed.

117 Hold Thou me up, and I'll be safe,
　　I'll on Thy *statutes* fix my eye:
118 Who err from *these* Thou 'lt set at naught,
　　For their deceit is their own lie.

119 The wicked purgest Thou like dross,
　　Thy *testimonies* I hold dear.
120 Trembles my flesh for dread of Thee,
　　And I Thy *judgments* greatly fear.

AIN.

121 Justice and *judgment* I have done,
　　Me not to my oppressors leave.
122 Be surety, Lord, for good to me,
　　Let not the proud me crush and grieve.

123 Mine eyes for Thy salvation fail,
　　Waiting Thy *words's* fulfillment long.
124 Deal kindly with Thy servant, me
　　Thy *statutes* teach, to make me strong.

125 I am Thy servant, make me wise,
　　May I Thy *testimonies* know.
126 'T is time, Lord, Thou should'st work, when men
　　Thy *law* make void and overthrow.

127 I, therefore, Thy *commandments* love,
 Above fine gold them estimate;
128 Thy *precepts* I esteem all right,
 And every lying way I hate.

PE.

129 Wondrous Thy *testimonies* are;
 In them my soul I exercise.
130 The entrance of Thy *word* gives light,
 And serves to make the simple wise.

131 I stretched my mouth and panted—for
 I longed for Thy *commandments* much.
132 Turn Thou to me for I Thee love,
 And do as Thou art wont to such.

133 Order my footsteps in Thy *word;*
 Let no iniquity have sway:
134 From man's oppression me redeem,
 So I Thy *precepts* will obey.

135 Make Thou Thy Face on me to shine,
 Thy *statutes* teach, by them me draw.
136 Rivers of tears run down mine eyes,
 Because men do not keep Thy *law*.

TZADDI.

137 Righteous and true, O Lord, Thou art,
 Upright Thy *judgments* are, and just.
138 Thy *testimonies* faithful are,
 On us enjoined that we may trust.

139 My zeal for Thee has me consumed,
   Because my foes Thy *words* forget.
140 Thy *word* is tried and very pure,
   Therefore my heart is on it set.

141 Though I am little and despised,
   Thy *precepts* I have loved from youth.
142 Eternal is Thy righteousness,
   Thy *law* is everlasting truth.

143 Trouble and anguish have me seized,
   Yet Thy *commandments* gladness give :
144 Right are Thy *testimonies*, make
   Me understand and I shall live.

KOPH.

145 With my whole heart I Thee invoke,
   Hear me and I'll Thy *statutes* keep ;
146 Save, and Thy *testimonies*, I
   Will cherish with affection deep.

147 I cry for help at early dawn,
   And for Thy *word* devoutly wait :
148 I shorten the night watches that
   I in Thy *word* may meditate.

149 According to Thy mercy hear,
   Just to Thy *judgments*, save alive !
150 For they are near, who, far from *law*,
   Ingenious wickedness contrive.

151 Thou too art near, O Lord, and Thy
   Commandments are immortal truth :
152 I have Thy *testimonies* known
   To be eternal from my youth.

RESH.

153 See my affliction, and me save;
   Naught from my breast Thy *law* shall drive,
154 Plead Thou my cause, and me redeem,
   According to Thy *word*, revive.

155 Salvation's from the wicked far;
   They've for Thy *statutes* no regard.
156 Great are Thy mercies, quicken me
   According to Thy *judgments*, Lord!

157 My foes are many, yet do I
   Not from Thy *testimonies* swerve.
158 I saw the faithless, and was grieved,
   That they did not Thy *word* observe.

159 Behold, how I Thy *precepts* love,
   After Thy mercy quicken me.
160 Thy *word* is from creation true,
   Thy *judgments* span eternity.

SCHIN.

161 Princes pursue me without cause,
   Awe of Thy *word* my heart appals :
162 And yet I at Thy *word* rejoice
   As one to whom great booty falls.

163 Falsehood I hate and I abhor,
    But love Thy *law* with all my might.
164 Seven times a day do I Thee praise
    Because Thy *judgments* are upright.

165 Great peace have they who love Thy *law*,
    Occasion have of stumbling none.
166 I have for Thy salvation hoped,
    And Thy *commandments* I have done.

167 I have Thy *testimonies* kept,
    And them I love exceedingly,
168 I all Thy *precepts* have observed,
    For all my ways are known to Thee.

TAU.

169 Let my cry come before Thee, Lord!
    True to Thy *word* me wisdom give:
170 Hear me, according to Thy word,
    Deliver me that I may live.

171 My lips shall praise Thee, for Thou wilt
    With knowledge of Thy *statutes* bless,
172 My tongue shall celebrate Thy *word*,
    For Thy *commands* are righteousness.

173 Be ready with Thy hand to help,
    For I've Thy *precepts* made my choice,
174 I've longed for Thy salvation, Lord!
    I greatly in Thy *law* rejoice.

175 Let my soul live to praise Thee, let
   Thy *judgments* help me; and O, when
176 I go astray like a lost sheep,
   Bring Thou Thy servant back again.

PSALM CXX.

I PRAYED the Lord in my distress,
   And He deferred not answer long:
2 "O Lord!" I cried, "deliver me
   From lying lips and guileful tongue."

3 What shall He give or do to thee,
   O tongue of infinite deceit?
4 Sharp arrows of the mighty, give!
   With burning coals of fiercest heat.

5 Woe's me that I in Mesech dwell,
   Among the tents of Kedar stay—
   Men of contention and of strife,
   Inclined to violence alway.

6 I've had my dwelling long with him,
   Who hated peace, and drove it far:
7 I am an advocate of peace,
   But when I speak, they are for war.

PSALM CXXI.

UP to the Hills I lift mine eyes.
   Whence comes my help? My help proceeds
From Him who made the earth and skies,
   Who at His board creation feeds.

3 He will not let Thy foot be moved;
   He will not slumber who thee keeps;
4 He, who o'er Israel beloved
   Still watches, slumbers not nor sleeps.

5 The Lord thy Keeper is, thy Shield;
6 The sun by day shall not thee smite,
   Screened by His hand—innoxious made,
   The moon shall not thee harm by night.

7 The Lord, who has thy safety been,
   Shall shield from evil, and watch o'er
8 Thy going out and coming in
   From henceforth and forevermore.

PSALM CXXII.

O I WAS glad then, when they said:
   "Let us together go,
A festal throng, up to God's House—
   His Dwelling here below."

2 Our feet are standing in Thy gates,
3 Jerusalem, that art
   Compactly as a city built,
   And fair in every part.

4 Thither the tribes go up; there they
   Before the Lord appear,
   (A law ordained for Israel)
   At stated times each year,

To tell His mercies, and give thanks
  In loud and joyful tones ;
5 For there are seats for judgment set—
  The house of David's thrones.

6 Pray for her peace, whose name is peace—
  Thine, fair Jerusalem !
  All they shall prosper who thee love,
  And peace shall fall on them.

7 Let peace within thy ramparts be,
  Prosperity be found
  Within thy palaces and homes,
  And everywhere abound.

8 I 'll for my friends' and brethren's sake,
  Say, Peace within thee be !
9 And for the sake of the Lord's House
  Seek thy prosperity.

PSALM CXXIII.

I UNTO Thee do lift my eyes,
  O Thou Who art enthroned in heaven !
2 As servants to their masters look,
  So I to Thee, till mercy 's given.

3 Have mercy on us, Lord, for we
  Are greatly sated with disdain—
4 Sated with scorn of our proud foes,
  Who scoff at us with lips profane.

PSALM CXXIV.

IF GOD had not been on our side,
  Let grateful Israel now say,
2 If God had not been on our side,
  So weak were we, so strong were they,
When men rose up 'gainst us to strive,
3 They then had swallowed us alive.

4 Deep waters then had us o'erwhelmed,
  And drowning flood gone o'er our soul,
5 Proud waters o'er our soul had gone,
  And we had perished as a whole.
6 Thrice blessèd be His Name for aye,
Who gave us not to them a prey.

7 Our soul has like a bird escaped
  Out of the fowler's fatal snare—
  The snare is broke, and we 've escaped,
  Thanks to the Lord's delivering care ;
8 He is our Helper, He who made
The heavens, and earth's foundations laid.

PSALM CXXV.

ALL who in Jehovah trust,
  They shall as Mount Zion be,
Which, immovable, abides,
  Fixed to all eternity.

2 As the firm-set mountains are
    Round about Jerusalem ;
So the Lord is evermore
    Round His people, guarding them.

3 For the rod of wickedness
    Shall not on the righteous rest,
Lest to sin they tempted be,
    By perplexing doubts oppressed.

4 To the good, O Lord, do good :
    But all such as turn aside
Shall as evil-doers fare.
    Peace on Israel abide!

PSALM CXXVI.

WHEN captive Zion God brought back,
    We were as those that dreamed :
We scarce could think it real, so
    Incredible it seemed.
2 Then was our mouth with laughter filled,
Our tongue with singing rapture thrilled.

The wondering nations said, " The Lord
    For them great things has done!"
3 The Lord has done great things for us,
    Our glad return begun :
4 Complete it, Lord, as after drouth
Come back the dried streams of the south.

5 The mourning souls that sow in tears,
    Shall yet in gladness reap :
6 Though he that goes forth bearing seed
    Upon his way may weep,
  He shall with singing come again,
  Bringing his sheaves in loaded wain.

PSALM CXXVII.

EXCEPT the Lord shall build the House,
    Man's labor is but fruitless pain ;
Except the Lord the City keep,
    The human watchman wakes in vain.

2 Vainly you eat the bread of toil,
    Rise early and late vigils keep ;
  Seeing to His belovèd God
    Gives time for needful rest and sleep.

3 Lo, children are a heritage,
    Which parents from the Lord acquire—
4 As arrows in a warrior's hand,
    Are sons of youth to aged sire.

5 O happy is the man, who has
    His quiver full, to him defend :
  They 'll not be shamed, when in the gate
    With adversaries they contend.

PSALM CXXVIII.

HAPPY the man who fears the Lord,
    That walks in His appointed ways!
2 Eating the labor of thy hands,
    Thou shalt be prospered all thy days.

3 Thy wife shall be a fruitful vine
    Within thy house: thy children be,
Like olive plants around thy board,
    An ornament and joy to thee.

4 Behold all those shall thus be blest,
    Who fear the Lord; the Lord shall them
Bless out of Zion, they shall see
    The welfare of Jerusalem.

PSALM CXXIX.

"THEY many a time," let Israel say,
    "From my youth up have me assailed;
2 They many a time have me oppressed,
    But have against me not prevailed."

3 The plowers plowed upon my back
    Long furrows, by the scourge produced;
4 The righteous Lord, He cut the trace,*
    And from the galling yoke me loosed.

5 Let all that Zion hate be shamed
    And backward turned; like grass chance-sown
6 Upon the house-tops which springs up
    And withers ere 't is fully grown;

---

* "Cord (not cords) that fastened the ox to the plow."—*J. A. Alexander.*

7 Wherewith who reaps fills not his hand ;
　Nor he who binds the sheaves his breast ;
8 Neither do they, which go by, say,
　"Jehovah's blessing on you rest."

PSALM CXXX.

OUT of the depths I call on Thee,
　　Hearken, O Lord, unto my prayer ;
2 Let me not unregarded sink
　In the deep waters of despair !

3 If Thou iniquities should'st mark,
　Who shall, O God, from guilt be cleared ?
4 Forgiveness is with Thee alone,
　To the intent Thou may'st be feared.

5 I wait, my soul waits for the Lord—
　By hope in His dear Name upborne—
6 Waits for His wished-for coming, more
　Than weary watchers for the morn.

7 Hope in the Lord, O Israel !
　For with the Lord is grace supreme,
8 And plenteous redemption—He
　Will thee from all thy sins redeem.

PSALM CXXXI.

NOT haughty is my heart ;
　　Not lofty are mine eyes ;
Myself, in matters great and high,
　I do not exercise.

2 I cherish humble thoughts;
   I've hushed my soul to rest;
  As a weaned child, whose cries are stilled,
   Leans on its mother's breast.

3 Hope thou, O Israel!
   In the Eternal One,
  From this time forth and evermore,
   And let His will be done!

PSALM CXXXII.

REMEMBER David's deep concern,
   O Lord, for Thy neglected Shrine;
2 How that he swore he would postpone
   All else to further one design.

3 "Surely," he said, "I will not come
   Into the tent in which I dwell,
  Ascend the couch on which I sleep—
4   But slumber from mine eyes dispel,

5 "Until I for Jehovah find
   A Place, and Tabernacle fit."
6 We heard of it at Ephratah,
   In Kirjath-jearim found we it.

7 We'll in His Tabernacles go,
   And at His footstool lowly bend;
8 Arise into Thy Resting Place:
   Ark of Thy Strength, O Lord, ascend!

9 Clothe Thou Thy priests with righteousness,
   And let Thy saints for gladness sing;
10 For David's sake. turn not away
   The face of Thine anointed king.

11 Jehovah has to David sworn—
   And from it He will ne'er turn back:
 "Of thine own offspring there shall be
   To sit upon thy throne no lack.

12 "If they will keep My covenant,
   My testimony that I teach,
 Their sons shall sit too on thy throne,
   And this to latest times shall reach."

13 So honored by Jehovah's choice,
   How far does Zion all excel!
14 "This is," He says, "My Resting Place,
   And here forever will I dwell:

15 "I will abundantly her bless,
   Her poor with bread will satisfy,
16 Her priests will with salvation clothe,
   Her saints with shouts shall fill the sky;

17 "I'll make a horn for David bud,
   A lamp for my Anointed trim;
18 His enemies will clothe with shame,
   And flourish shall his crown on him."

PSALM CXXXIII.

How good and pleasant 't is
    For brethren to agree—
To dwell in unity of love,
    From strife and envy free.

2 'T is like the precious oil,
    Poured out on Aaron's head,
That flowing down on beard and dress,
    A grateful fragrance shed.

3 'T is like the drops of dew
    Of Hermon, falling bright
On Zion's consecrated Hill,
    The jewels of the night.

For there Jehovah doth
    Selectest influence pour:
He there His blessing doth command,
    Ev'n life forevermore.

PSALM CXXXIV.

"Lo, we you greet! Jehovah bless,
    All ye, His servants, made to stand
Here in Jehovah's House by night,
2   Raise to the Holy Place your hand

3 "And bless Jehovah!" "Welcome here,
    Ye pilgrims! seeking heavenly aid;
May out of Zion He you bless
    Who heaven and earth and all things made."

PSALM CXXXV.

HALLELUJAH ! Praise ye Jah ;
    Ye, His servants, standing there
2 In the courts of the Lord's House, .
    His Eternal Name declare !

3 Praise ye Jah, for He is good ;
    Music make to His dear Name ;
4 Jacob for Himself He chose—
    His electing grace proclaim.

5 For I know Jehovah 's great,
    High above all gods ; that He
6 Works His will in heaven and earth
    And th' abysses of the sea ;

7 Causes vapors to ascend ;
    And makes lightnings for the rain ;
  From His store-house brings the wind,
    Then commands it back again.

8 He all Egypt's first-born smote,
    Both of man and beast, and sent
9 Signs and wonders in her midst
    To make Pharaoh relent.

10 He great nations smote, and slew
    Mighty kings in many fights—
11 Og of Bashan ; Sihon, king
    Of th' opposing Amorites.

All the kings of Canaan slew,
   Executing righteous doom ;
Drove the dwellers from the Land,
   For His people to make room.

12 All the Land to Israel gave,
   For a lasting heritage :
13 Everlasting is Thy Name,
   Handed down from age to age.

14 For Thou wilt Thy people judge—
   For Thy servants' sake, repent,
When Thy purpose shall be served
   Of paternal chastisement.

15 Idols of the nations are
   Gold and silver, man-begot ;
16 Mouths have they, but have not speech ;
   Eyes have they, but sight have not.

17 They have ears, but do not hear ;
   In their mouths they breath have none ;
18 They that made shall be like them,
   They that trust in them, each one.

19 House of Israel, bless the Lord !
   House of Aaron, sound His fame !
20 House of Levi, render praise !
   And all fearers of His Name !

PSALM CXXXVI.

PRAISE the Lord for He is good,
O ye faithful brotherhood!
For His mercy firm and sure
Doth from age to age endure.

2 Lift to Him your hymns of laud,
Who of gods alone is God.
    For His mercy firm and sure
    Doth from age to age endure.

3 Tune Him thanks with sounding chords,
Who doth reign the Lord of lords,
    For His mercy firm and sure
    Doth from age to age endure.

4 Who alone great wonders doeth,
And creation thence ensueth.
    For His mercy firm and sure
    Doth from age to age endure.

5 Who by wisdom made and bent
Overhead the firmament.
    For His mercy firm and sure
    Doth from age to age endure.

6 Who the earth on nothing hung,
And in empty space it flung.
    For His mercy firm and sure
    Doth from age to age endure.

7 Who when darkness did entomb,
Made great lights to chase the gloom—
    For His mercy firm and sure
    Doth from age to age endure.

8 Made the sun to rule the day,
And the joy of life convey—
    For His mercy firm and sure
    Doth from age to age endure.

9 Moon and stars to rule the night
With a soft and mellow light.
    For His mercy firm and sure
    Doth from age to age endure.

10 Who smote Egypt's eldest born
Making the oppressor mourn:
    For His mercy firm and sure
    Doth from age to age endure.

11 Brought out Israel free from harm
12 With strong hand and outstretched arm.
    For His mercy firm and sure
    Doth from age to age endure.

13 Who the Red Sea cleft in two
14 And made Israel pass through—
    For His mercy firm and sure
    Doth from age to age endure.

15 But pursuing Pharaoh
   And his hosts did overthrow.
      For His mercy firm and sure
      Doth from age to age endure.

16 Who His chosen people led
   Through the wilderness, and fed.
      For His mercy firm and sure
      Doth from age to age endure.

17 Many kings did smite and slay
18 Great and famous in their day:
      For His mercy firm and sure
      Doth from age to age endure.

19 Sihon—king in Heshbon dwelling—
   Friendly words of peace repelling;
      For His mercy firm and sure
      Doth from age to age endure.

20 Og of Argob, land of stone,
   King of mighty bulk and bone;
      For His mercy firm and sure
      Doth from age to age endure.

   Wrested from the Canaanite
   Other kingdoms in sore fight;
      For His mercy firm and sure
      Doth from age to age endure.

21 These to Israel did deliver
   For a heritage forever.
      For His mercy firm and sure
      Doth from age to age endure.

23 Who when our estate was low
   Help remembered to bestow.
      For His mercy firm and sure
      Doth from age to age endure.

24 From our enemies hath freed
   In the hour of bitter need.
      For His mercy firm and sure
      Doth from age to age endure.

25 Who to all flesh giveth food
   And abundance of all good.
      For His mercy firm and sure
      Doth from age to age endure.

26 Let our thanks to Him be given
   Israel's God, the God of Heaven!
      For His mercy firm and sure
      Doth from age to age endure.

PSALM CXXXVII.

BY the rivers of Babylon there we sat down;
   When we thought upon Zion our tears gan to flow;
We wept when we thought on her faded renown,
   And remembered the days of the dear long ago.

2 We hanged up our harps on the willows, that seemed
      With branches low bending to share in our grief ;
   Homesick and despondent, unceasingly streamed
      Our fast flowing tears, which yet brought no relief.

3 Our captors unfeelingly asked of us songs,
      And they that tormented us asked of us mirth :
   "A song sing," they said, "that to Zion belongs,
      A favorite song of the land of your birth."
4 But how can we sing the Lord's song in a land
      Far from thee, O Jerusalem! strangers among?
5 If less than most dear I thee hold, let my hand
      All its cunning forget, and be palsied my tongue!

7 Remember it, Lord, against Edom, who said
      In the day of Jerusalem's utmost distress :
   "Now raze it, now raze it, ev'n down to its bed !"
      Who aided the foe, and who wished him success.
8 O daughter of Babylon! desolate made,
      He happy shall be, who thy many proud mocks
   And merciless doings shall thee have repaid,
9   Thy little ones dashing against the hard rocks.

PSALM CXXXVIII.

I GIVE Thee thanks with my whole heart,
   Before the gods Thy praise will sing,
2 Will towards Thy Holy Temple bow,
   And bless Thy Name for everything—
Thy mercy and Thy truth, whereby
Thy promise Thou dost magnify.

3 Thou didst me answer when I called,
   And with Thy strength didst me make bold;
4 All kings shall Thee acknowledge, Lord!
   When they Thy sayings shall be told:
5 They of Thy ways shall sing, thy great
   And proper glory celebrate.

6 Though Thou art high, Thou dost regard
   The lowly, and their prayers dost hear;
   But dost the haughty know afar,
   And on them look with eyes severe;
7 If faint I sink, Thou wilt revive,
   Mid deaths and dangers save alive;

   Wilt 'gainst the wrath of foes stretch forth
   Thine arm, and save with Thy right hand;
8 Wilt perfect that which me concerns,
   Till all begun complete shall stand:
   Thy mercy is forevermore
   Work of Thy hands, O give not o'er.

PSALM CXXXIX.*

LORD, with all-seeing eyes
   Thou hast me searched and known;
2 My acts of rising and of rest,
   My doings when alone.

---

* This wonderful Psalm seems like a scientific anachronism. One finds it difficult to believe that this production, evincing apparently the utmost familiarity with all the facts and discoveries upon which our latest Geologies, Anthropologies and Biologies are based, was written 3,000 years ago and not yesterday. Certain it is, that it discourses upon the prevailing doctrine of Evolution (Evolution as taught by Agassiz, not by Spencer) with the ease and knowledge of the profound

My budding thought afar
   Is open to Thy gaze;
3 Thou compassest my path, and art
   Acquainted with my ways.

4 No word is in my tongue
   Thou dost not understand:
5 Thou hast beset me on all sides,
   And on me laid Thy hand.

6 Such knowledge is too high,
   Too wonderful for me:
7 Where shall I from Thy Spirit go?
   Or from Thy presence flee?

8 If I ascend to heaven,
   Or make my bed in hell,
   Thou art there present—in the height
   And in the depth as well.

est adept in modern science. In verses 15-18, man is traced back to his rudimentary beginnings; and no writing could speak with greater plainness and scientific precision of the Geologic prophecies which the fossil-bearing rocks contain, significant of the coming man. However we may explain it, there it is, set forth in our English Version made well nigh 300 years ago, by translators who were ignorant of the meaning of the words they employed, and which have been a puzzle to all commentators since. We read, "My frame was not hidden from Thee when I was made in secret, and curiously wrought in *the lowest parts of the earth*. Thine eyes did see my substance yet being imperfect, and in Thy book (book of Nature whose leaves are the earth's strata) all my members were written, which in continuance were fashioned, when as yet there were none of them," etc. Who gave the Hebrew poet such an insight into the mysteries of anatomical structure as to enable him to discover in the ossicles that go to make up the fin of a fish typical anticipations (homologues) of the bones of the human hand?

9 If me to farthest seas
　　The wings of morning bear,
10 The hand that leads and holds me here,
　　Shall lead and hold me there.

11 If I say: "Sure the dark
　　Will cover me from sight,"
12 The darkness hideth not from Thee,
　　The dark is as the light.

13 I in my mother's womb
　　Was woven and arrayed:
14 For I am fearfully contrived,
　　And wonderfully made.

15 My frame, the crowning work
　　Of Thy creative plan,
　Was seen, though hid in thousand forms
　　Prophetical of man,

　When I was darkly made,
　　And curiously wrought
　In lowest depths of earth, and stood
　　The symbol of Thy thought:

16 My members in Thy book
　　Were written every one,
　And fashioned were unceasingly
　　When of them there was none.

17 How precious are Thy thoughts;
   The sum of them how grand!
18 If I should count them they are more
   In number than the sand.

   In Thy safe arms I lie,
     And nightly slumber seek:
   When I awake I'm still with Thee,
     Thy kiss is on my cheek.

19 Thou wilt the wicked slay;
     Depart, ye men of blood!
20 They speak against Thee wickedly,
     The enemies of good.

21 Do not I hate all those,
     Jehovah, that hate Thee?
22 With perfect hatred I them hate,
     I count them foes to me.

23 Search me and know my heart,
     So prone to self-deceit,
24 And in the everlasting way
     Direct my wandering feet?

PSALM CXL.

DELIVER from the evil man,
   The man of violence, O Lord!
2 From them who 'gainst me mischief plot,
   And stir up wars—defence afford.

2 Their tongue is, like a serpent's, sharp :
4   Their lips an adder's poison hide :
5 The proud ones have laid traps for me :
    Have spread a net my path beside.

6 Thou art my God : vouchsafe to hear
    My supplication, Lord, I said ;
7 The strength of my salvation, Thou
    In battle covered hast my head.

8 Give not the wicked their desire ;
    Defeat the evil they intend ;
9 To shame them, let on their own head
    The mischief of their lips descend.

   The Lord is sure to recompense :
10   He shall live coals upon them rain,
   Plunge them in fire, cast in deep pits,
    So that they shall not rise again.

11 The man of evil-speaking tongue
    No settled place on earth shall know ;
   The violent and wicked man
    Evil shall hunt to overthrow.

12 Jehovah will, I know, maintain
    The sufferer's cause, the needy's right :
13 The righteous shall give thanks to Thee,
    The upright dwell in Thy dear sight.

PSALM CXLI.

O LORD, make haste to me, and let
   My prayer like incense to Thee rise;
And let th' uplifting of my hands
   Be as the evening sacrifice.

3 A watch, Lord, set before my mouth,
   And keep the portal of my lips;
4 My heart to evil disincline,
   So tempted and so prone to slips.

  Let me all forms of evil shun,
     Avoid the doer and the deed—
  Give for the proud a wise distaste,
     Nor let me on their dainties feed.

5 When me the righteous smites, it shall
   A kindness be, and proof of love;
A grateful oil be on my head,
   When he shall faithfully reprove,

  For still my prayer for them shall rise:
6 When overthrow their judges meet—
  Hurled down among the rock--then they
    Shall hear my words, for they are sweet.

7 As when one ploughs and cleaves the earth,
   At Sheol's mouth our bones are spread—
Frequent as sheaves on fields just reaped
   The scattered bodies of the dead.

8 For that mine eyes are unto Thee,
  O God, the Lord, in whom I trust,
 Leave me not destitute, a prey
  To machinations of th' unjust.

9 Keep from the snares they laid for me,
  From nets and gins of every shape;
10 Bad men make fall in their own traps,
  Whilst I meanwhile unharmed escape.

PSALM CXLII.

1 TO Jehovah cry
   With supplicating moan;
2 I pour before Him my complaint,
   My trouble I make known.

3 Then when my spirit faints,
   Thou, Thou my path dost know,
  And how they 've hid a snare for me
   Along the way I go.

4 Look to the right, and see,
   I 've no defender there;
  Refuge has failed me, there 's no man
   That for my soul doth care.

5 I cried to Thee, I said:
   "Thou art my Refuge, Lord!
  My portion in the land of life,
   And my supreme reward."

6 For I'm brought very low,
    Attend unto my cry—
From my pursuers save, for they
    Are mightier than I.

7 My soul from prison bring,
    To render thanks to Thee;
The righteous shall me gather round
    When Thou shalt favor me.

PSALM CXLIII.

JEHOVAH, hear my prayer,
    Which I to Thee address;
According to Thy faithful word
    Answer in righteousness.

2 Not at Thy judgment-bar
    Do Thou Thy servant try;
For no man living righteous is
    Before Thy searching eye.

3 The foe has vexed my soul,
    And has my life brought low;
Has made me dwell in darkness, like
    The dead of long ago.

4 Therefore my spirit faints,
    My heart is desolate;
5 I recollect the days of old,
    Thy doings meditate.

I muse upon Thy works,
6   I stretch toward Thee my hand;
My soul for Thee is thirsty, like
    A dry and weary land.

7 Send speedy answer, Lord,
    My spirit fails for it;
Hide not Thy Face, lest, dying, I
    Go down into the pit.

8 Me in the morning make
    Thy loving-kindness know;
Cause me to understand the way
    Wherein I ought to go.

9 Lord, free me from my foes:
    I hide myself with Thee—
10 Teach me to do Thy will, my God,
    Thy Spirit guiding me.

11 For Thy Name's sake, O Lord!
    Me quicken and relieve;
12 My foes destroy, the foes of right,
    Who vex my soul and grieve.

PSALM CXLIV.

THRICE blessèd be the Lord, my Rock,
    Defender of the Right!
My hands He for the battle trains,
    My fingers for the fight.

2 My Goodness, Fortress and High Tower,
   Deliverer and Shield,
   My Trust, He Who my people makes
   Subjection to me yield.

3 Lord what is man that Thou shouldst know
4   Or think of him? A breath—
   The shadow of a flying cloud
   Swept by the wind of death.

5 Thy heaven of heavens, Jehovah, bow;
   In majesty come down;
   The mountains touch so that they smoke;
   And, from Thy gathered frown,

6 Cast lightnings forth, and scatter them—
   Confounding arrows hurl;
7 Stretch out Thy hand from highest heaven,
   And snatch me from the whirl

   Of whelming waters; from the hands
   Of aliens threatening nigh;
8 From those whose mouth deception speaks,
   And whose right hand's a lie!

9 I'll then a new song unto Thee
   Indite and sing, O Lord!
   I will sing praises unto Thee
   Upon the decachord.

10 Thou dost salvation give to kings,
    From hurtful sword dost free
  Thy servant David : Wherefore, Lord,
11   Deliverance give to me,

  Out of the hands of aliens, those
    Whose false mouths testify,
  And whose right hand is lifted up
    To solemnize a lie—

12 So that our sons may be as plants,
    To ripeness grown full soon ;
  Our daughters be as corner-stones
    For a fair palace hewn ;

13 Our garners be heaped high with corn ;
    Our flocks be multiplied,
  By thousands and ten thousands, spread
    O'er vale and mountain-side ;

14 Our oxen drawing loaded wains,
    Men's eyes delighted greet ;
  No breaking in, no going out,
    No outcry in the street.

15 Happy the people, who are thus
    Honored of God as His !
  Happy the people, happiest known
    Whose God Jehovah is !

PSALM CXLV.

I WILL Thy Name extol,
  My God, O King, and bless;
2 Each day Thy love recall,
  Perpetual praise express.
3 The Lord is great, too great to tell,
  His greatness is unsearchable.

4 One generation shall
  . Unto another bear
  Thy fame terrestrial,
    Thy mighty acts declare;
5 Thy glorious majesty and state
  And wondrous works I will relate;

6 And men shall tell in verse
    The might of Thy dread acts;
  Thy greatness shall rehearse,
7   Enlarge upon the facts
  Of Thy great goodness from of old,
  And righteous judgments manifold.

8 The Lord is full, we know,
    Of love to all that live:
  To anger He is slow,
    And ready to forgive;
9 High over all, His mercies span,
  Like the dear sky, the race of man.

10 Thee all Thy works shall praise:
    And all Thy saints shall bless—
11 The glory of Thy kingdom blaze,
12   Acts of almightiness:
13 Thine empire stable is and vast,
   Thy kingdom shall forever last.

14 Thou notest each man's state,
    And raisest those that fall;
15 All eyes upon Thee wait,
    And Thou dost feed them all;
16 Thine open hand hath full supply,
   And every want doth satisfy.

17 The Lord is just and pure,
    In all His works and ways;
18 His grace is near and sure,
    To him who truly prays—
19 To them who fear Him, that they crave
   He will fulfill; and hear and save.

20 All who Jehovah love,
    They safety shall enjoy;
   But all the wicked He
    Will finally destroy:
21 My mouth His praises shall proclaim—
   Let all flesh bless His Holy Name!

PSALM CXLVI.

Hallelujah!

PRAISE Jehovah, O my soul!
　　I will praise Him while I live:
2 While I shall have being, I
　　Will melodious praises give.

3 Not in princes put your trust,
　　Not on mortal man rely,
4 Breath departs, on that same day
　　His own projects with him die.

5 Happy he whose help and hope
　　On the Lord his God are laid—
6 Him, Who heaven and earth and sea
　　With their countless people made;

　Keeping truth forevermore;
7 　Doing justice for th' oppressed;
　To the hungry giving bread;
　　Freeing prisoners distressed.

8 He the blind restores to sight;
　　He the burdened soul upbears;
　He the righteous loves, and He
6 　For the friendless stranger cares.

　He the fatherless relieves,
　　And the widow; but the way
　Of the wicked crooked makes—
10 　Dear and endless is His sway!
　　　Hallelujah!

PSALM CXLVII.

HALLELUJAH! It is good
　　Praise to sing unto our God:
Comely is it and thrice fit
　　Him to celebrate and laud.

2 He rebuilds Jerusalem:
　　Back from exile Israel brings:
3 He the broken-hearted heals,
　　And relieves their sufferings.

4 Tells the number and the names
　　Of th' uncounted stars of night;
5 Great and mighty is our Lord
　　And His knowledge infinite.

6 He the lowly raises up,
　　Casts the wicked to the ground;
7 With thanksgiving sing to Him,
　　On the harp His praise resound.

8 He the heaven o'erspreads with clouds,
　　For the earth preparing rain;
And He makes the grass to grow
　　On the mountain and the plain.

9 To the beast He gives his food;
　　Answers the young raven's cry;
19 Him nor strength of horse nor man
　　Pleases—foot nor cavalry.

11 He is pleased with them who fear,
    Them that in His mercy hope;
  He will make them wise and strong
    With the enemy to cope.

12 Praise the Lord, Jerusalem!
    Praise thy God, O Zion! He
13 Strengthened has thy gates, thy sons
    Blest has in the midst of thee

14 Peace He in thy borders makes;
    Fills thee with the fat of wheat;
15 His commandment sends He forth,
    Runs His word on swiftest feet.

16 Snow He gives like wool: hoar frost
    Spreads like ashes o'er the land;
17 He His ice, like crumbs, casts forth—
    Who before His cold can stand?

17 He sends out His timely word,
    Causes a warm wind to blow,
  And He melts them, so again
    The congealèd waters flow.

19 He His word to Jacob shows,
    Makes His laws to Israel known,
20 To no other nation He
    Has such grace and favor shown.

PSALM CXLVIII.

HALLELUJAH! all unite!
   Praise Jehovah in the height;
From the heavens let praise arise
To the Maker of the Skies.

2 Praise Him, all ye angels bright;
3 Praise Him, all ye stars of light;
Praise Him, sun and moon, whose rays
Beautify the nights and days.

4 Praise Him, as ye upward soar,
Heaven of heavens, forevermore;
Praise Him, waters of the sky,
Stored in airy depths on high.

5 Let them praise Jehovah's Name,
For He spake and forth they came;
6 Stablished them by a decree
Which can never broken be.

7 Praise Jehovah from the earth;
Praise the power that gave you birth,
All ye monsters of the main,
All the ocean's depths contain.

8 Praise Him, fire and hail and snow;
Mists, and stormy winds that blow
Over sea and over land,
Executing His command;

9 Mountains, and ye uplands all,
  Fruitful trees and cedars tall,
10 Savage beasts, and flocks, and herds,
  Creeping things, and wingèd birds,

11 Monarchs, exercising sway,
  And all peoples these obey,
  Champions of their country's cause,
  Princes, judges of the laws,

12 Youths and maidens, elders sage,
  Children, too, of tender age—
13 Make Jehovah's praises known
  For His Name is great alone.
                    Hallelujah.

PSALM CXLIX.

HALLELUJAH ! A new song
  Let the congregation sing ;
2 Let the sons of Zion joy
  In their Maker and their King ;

3 Let them praise Him in the dance,
  With the timbrel beating time ;
  Tune His praise to pulsing wires,
  And the harp's melodious chime.

4 For Jehovah pleasure takes
  In His people from on high ;
  In due time He will the meek
  With salvation beautify.

5 Let His honored saints exult,
  On their beds sing to the Lord—
6 God's high praises in their mouth,
  In their hand a two-edged sword,

7 Punishment to execute
  On the nations that environ;
  Bind their kings and nobles with
  Fetters strong and chains of iron.
                    Hallelujah.

PSALM CL.

HALLELUJAH! Praise the Lord,
  Earth and heaven, in sweet accord:
Praise ye Him with voices clear
In His Sanctuary here.

Praise Him in the firmament,
Reared by power omnipotent:
2 Praise Him for His works of might;
For His greatness infinite.

3 Him with sound of trumpet sharp;
  Him with psaltery and harp;
4 Him with timbrel and with dance,
  Joined in pleasing consonance;

Him with strings, with lyre and lute,
Piercing pipe and warbling flute,
5 Clanging cymbals, every thing
6 Musical accompanying—

Praise Him with uplifted palms ;
Praise Him in perpetual psalms ;
Let each creature that hath breath ;
Praise the Lord of life and death !

>   HALLELUJAH !

>   Sit laus Patri cum Filio,
>   Sancto simul Paraclito,
>   Nobisque mittat Filius
>   Charisma Sancti Spiritûs.

Praise to the Father with the Son
And Comforter, dear Three in One ;
And may the Son on us in love
Send down the Spirit from above.

Errata.

Introduction, p. xi, line 13 from top, *for* " thus " *read* then.

Introduction, p. xviii, line 10 from top, *for* 1605 *read* 1695.

Introduction, p. lv, line 9 from top, for *Qui* read *Cui*.

Psalm xix, p. 33, line 8 from top, *for* in *read* is.

Psalm xli, p. 77, Note, line 9 from bottom, *for* Ps. 102 *read* Ps. 101.

Psalm lvi, p. 105, line 5 from top, *for* In God I'll trust, etc., *read*—

> In God I trust, Jehovah's word
> Theme of my praise shall be ;
> Because I trust, I will not fear
> What man can do to me.

Psalm lxxviii, p. 150, after verse 22, line 8 from top, insert the following :

> [23] Yet to the clouds command was given,
> And opened were the doors of heaven,
> [24] Manna to eat was on them shed—
> [25] Celestial corn, angelic bread.
>
> [26] He made an east wind blow with force,
> Guided a whirlwind in its course,
> [27] Rained on them quails, as dust or sand,
> [28] That filled with flesh each hungry hand.
>
> [29] Their sinful lusting not denied,
> They ate till they were satisfied ;
> [30] Then mid the glut on viands new,
> [31] God smote them, and their strongest slew.

INDEX.

PSALM.		PAGE.
49	All men, where'er ye dwell, give ear—	90
125	All who in Jehovah trust,	257
42-43	As the flying hart, pursued,	78
37	At evil-doers do not fret :	66
67	Be merciful and bless,	121
57	Be merciful to me, O God !	105
56	Be merciful, O God, to me,	104
14	Besotted pupil in that school,	20
119	Blest are the perfect in the way,	239
32	Blest is the man, who stands forgiven	56
86	Bow down Thine ear, O Lord, to me,	164
137	By the rivers of Babylon there we sat down ;	270
4	Delay not answer when I call,	4
59	Deliver me from those,	108
70	Deliver me, O God !	131
140	Deliver from the evil man,	275
127	Except the Lord shall build the House,	259
45	From my heart's fountain, my great theme	83
55	Give ear unto my prayer, O God !	101
5	Give ear unto my words, O Lord !	6
107	Give Jehovah thanks, for He	217
105	Give to Jehovah thanks and praise !	208
29	Give to the Lord, ye sons of might,	50
48	God is great, and only great :	89
46	God is our Refuge and our Rock,	86
68	God shall arise and scatter them,	122
149	Hallelujah ! A new song	289
148	Hallelujah ! All unite !	288
147	Hallelujah ! It is good	286
113	Hallelujah ! Praise accord,	231
135	Hallelujah ! Praise ye Jah ;	265

PSALM.		PAGE
150	Hallelujah! Praise the Lord	290
112	Hellelujah! This attest	229
41	Happy is he whose heart unlocks	75
128	Happy the man who fears the Lord,	260
51	Have mercy, my offended God;	97
51	Have pity on me, Lord!	94
102	Hear, O Jehovah, let my cry	191
73	Hear, O my people, I will tell	148
61	Hear Thou, O God, my cry;	112
17	Hear Thou the right, O God!	24
12	Help, Lord, for these are evil days;	19
109	Hold not Thy peace, God of my praise!	224
133	How good and pleasant 'tis	264
57	How is it, judges, ye sit dumb,	107
13	How long wilt Thou, Lord, me forget?	20
84	How lovely are Thy Dwellings, Lord!	161
124	If God had not been on our side,	257
138	I give Thee thanks with my whole heart,	271
18	I love Thee, Lord! my Strength,	26
77	I'll lift my voice to God,	146
76	In Judah God is known; His Name	144
31	In Thee, O Lord, I put my trust—	53
120	I prayed the Lord in my distress,	254
71	I put my trust, Lord! in Thy Name:	132
11	I put my trust in God my King:	17
39	I said, I will take heed, that I	72
142	I to Jehovah cry	278
123	I unto Thee do lift my eyes,	256
40	I waited for the Lord till He	73
34	I will bless the Lord, and raise	60
30	I will extol Thee and adore,	51
145	I will Thy Name extol,	283
9	I with my whole heart will praise,	12
143	Jehovah hear my prayer,	279
97	Jehovah reigns: let earth rejoice;	186
99	Jehovah reigns, the Mighty God,	188
24	Jehovah's right to all extends;	42
110	Jehovah said unto my Lord:	227
26	Judge me, O Lord! to Thee I dare	46
83	**Keep** silence not, O God!	159

INDEX.

PSALM.		PAGE
95	Let us to Jehovah raise.	183
88	Lord God of my Salvation, I	167
94	Lord God of recompense,	180
7	Lord, my God, in Thee I trust	8
90	Lord, Thou hast been our dwelling-place,	174
10	Lord, why standest Thou afar?	15
139	Lord, with all-seeing eyes	272
134	Lo, we you greet! Jehovah bless,	264
20	May God thee answer in the day	34
108	My heart is fixed, my heart is fixed	222
22	My God, my God, O why	36
62	My soul is silent unto God,	113
73	My tongue was loosed, I broke the spell,	138
101	Mercy and judgment will I sing;	190
121	Not haughty is my heart;	261
115	Not unto us, but glory give,	232
47	O all ye peoples, clap your hands;	88
100	O all ye lands, unite your joys:	189
103	O bless the Lord, my soul!	194
1	O happy is the man who hath	1
63	O God, my God, Thou art	114
64	O God! hear my complaint and prayer	116
72	O God! supremest Source	134
44	O God! we with our ears have heard,	81
74	O God, why dost Thou cast us off?	141
122	O I was glad then, when they said:	255
3	O Lord! how many foes	3
141	O Lord, make haste to me, and let	277
8	O Lord, our Lord, in all the earth,	11
104	O Lord, my God, Thou art	196
104	O Lord, my God, Thou art	202
87	On consecrated ground,	166
117	O praise the Lord, His name extol,	236
118	O thank the Lord, for He is good—	236
130	Out of the depths I call on Thee	261
65	Perpetual worship for Thee waits	117
111	Praise Jehovah! I will bring	228
146	Praise Jehovah, O my soul!	285
136	Praise the Lord for He is good,	267

PSALM.		PAGE.
106	Praise ye the Lord, for He is good	212
54	Preserve me by Thy Name, O God!	100
16	Preserve me, for in Thee I trust,	22
6	Rebuke me not in anger, Lord!	7
33	Rejoice, ye righteous, in the Lord,	58
132	Remember David's deep concern,	262
80	Shepherd of Israel, give ear—	155
81	Shout to the Lord, our Strength	156
66	Shout unto God, all lands,	119
98	Sing a new song of matchless charm!	187
96	Sing to Jehovah a new song,	184
38	Spare me! howe'er deserved,	70
35	Strive Thou with those who strive with me;	62
69	Succor, O God! and save	127
79	The heathen in Thine heritage,	153
21	The King shall in Thy strength rejoice,	35
27	The Lord my Saviour is, and Light	47
23	The Lord my Shepherd is,	41
23	The Lord is my shepherd, I never shall want	42
89	The mercies of the Lord	169
82	The Mighty God of Heaven	158
50	The Mighty God, the Lord of all,	92
19	The rolling skies with lips of flame	32
53	"There is no God"--the fool hath said,	99
129	"They many a time," let Israel say,	260
60	Thou, God, hast cast us off;	110
85	Thou hast, O Lord, in former years	163
144	Thrice blessed be the Lord, my Rock,	280
92	To give Jehovah thanks,	178
25	To Thee I lift my soul—	43
28	To Thee, O Lord, I lift my cry—	49
121	Up to the Hills I lift mine eyes,	254
75	We give Thee Thanks, O God!	143
126	When captive Zion God brought back	258
114	When Israel, held in bondage long,	231
36	Wickedness within the heart	64
91	Who has his refuge in the sky,	176
15	Who shall inhabit, Lord, Thy tent?	21
52	Why boasteth thou thyself in mischief, mighty man?	98
2	Why do the nations rage,	2

www.ingramcontent.com/pod-product-compliance
Lightning Source LLC
Chambersburg PA
CBHW050835230426
43667CB00012B/2004